Conscious  *Coaching*

The
Art & Science
of
Building Buy-In

Brett Bartholomew

Copyright © 2017 Brett Bartholomew

Bartholomew Strength LLC
19310 Atlas Street
Omaha, NE 68130

www.bartholomewstrength.com

Ordering Information:
Quantity sales: Special discounts are available on large quantity purchases by corporations, universities, associations, and others. For details, contact the author via email with the subject heading "Quantity Sale Inquiry" at the email address below:

info@bartholomewstrength.com

ISBN-13: 978-1543179477
ISBN-10: 1543179479

DEDICATION

To my family—especially my wife—and my closest friends,
thank you for always believing in me. And to my mentors,
editors, and colleagues who contributed their time and
effort to this project, thank you for being a part of it.

TABLE OF CONTENTS

FOREWORD

I am delighted to write this foreword, not only because Brett Bartholomew has been a friend and colleague for many years, but also because I believe deeply in the value of providing coaches with solid material aimed at helping them better understand the "art" of communication. It turns out that the "art" of communication is every bit as much a science as that of the physical training of the body. *Conscious Coaching: The Art and Science of Building Buy-In* is a detailed exploration into the science behind the art of communication, and a critical addition to the toolbox of all coaches.

Brett is the perfect person to write this book. He's paid serious dues in his evolution as a coach, working his way up from unpaid intern, to graduate assistant, to team coach, and now works in world-class training centers, coaching top athletes as well as military men and women. Brett is known for his ability to connect with everyone around him—he doesn't just live *Conscious Coaching*, he researches, speaks, and teaches about it, too. That's why I was so excited when I heard he would be coalescing his firsthand experiences and findings into a single book.

This book is needed, and its time is now.

In my own role as an educator, coach, center director, and endless researcher in sport for over 40 years, I have had the honor and distinct pleasure of traveling around the world, meeting with many top-shelf practitioners in sport.

Even after visiting hundreds of nationally and internationally top-performing organizations in a variety of settings, and meeting and learning from thousands of successful leaders in sport performance, I was still excited to learn of Brett's treatise discussing what many call the "soft side" of coaching. The topic is wanting for a good, thorough, and comprehensive treatment.

A current issue in sport is what I call the problem of modernity. We have a tendency to rely on mainstream information, technology, and science to alter behavior and enhance performance. In doing so, we often pick specific areas and put our focus there, unfortunately overlooking a more balanced approach. Brett bridges this gap because for him, it's not about science or art. It's about science and art.

Conscious Coaching provides insight into the practice of individuals who excel consistently at the highest levels of administering sport performance. At the same time, *Conscious Coaching* overviews the latest research on the foundational elements of building buy-in. After reading this book, coaches will no doubt improve relationships with their athletes—and improved relationships mean improved performance.

This book details the four components of the coaching compass: buy-in, relationships, social intelligence, and time. It explores why it is not just enough to know your athletes; you also have to know yourself. Brett offers strategies to enhance your day-to-day coaching and also shares his thoughts on how to achieve longevity—and build a legacy—in your career.

Brett writes that ego is often the enemy in coaching. He practices what he preaches by including thoughts from other well-respected coaches and researchers to produce a powerful resource that belongs on the bookshelf of every high-performance coach.

It is my hope that this book helps coaches and performance staff members learn, teach, and practice the art of *Conscious Coaching*. There is compelling evidence that a core teaching practice like *Conscious Coaching* can be learned, but not without serious and sustained effort. The effort is worth it! What better way to strengthen the quality of teaching and learning in our workplaces than by being engaged in *Conscious Coaching*? Read on, and I'm convinced you'll find the answer is that there is no better way.

Dan Pfaff
Head Coach, ALTIS
10 Olympic Games
49 Olympians (9 medalists)
51 World Championships competitors (9 medalists)
57 national record holders

INTRODUCTION

By wisdom a house is built; and through understanding it is established.
—Proverbs 24:3 (New International Version)

For far too long, performance coaches, both current and aspiring, have found themselves at various stages of their career asking: "What books or articles should I read to learn more about _____?" The blank, of course, is usually filled with some combination of science-based topics including speed, agility, periodization, energy-system development, movement screening, plyometrics, strength training, nutrition, and recovery. In addition to this ongoing search for technical knowledge, performance coaches are also constantly questioning what credentials or certifications they should attain and what conferences and workshops they should attend. Taken together, performance coaches are hungry to improve their technical skill set, build their science-driven knowledge, and develop their "coaching compass," or the set of principles and general path they'll follow. When this insatiable appetite for learning is a coupled with a devotion to serve athletes and teams (a 24-7 job in and of itself), it becomes easy to see how the modern-day performance coach is often overwhelmed with information.

Thus, we find ourselves indulging in a circuitous cycle of scouring countless books, articles, and podcasts to store in our digital or physical hard drives. When we create the time to dive in—often sacrificing sleep and family time to do so, something we'd never willingly advise our athletes to do—we learn about the myriad of ways to make athletes bigger, faster, stronger, and more powerful; the latest and greatest approaches to movement assessments and injury prevention; and how to optimize nutrition and recovery. By the time we have finished reading stacks of research, attending conferences and debating with one another, we find our toolbox full of strategies for successfully dealing with programming, but almost empty when it comes to strategies for successfully dealing with people. Ask a performance coach to recite the history of a specific training method or discuss the originator of a particular theory and they will talk your ear off for hours. But ask them to name thought leaders on influence, communication, and human interaction, or to describe how everything from our environment to our body language affects those around us, and you'll struggle to find someone who is up for the task. This is unfortunate because athletes are not robots. They are people. And in order to get athletes to move physically, we must first get people to move psychologically and emotionally. Recent technology may be advancing what we are able to measure and manage, but the best training programs are not driven by technological connection. They are driven by human connection. Put simply: there is no gadget that can inspire and ignite an athlete like an emotionally-tuned coach can.

Unfortunately, while it's obvious that performance coaches (which I also refer to as strength and conditioning coaches throughout this book) have many resources to enhance their knowledge of physiology and physical training, they often lack the appropriate resources to hone their ability to create effective "buy-in" with their athletes from a psycho-social (or even psychological) standpoint. Every day, strength and conditioning coaches talk to their athletes about proper training and recovery, but they don't always communicate in a language or manner that the athlete understands or connects with on a personal level. Because of this, far too often athletes fail to engage at the intensity required for them to obtain the full benefits of their training. Instead, these athletes go through the motions on autopilot simply because their training is "required" and has been routinized as part of their day-to-day sporting lifestyle. Other athletes train without a full understanding of the purpose of their program, which leads to confusion and a sub-standard effort compared to what is possible when an athlete and coach are fully aligned and working in harmony. As a result, potential is often left untapped, athletes become apathetic, and many highly skilled coaches find themselves frustrated with their inability to convince athletes to "care." Even the best physiological programming is useless if it can't be properly implemented.

The interpersonal dynamic between coach and athlete is central to the coaching process. Thousands of coaches, including myself, have longed for a book that explains how to master this side of the coaching equation. A book that teaches us how to enhance athlete engagement through a better knowledge of their behavior. A book that shows us how we can truly get inside the mind of an athlete to gain a clearer understanding of their perspective. A book that we can lend to an intern, young coach or even seasoned veteran to assist them in lighting the internal spark within an athlete, which, of course, is every bit as important as targeting accurate loads for strength and hypertrophy. A book that explains how to manage a difficult athlete or organizational culture, or how to effectively build trust and adapt communication styles to individuals with diverse sporting, socioeconomic, and psychological backgrounds.

One might think this book would have already been written. The study of effective communication is anything but new. It spans nearly 5000 years, with classics like the Precepts dating back to Egypt in 2675 BC. Today, we have entire academic departments dedicated to communication and behavioral science. Even so, when it comes to easy-to-access and practical information geared toward maximizing athletic performance, there is next to nothing. Sure, you might point to the "self-help" or "leadership" aisle of your local bookstore as a destination for this type of material, but such books are strong on rhetoric and idealism and weak on science, and certainly don't address the realities of working in a high-performance athletic environment. And while there are plenty of memoirs of world-championship coaches and motivational tomes relating to athletics, hardly any of them focus exclusively on human behavior and how to influence it in athletes.

This book strives to fill the gap.

I wrote this book to remind fellow strength and conditioning coaches of the critical importance of recognizing, remembering, and optimizing the human element of what we do. In order to maximally enhance performance, delivering no -nonsense, evidence-based training techniques is a must. But it's also important that we communicate at an elite level, as a training program is only as good as an athlete's willingness to buy into it.

In the pages that follow, you'll find tools that will help you improve your ability to close the gaps that may exist between your athletes' internal drives and your personal coaching practices. You'll learn about the science of communication and behavior change in a manner tailored to strength and conditioning coaches. And most importantly, you'll see via numerous examples—including those from the experience of some of the world's best performance coaches—of how this science can be applied in day-to-day coaching. And although this book was written with the strength and conditioning coach in mind, the insights uncovered transcend domains and can be put to good use by just about anyone in the business of motivating other people.

What this book will not do is claim to have all the answers, nor will it peddle any quick fixes. Coaching is a journey, a hands-on process in which there are no shortcuts. Along those lines, the concepts in this book are only as valuable as your willingness to act on and personalize them in a way that fits with your unique coaching style. I promise that I'm not withholding any "secrets." This book contains all of the knowledge I've amassed through research, relationships, and practice. But it's worth reiterating that this book's real value doesn't just come from reading it, but also from bringing what you learn to life in your interactions with the athletes you coach. And, as you're about to learn, the first step in doing so is understanding the destination we are striving for: becoming what I call a Conscious Coach.

Becoming a Conscious Coach

The style and skills of strength and conditioning coaches span a wide spectrum. On one extreme, there are uneducated and unregulated coaches who run amuck, applying training techniques that don't fall in line with best practices and also put athletes in harm's way. These individuals are master swindlers, peddle quick fixes, and almost always fail to see long-term results and performance improvement. On the other end of the spectrum, there are coaches who are informational cookie monsters. These coaches believe that the science of training alone is the key to their success. They think out every last detail of their training program but cannot figure out for the life of them why their athletes never seem to stick to it.

Somewhere in between lies what I call a Conscious Coach. For a long time, I used the term "master coach," but I stopped using it after reading a quote from writer Ernest Hemingway. *"We are all apprentices in a craft in which no one ever becomes a master,"* he wrote. Hemingway hits the nail on the head. There is no such thing as a "master coach." The best coaches are the best not because they think of themselves as a master, but because they always want to keep learning. So, the term Conscious Coach was born.

A Conscious Coach is someone who sees the big picture and is able to balance the science and art of coaching. Someone who understands all the technical material but is also comfortable adapting it for a given athlete's needs. *Conscious Coaching* is about figuring out an athlete's purpose and matching it with an evidence-based coaching process. It's focused on understanding what really drives our athletes from the inside out so that there is a shared enthusiasm for what we're trying to accomplish, the level of effort and dedication necessary in order to make it happen, and how we can best surmount and adapt to the obstacles that we'll inevitably encounter along the way. Pay close attention to Conscious Coaches at work and you'll notice everything they do is strategic yet natural: from the way they alter their tone of voice, to how they explain a drill or exercise, to where they stand in relation to an athlete, to how they hold their own bodies.

Conscious Coaches don't coach to athletes—they coach with athletes. When a Conscious Coach is at work, you won't find any evidence of an authoritarian relationship. *Conscious Coaching* occurs through a connection. Conscious Coaches teach athletes how to teach themselves by enhancing an athlete's awareness of the training method and its desired outcome. At the same time, they focus explicitly on building rapport with their athletes through small talk, humor, and inviting questions. Conscious Coaches understand that successful training is more than just the sum of various physical drills and exercises. Success depends upon the interactions of the physical, psychological, emotional, and social components of a training program. Thus, a Conscious Coach must understandably be comfortable with all of those elements. It is my opinion that the attainment of this diverse skill set is what helps performance coaches turn what is otherwise a lifeless training program written on paper into a catalyst for physical transformation.

Conscious Coaching relies foremost on trust. The coach-athlete relationship needs trust to survive in the same way humans need oxygen. When you combine trust with an understanding of how to more effectively communicate with those around you, the outcome is almost always positive. Trust, combined with strong communication skills, is an alchemy for excellence. It's a mixture that allows you to gain a sense for what makes an athlete tick so you can design an evidence-based program with that information in mind and communicate it in a way that makes sense to, or strikes a chord within, the athlete. It is a skill set that current and future performance coaches will need to build and acquire if they want to truly impact lives within—and beyond—the world of sport. We spend so much time learning about the history of an athlete's body (e.g., previous injuries, mobility limitations, etc.) but far too little time learning about the history of an athlete's mind. Perhaps that's because in many ways, learning about the history of someone's body is easier than learning about the history of their mind. The latter requires trust.

Want to set yourself apart from others in the industry for the right reasons? It's worth remembering that in the eyes of the athlete, the successful demonstration of this balanced skill set, of the alchemy of excellence, is what will help you do so. This all makes sense to us intuitively, yet many struggle with this or lose their way at some point in their career and we often don't know why. This is in part because building trust and communicating effectively are not skill sets that are clearly defined or understood, let alone adequately taught, developed, or passed down by elite-level coaches.

Instead, we often refer to issues within this domain as the "art of coaching," pair it with vague descriptions of what that means, and then stop right there. This makes for a nice presentation and draws a decent crowd at a conference, but it does not adequately do the term justice.

We act as if the art and the science are separate entities, when in reality the two are inextricably linked more than most understand. As a matter of fact, there is a science to the art itself. The roots of the "art of coaching" are found in the science of connecting with others and making the information that we share with them more meaningful. This is true whether we are meeting someone for the first time, coaching them during a training session, or consoling them in the midst of a hardship. It's also true whether we are working with an NFL MVP, an Olympic-caliber boxer, or a 55-year-old woman trying to lose a few pounds. In all of these cases, successful interventions begin with successful interactions. And in order to understand what makes for a successful interaction, we must learn how to blend the latest insights from the academic literature regarding behavioral science into our unique coaching situations. Our ability to become Conscious Coaches depends on it.

CHAPTER 1
MAPS & MEANINGS

"A map does not just chart, it unlocks and formulates meaning; it forms bridges between here and there, between disparate ideas that we did not know were previously connected."
—Reif Larsen, *The Selected Works of T.S. Spivet*

When you look at a standard road map, what do you see? Generally, you'll find a variety of destinations that are connected by highways, interstates, and other roads or bridges. There is almost always more than just one way to arrive at the majority of destinations; some routes are more direct, while others are more scenic. Which route you take usually depends on factors like comfort, safety, and duration. I've always looked at the training modalities I choose when designing sessions for my athletes like I do the roads on a map. While all modalities I use are based on sound science, and all will eventually help an athlete arrive at his or her destination (a specific physiological adaptation, or, for skill sports, the improvement of a capability), they differ based on an athlete's unique situation. It wasn't until later in my career, however, that I realized the same analogy holds true when it comes to the teaching and communication strategies I use with my athletes.

Over the course of your career coaching, managing, teaching, and leading others, you will surely have to navigate a multitude of these metaphorical roads. Many will be laden with physical and psychological cracks, bumps, detours, and obstacles. This is nothing to be worried about as long as you have both the awareness required to identify them ahead of time and the driving skills necessary to move around and/through them. For a Conscious Coach, no matter how difficult or damaged the terrain, there is always a way to get to where you need to go, to get back on route.

Principles and Strategies

Understanding the roads and the topography you will cover are important, but the fact is that detours will inevitably arise. These unexpected circumstances cause our internal GPS to "re-calculate" and make what was once a direct route a bit more circuitous. If calibrated correctly, our internal GPS finds us another route that we can take in order to achieve our goal. But calibration is key. And calibration depends on a well-functioning compass. Without this tool, our map is much less valuable. Your ability to effectively use a compass in no small part determines where you end up should you find yourself lost, stranded, or confused. The cardinal directions on our coaching compass are signified by the four elements of what makes a Conscious Coach an effective teacher and communicator: Buy-In (trust), Relationships, Social Intelligence and Time.

The following subsections will equip you with a working knowledge of each of these concepts. Pay close attention, as you'll see these concepts appear repeatedly throughout the book. They are critical to *Conscious Coaching*. When paired with the proper knowledge surrounding the science of the human body, the concepts are what separate good coaching from great coaching. Given that the term "buy-in" is the most over- and incorrectly used of the bunch, let's start there.

Buy-In

Ask any coach at nearly any level of sport about the key determinants of success when they first begin working with a group of athletes and within five minutes they will likely mention the term "buy-in." Buy-in is a coveted commodity for coaches, and true buy-in comes by first establishing relationships based upon trust and understanding. In fact, that's all "buy-in" really is: trust. Trust is invaluable to human existence. We rely on it all the time, often without even realizing it. Trust is how we know that our car's brakes will work when we need to avoid an object in the road, that our paychecks will arrive on time so that we can pay our bills, and that our closest friends and family will be there for us should disaster strike. Trust is the impetus for growth, progress, and action. In coaching, trust is built in much the same way that we create an old-school camp fire. There are no shortcuts. Trust, like a campfire, must be laid down stick by stick. Trust should ignite a slow and steady burn that illuminates a clearer path for us to travel. When we have a trusting relationship with our athletes, we don't light a flame in them—we burn with them, stoking their embers in an incredibly powerful way.

Some may scoff at the term "buy-in." If it's trust that we are talking about, why not just use that term in the first place? After all, do we really need another "frankenword" when we could just as easily call it what it is? I can appreciate why some may have a knee-jerk reaction when they hear the term and why some may believe it has a snarky connotation to it. The truth is that while "buy-in" is certainly not a negative term, if used incorrectly or too often, it can indeed conjure the notion that we are trying to sell someone something they may not want, trying to connive and convince our athletes to submit to our grand plans. Still, it's important not to relent to primitive or emotional responses. It is the context with which we surround our words, rather than the words themselves, that we should be focused on. I use the term "buy-in" throughout the book, regardless of the emotions it may invoke. Whether or not you agree with the phrasing, the term "buy in" is not going away, so you must learn to look at it differently and bring it to life through improved context and communication.

The key thing to focus on throughout our careers and time working with athletes is not the nuances of nomenclature but rather that true buy-in will always be built on a bedrock of trust. The two are intimately interwoven. Other coaches often ask me how I go about "getting" buy-in with my athletes. There is no misunderstanding on my part as the majority of these questions are coming from a good place, but I try to make it clear that buy-in is not something you can "get," permanently possess, or otherwise passively receive. Rather, it is a feeling that is built over time and must be maintained through a combination of loyalty, results, and consistent positive actions.

True buy-in is initially constructed from the ground up, through the connections that we make with our athletes as individuals. It is maintained via mutually earned respect and our ability to communicate and consistently bridge the gap between the training science that we all know and love as coaches and the way that our athletes perceive it when the actual training takes place. Buy-in is central to *Conscious Coaching* as it enables us to better connect with those we teach, serve, and lead.

"But how do I do that when time is a major factor?" is a question you might be asking yourself. I warn fellow coaches that we must tread carefully with that excuse. Many of us in the strength and conditioning world seem to take great pride in talking about how we are the year-round workhorses—first one in the building, last one out—and that we spend more time with the athletes than any other coach on the team. Given that, how can we say that we don't have the time? Nobody is insinuating that we tell the athletes to "pull out the couch," as my former colleague Joel Sanders liked to put it. This doesn't have to be some deep psychotherapeutic exploration of their darkest secrets. Just have a conversation! Dale Carnegie taught us that relationship building starts through first demonstrating interest in others. If buy-in is critical to working with athletes to accomplish their goals, it follows then that relationships are critical to buy-in.

Relationships

A relationship includes both the interdependence of two individuals working together to achieve a common goal(s) and a level of understanding between them (Knowles, Shanmugam, Lorimer 2015). In the sporting realm, it has been described as a "social vehicle" for the often long road to performance success, with positive relationships enhancing this experience and negative relationships prolonging or disrupting both progression and personal development (Knowles, Shanmugam, Lorimer 2015). Dr. Sophia Jowett, whose primary research revolves around the confluence of interpersonal relationships within the worlds of sport and coaching, believes that the relationship between a coach and an athlete can be conceptualized by the elements of both success and effectiveness (2005). Success relates to skill development and competition results, and effectiveness focuses upon personal satisfaction and the development of a rewarding bond. Relationships serve as the foundation of the influence that we have on others and that they have on us, while a humans' ability to form relationships was critical to our species' survival in the hunter-gatherer days. Many evolutionary psychologists posit that our ability to cooperate helped elevate us to the top of the food chain. If one person or tribe made a big kill, they would share it with others because in the future they might depend on others to share their food with them. Bonds were key to our survival. If you follow sporting culture you realize that this hasn't changed much, despite not having to go any further than the nearest COSTCO for a super-sized surplus of food. The success of individual coach-athlete relationships, teams, and even governing bodies depends largely on relationships. (For further detail on 3+1C, a scientific framework for developing relationships, see the appendix.)

Social Intelligence

The definition I use for social intelligence is inspired by internationally recognized social scientist and professor, Dr. Ross Honeywill. Social intelligence, according to Honeywill, refers to the exclusive ability of humans to navigate, negotiate, and influence social relationships and environments. Other authors such as Daniel Goleman, Robert Greene, and E.L. Thorndike (the originator of the term in 1920), have written about social intelligence. While all of these individuals have made solid contributions to our understanding of social intelligence, they have not discussed in great detail how social intelligence plays a strong daily role in the world of performance coaching—specifically, working with athletes from various backgrounds and pinpointing specific strategies that can be utilized to influence those interactions. In their 2014 book, The Upside to Your Dark Side: Why Being Your Whole Self – Not Just Your "Good" Self – Drives Success and Fulfillment, authors Todd Kashdan & Robert Biswas-Diener take a different route. Instead of using the term "social intelligence," they use the "social agility," which they define as the ability to recognize how one situation differs from another, and how to adjust our behavior to match these changing demands. Both definitions mentioned so far, along with many of their derivations, essentially boil down to having "people smarts." The research supporting these definitions is both recognized and appreciated, and it's up to us as coaches on the ground floor to advance it in a coaching environment.

Personally, I've always believed that one of the most overlooked signs of true intelligence is an individual's ability to avoid getting hung up on minor or irrelevant points. To properly illustrate this point, imagine yourself enjoying a day of barbecuing and hanging out with friends and family. The sun is out, you have a cold drink in your hands, and you're surrounded by people you love. The day couldn't be more perfect. Now imagine that your friend, let's call him Jim, begins to tell you a story about a recent event in his life. He tells you that he and a co-worker have started playing pickup basketball three times a week after work to break up his otherwise monotonous and sedentary routine. Even though you may not particularly care, or like basketball yourself, you are genuinely interested in listening to Jim's story because you think it's great that he's found something new that he enjoys. Now, imagine Jim starts telling you about the color of his shirt, his friend's favorite shoes, the number of points they average each game, the precise time in which they play, and the cost of the basketball they play with.

Do any of these details enhance the nature of the story? Likely not. Similarly, how would you expect Jim to react if you were to ask him such questions? He may oblige and give you a response, but would likely wonder why on earth you are asking these irrelevant questions. Yet many "intelligent" people get caught up in trivialities and miss the main point of a message. In their book, Made to Stick, authors Chip and Dan Heath refer to this as the "core" of the message. Displaying a compulsion for correcting others or an obsession for accuracy on minutia in social settings is the quickest way to go down a relational dead end: you will accomplish nothing other than gaining a reputation for being annoying or vexing. This is the antithesis of social intelligence.

The hallmark of a socially intelligent individual is one who can blend in with nearly any social setting. Many within our profession (and those like it) have yet to learn that it's not about being the smartest person in the room, but rather being the person who is the most capable of reading the room, and then doing something meaningful with the information you gather by speaking in a language that others can relate to and understand. Communication skills such as reflective listening, open body language, paraphrasing, humor and observation help us to more effectively build this necessary and influential rapport. We naturally seek and direct our attention toward things that affirm or validate our status, perceived uniqueness, concerns, or interests. Humans are unique from any other species in this manner. Dr. Thomas de Zengotita, a former professor of anthropology at Columbia University who now teaches at Dalton School and the Draper Graduate Program at NYU while also serving as a contributing editor at Harper's magazine, has stated that while "all mammals want attention, only human beings need acknowledgement" (Parr, 2015). In fact, you will stimulate physiological responses that trigger feelings of connectedness and relaxation just by listening to and acknowledging someone. This is advantageous when trying to capture someone's attention and make them more receptive towards your message. We will discuss the concept of emotional payments in Chapter 4, where you'll learn how to best capitalize on various strategies for eliciting this type of response on behalf of the listener.

The ongoing practice of carefully observing, relating and then communicating (both verbally and non-verbally) is what makes one truly socially intelligent or agile, but what exactly does communication mean? Think of communication as having two distinct elements: content and relation (DeVito 1986). When we first begin to communicate with another person, we are biased in the sense that both parties tend to be most focused on the information they are trying to convey to the other person. This is evident when you stand in front of your athletes to let them know the details surrounding a morning workout or tell your significant other about a promotion that you received after getting off the phone with your boss. This is also usually commonplace in most debate scenarios, in which one party will be stating their case while the other may be listening for key details from which they can base their reply or rebuttal. They are usually thinking about what they are going to say next, either to counter the points made by the other party, or to compliment them. It is certainly not uncommon for a significant degree of sub-vocalization to occur at the exact same time that the other person is speaking. Sub-vocalization is what happens when we say words in our head while reading or listening to someone or something. This form of "silent speech" can often be quite disruptive to the point that we nearly disengage from the moment and muffle any input that would otherwise be important to achieving a higher level of understanding.

In the above scenarios, the information we are eager to get off the tip of our tongues is an example of the content element of communication. This element of communication is the primary means by which we as coaches transmit or package technical and tactical information to our athletes, and thus it is crucial in developing our athlete's enhanced competence and performance (Poczwardowski, Barott, and Henschen 2002). This element is typically seen in the coaching setting through our verbal instructions or our physical demonstrations of a particular skill or drill. Due to the nature in which content-oriented communication can and does influence performance results, it is essential in creating a successful coach-athlete interaction. But, it's only half the battle.

Relation, the other half, is the WAY in which two or more individuals exchange information. Think of this as the way in which we deliver our previously packaged message to our audience via analogies and metaphors—

the use of which I refer to as "talking in color," since they make our message far more vivid and lively—and how we vacillate our tone of voice. The very notion of delivery (as used in the prior sentence) is a relational metaphor as we all can relate to having to choose between several different options whenever we order something online. After we order an item, the way in which it ultimately arrives into our arms is based on our individual preference of how and when we choose to receive it. Also included within the relational element is our body language, which includes things like eye contact, facial expression, and other non-verbal gestures that comprise up to 70 percent of all perceived communication (Burke 2005). The relational element of communication is typically more challenging to get right versus the content element, and it is one of the key areas in which Conscious Coaches separate themselves from the pack. This is also true for managers and teachers of all kinds. For example, two coaches can both have the same level of technical/tactical knowledge when teaching a concept or demonstrating a skill, but a Conscious Coach is able to deliver the message in a more expedient and personal manner. This involves flexing on relational elements of the message depending on the audience. To this point, the mantra I often give my interns or volunteer coaches to help them remember that there is much more to coaching than rote memorization or regurgitation is this: "Don't just teach the lessons, tell the stories." Information is most powerful when it is personal. This proverb speaks to the notion that HOW we communicate with others is often more important than the information by itself, and can profoundly influence how others respond to that communication (Montgomery 1988).

Time

Now that we've explored buy-in, relationships, and social intelligence—along with several of their subcomponents—the time has come (excuse the pun) for us to analyze the concept of "time" as it pertains to our coaching compass. Time as it's depicted within the coaching compass refers to the notion of having patience. Early in my career I was once told that patience was a "conquering virtue," meaning that it helps us to avoid the poor decisions that we so often tend to make when we act out of insecurity, ego or anxiety. I had never thought of time in this way until I heard it phrased in that manner. Young and eager to make a difference, I would often try too hard too early in the process, overly eager to "get" buy-in from my athletes instead of being patient and truly building it. I'd get frustrated and search for ways to hasten the process. The reality was that there wasn't anything I could do other than be consistent in my messaging, my practice, and my actions in proving to my athletes that I cared and had their best interests at heart. I understood what patience was, but being someone who has never taken a passive approach toward any part of my life, and certainly not my career, I had trouble waiting for anything to happen. In other words, I didn't even have enough patience to want to be patient! The entire process felt akin to that of having a pebble in your shoe while hiking a steep mountain and having to wait until a stopping point to get it out.

I had spent nearly an entire year in a hospital (more on that in a few pages) and I wanted to help others avoid the mistakes I'd made. During my time laid up, I began to acquire vast knowledge regarding the science of strength and conditioning, and I was eager to share it. But, in my mind, I needed to do it all right away. It wasn't until I stumbled upon a quote by author and speaker Joyce Meyer that I was put in my place and began to understand the power of patience with a new perspective. Meyer defined patience as not simply the ability to wait, but rather "how we behave while we're waiting." This quote is one of the best I've come across because it defines a word in a simple yet effective way, but also references the kind of behavior that goes along with the acquisition of a trait in its truest form. The best of anything cannot be rushed: cooking, architecture, training, art, and of course, our relationships with others. There's a reason why the best-tasting food cooks the longest; it allows all of the ingredients to blend together in order to bring out the true essence of the dish—and with it, a more satisfying end result.

Patience as it pertains to relationship management demands a combination of consistency, care, and the ability to let go. I've learned that, as a leader, sometimes the best thing you can do is to let go of a certain situation at a given time. People have to be ready to step up to the plate themselves at some point and no matter what you try to do you cannot force the desired endpoint—whether it is a relationship or specific training lesson learned. Athletes can be led, guided, and even loved, but may not be ready for change or to award trust at the same time that you are. This is a key piece of the transtheoretical model, which, born out of psychological science, discusses "stages of change" that an individual must undergo before being ready to adopt a new behavior or action. Understand that letting go is not the same thing as giving up. Sometimes moving forward requires letting go, so that when you come back the connection is more intimate.

Knowing when to step back is largely a matter of empathy. Empathy is one of the strongest leadership traits there is, and a powerful component of patience in and of itself. We will discuss the influential power of empathy further in Chapter 4. Cautionary advice for those who don't wish to practice the virtue of patience: try too hard and you will end up overcompensating in a manner where you not only will look foolish, but may even alienate or deteriorate the relationship or level or respect the athlete had for you in the first place.

Similar to chess masters, elite coaches are able to focus on the long play and see each step as a strategic move necessary to achieve an ultimate outcome. While we wait, we must continue to observe. Our vision within this capacity is not immediate, and it may take time to see what we need to do or say. Don't be afraid to distance yourself from the interaction and see how the game continues to play out. If you are met with a situation in which you feel absolutely stuck, allow your inner evaluator to turn off and remember to relax and go with the flow. This will allow the athlete the opportunity to engage on their own terms, and in doing so, they will provide you with insight as to what they care about or as to how they communicate. In other words, patience is a virtue.

Finding Our "True North"

With our coaching compass now in place and a newly calibrated viewpoint surrounding the importance of the micro-elements (Buy-In, Relationships, Social Intelligence, and Time), we now need to take a baseline inventory of ourselves. All of this talk about enhancing connections through knowing and understanding our audience is great, but how do we give it more meaning so that we can start putting this information to better use? It's key to remember that whenever we aim to influence others, we must first begin with a better understanding of what is influential about ourselves. The phrase "know your audience" is only helpful if you are confident that you have the necessary tools in order to successfully interact with them. If a stand-up comedian accidentally wanders onto the stage in which a symphony is about to perform, knowing that the crowd is expecting to hear music as opposed to the slapstick humor is pointless and problematic. The comedian has the tools for comedy, not music. We are the navigators and the guides, and therefore we must know what traits we possess ourselves so that we can leverage them in order to lead others in an optimal way. When an individual is able to identify their own communication style and tendencies, they possess the power to successfully navigate any social situation, whether it be a casual conversation or a speech delivered to a large crowd. This discovery process does not come easily and may in fact elude you at first, but with a bit of focused reflection and deep introspection, we can all more successfully excavate our own coaching identity.

CHAPTER 2
KNOW THYSELF
TO KNOW THY ATHLETES

"Study the heart and mind of man, and begin with your own." —
Lord Chesterfield

Do you remember when it first hit you? Many of you may recall your basement weight-room sets or the first "muscle rag" you ever purchased. At 14 years old, I would snag my dad's fitness magazines and scour the pages of just about anything else I could get my hands on, tearing out articles on everything from the "best" supplements to take, to new ways to stimulate or "shock growth" into different muscles. I would try every training program under the sun while laboriously writing down every detail in a spiral-bound training log. When I was done reading the magazines, I'd take pages from my favorite articles and place them carefully in plastic page protectors, inserting them into a large three-ring binder that was labeled "SIZE, STRENGTH & MASS BUILDING." To this day, I still have this black binder on the bookshelf next to my bed. My story is likely not unique to many of you, my fellow coaches. Over time, the hours spent in my bedroom late at night tearing out these pages were replaced by countless hours actually training others and later on, continuing my research inside of the small, musty office/storage space that I inhabited as a graduate assistant strength and conditioning coach at Southern Illinois University-Carbondale. Sitting under the pale glow of an incessantly buzzing fluorescent light, I searched through scientific databases and online journals, as well as countless blogs and websites, searching for anything I could find that would help me learn the best ways to train my athletes and stay on top of the latest findings and techniques. This office was so small that you would have had to leave the room in order to change your mind, but it served as the home and foundation for what became the bedrock of principles that I still abide by today. Many of you can probably relate with the long and arduous path of internships, volunteer roles, and part-time jobs that precede the blessing of actually getting a paid position as a full-time coach.

Details surrounding the blue-collar nature of common early experiences within the field—such as the early mornings, late nights, side jobs, sleeping in a car, set-up and cleaning duties, competitions, food and money scavenging, resume writing, and continual learning—have been well chronicled by a large number of other authors who have come before me, so I will spare you the fine details regarding my own professional sequence. This omission is not just out of respect to the aforementioned authors who have captured the essence of early professional struggles so well but also because, quite simply, it is not what got me here today. It is also my opinion that it's not the most important part in your journey, either. The details of our professional paths may provide others with information, but it's the details of our personal journeys outside of the weight room that provide insight to our true origins and coaching identities. Any time I am fortunate enough to speak at a conference or an event, I make it a point to state to others in the field that if you have identified your training philosophy before you have identified your coaching identity then you have misplaced your priorities. Exploring our past enhances our understanding of the present, and helps us to better refine our approach in the future.

At times, strength and conditioning can be a proud field in that those who inhabit it constantly display an indomitable will and a Superman persona. In a field that literally emphasizes the word "strength," we despise anything that could be perceived as weakness. But is it strong to feign perfection for the sake of perception? At what point did experiencing personal struggle in our past or present become something that we should be ashamed about or feel that we need to compensate for? I was always taught that when you get into a fistfight, it's not the guy that is bigger, taller, stronger, or more powerful that you should fear; but rather the guy that isn't fazed by the sight or taste of his own blood. In our field, if you want to be great, you better expect bruises and learn to love your battle scars.

Overcoming adversity means that you've gotten to know yourself on another level through pushing, progressing, and persevering through what, in the moment, may have seemed like a very negative situation. I believe that this sort of struggle begets strategy, and that it is in these times of adversity that we become who we are — both as people and as coaches.

The next part of this chapter contains the story of my own struggle: A no-holds-barred account of something that I used to shy away from discussing openly. I guess I never thought it would matter to anyone else but me, not to mention, I wasn't sure what others would make of it. I never wanted to explain myself and there was never any "quick" way to tell it, but the truth is that in order for someone to understand both the roots of where my natural intensity comes from and the way that I go about both coaching my athletes and living my life, they need to know about my past, a past in which I almost lost my life.

The experience that I am about to share with you brought extreme clarity to my longterm goal of helping others, and I hope it helps you to reconnect with a moment of your own past that influenced you in a similar way. Remember, without first knowing ourselves, we'll never be able to apply the tools of the coaching compass effectively.

Setting the Table:
How Struggle Begets Strategy

"Vires Acquirit Eundo" We Gather Strength as We Go.
-Virgil

There I stood in a hallway on the 8th floor of a hospital in Minneapolis, Minnesota, staring out the window. Barefoot, hospital gown wrapped tight, bandage around my arm from the morning blood draw. I stared out at a colorless landscape in the middle of winter. If you grew up in the Midwest or a part of the world with similar weather patterns, you know what this looks like: endless gray skies, bare trees, and grass frozen as if it had been terrified. The color palette of a Midwest winter consists almost entirely of grays, browns, and the white of snow when it falls. Oh, and it gets very cold. Growing up there, you complain about it a lot, but at the same time it hardens you and gives you strength. Midwesterners know how to persevere and overcome the familiar melancholy that can be brought about by these all too common gray days. You get used to it and learn that regardless of the weather outside, there is work to be done and life to be lived. You plow forward. After all, spring is just a few months away, right? At this particular moment in my life, however, the warmth of spring was not on my mind.

It started toward the end of my freshman year in high school. I had grown up playing baseball and football and as early as I can remember, my core group of friends had been my teammates. The spring and summer were filled with baseball and the fall and winter typically belonged to football. If we weren't playing in actual competitions or official practices, we could be found at the local park playing pickup games. I wasn't destined to be a professional athlete in either sport, or even a Division 1 collegiate athlete, but I was an above average player in both baseball and football and have always had a mean competitive streak, especially when it comes to competing against myself. During baseball season, we would play around 80 games in nearly 80 days and if I struck out more than 8 times during the season I would obsessively refine my swing in the batting cages. I took the same approach during the years that I played football. Practices and two-a-day workouts were never enough. I would wake up early and run hills, lift weights at our local gym later, and follow that with countless pushups and situps each night before I went to bed. The rule was that I always had to get them in before midnight, even if that meant finding ways to sneak them in when sleeping over at a friend's house so that they didn't think I was crazy. I had convinced myself that they wouldn't understand because their dedication likely didn't match mine, and at the end of the day, I simply didn't want to explain myself.

I've always been infatuated with seeing how far the human body can go. It was a curiosity that started early. In addition to my dad's magazines, whenever I had to go with my mom to the mall, I'd hit the bookstore and bury myself in the "health and fitness" section, killing time while she shopped. Unlike many other strength coaches, I didn't have a mentor when it came to training. No one guided me through the process. Our high school strength coach would sit in his office while a menagerie of awkward high schoolers gathered around the platforms to see who could perform the heaviest lifts with little to no regard for proper technique. Even then, at that young age, something felt intuitively wrong about a lot of the stuff my friends and teammates were doing. I felt their style of lifting was reckless, so I only did the lifts that I was familiar with, augmented by my own workout, which was inspired by whatever I had read in the magazines or books I had sifted through recently. I had no idea what I was doing, but at least it seemed to follow some kind of logical progression. Sitting here today, knowing the full value of asking questions rather than pretending, out of insecurity, to have all of the answers, I would love to tell you that I had the maturity and train of thought to just go ask the coach at school what to do. But I didn't. Instead, I wrote it off and moved forward with the inaugural version of what would later become Bartholomew Strength and its associated ventures.

Playing youth sports afforded me with automatic friendships. After all, there are only two options when you see the same group of people almost every day: you either hang out all the time or split up into groups. Over the course of time, we ended up doing both. From ages 10 to 14, the guys on my baseball team and I were inseparable, but the majority of them ended up going to a different high school. I lived further out on the west side of town, which placed me in a different school district. My parents were divorced and had joint custody of me and my brother. The arrangement was such that we would stay with my father on Tuesdays and Thursdays and my mother on Mondays, Wednesdays, and Fridays. The weekends would switch off, and if it seemed like I was packing a bag every night, it's because I was. Eventually, as I entered high school, I wanted to have more stability and not have to move back and forth all the time. At this stage in my life, all I wanted to worry about was school, sports, girls, and hanging out with friends—not what I would need to throw in my duffel for the next day. This led to a decision that remains one of the most difficult things I have ever done: I told my parents that I wanted to live with one of them full-time. My mother lived closer to my high school and it was easy to have friends at her place (based on where they all lived), so I had to tell my father the bad news. I'm not afraid to admit that I had tears in my eyes as I dialed the phone. I was 16 years old and didn't want my father, someone I have always had a good relationship with, to think I was choosing my mother over him. I certainly didn't want him to think that I didn't love him anymore. Rather, I just wanted him to understand that this new arrangement would make things a bit easier on me, and even though it hurt him at the time, ultimately, he did. Thankfully my parents did not live too far away from one another so it was easy to make arrangements to see him through our mutual involvement in sports, Nebraska football games, and other activities. At one point during my teenage years things with both parents were tough, but despite everything that our family has gone through, I'm thankful that we've always found a way to overcome tough losses and difficult decisions. We have faced dark times but have always found a way to reconcile, regroup, and move forward together.

After moving in with my mom full-time and finishing my first year of high school, things seemed to fall into a rhythm. I made new friends. Football and baseball helped me fall into new social circles. As my sophomore year came along, however, things looked less promising in my new social circle. Enter: drugs. To this day, neither drugs nor alcohol have ever had much appeal to me. But these were my new friends, and I was scared to abandon them and desperate to fit in. So, instead of sticking out like a sore thumb, I walked around at parties with an empty can or a full glass in my hand so that I never got questioned. I could deal with this stuff, but eventually casual get-togethers at a friend's pool turned into people smoking marijuana or doing cocaine in their parents' basement. I'll never forget the image of seeing a lifelong childhood friend passed out in his parents' bedroom after overdosing on cocaine. In that moment, it became evident it was time for me to get out of that social group and go my own way.

It wasn't just my new friends. Around this time, alcohol and drug abuse became major issues throughout my high school. The administrators didn't have any clue, which always baffled me. With the stress of separating myself from my friends and their newfound hobbies, compounded by dealing with changes on the home front, I turned to training as my outlet. We all have an escape in life that makes us feel euphoric, helps our thoughts flow more freely and makes every issue in life easier to deal with. For me, this was training. I was never the fastest kid on the team, or the guy that hit all the home runs, but for whatever I lacked in natural top-end talent, God blessed me with a capacity and ethic to do work that made up for it. Anyone who truly knows me or has trained with me can vouch for that. By turning to this escape and focusing on strengthening my body, training constantly and eating the way the magazines told me to eat (which at that time essentially amounted to "eat nothing," since we were in the midst of both the low-fat and low-carb fads), I thought that I was distancing myself from the kids at my school who were doing drugs. But in reality, I was becoming hooked on one of my own.

My two to three daily workouts became longer and more intense. I would find absolutely any way I could to burn calories or strengthen my body in hopes of getting an edge and making sure I left no resource in my body untapped. I had so much pent-up emotional energy and determination to see how far I could push my limits. Sometimes after a 2-hour lower-body workout, I would run 13-18 miles in no particular direction just to see where I would end up and how far I could go before physically gassing out. On Friday nights, when I knew my friends were out partying, I would drive to a local 24-hour gym at 10:30 or 11 PM and run for an hour on the treadmill, followed by sprints, and another 60- to 90-minute strength-training session. By the time I got home, it would be almost 2 AM and I would still do my routine of pushups and situps before finally going to bed. It was pointless, but at that moment in my life I didn't know any better. I was high on the notion that I was getting better and pushing my potential while my peers were messing up their bodies (with drinking and drugs). With each training session I became more obsessed with finding and correcting my own weaknesses. The perfectionist in me forever tried to expose new areas to develop and improve. I was completely hell-bent on bulletproofing myself, building myself up. Yet I had no idea how vulnerable and broken down I was.

THUD. My face hit the ground. Seconds later, I was surrounded by bystanders. I had passed out while running laps around our school track. If it wasn't evident at that point in time that my body was starting to shut down, it soon would be. At school, the talk about me shifted from "Wow, look how strong and cut Brett is!" to "Is he OK?" or "What's wrong with him?" In less than a year I had dropped from an already lean 135 pounds down to just over 100. It was never my intention to lose weight, but rather a byproduct of depression turned to obsession. What began as an outlet and a desire to gain a competitive edge—my relentless training—turned into a systemic wasting away of my body, and even my mind in some regards. The combination of physical stress and malnutrition severely affected my cognitive abilities. I developed patterns of Obsessive Compulsive Disorder. I was addicted to training and to what I thought was healthy eating. Looking back, while I am certainly to blame, I didn't do this to myself out of intent. I was utterly confused on how to train and eat because so much of what was in the magazines was garbage. Still, how could I have let this happen? I completely lacked awareness of what was happening; I was in a state of autopilot, manning the controls with a desire to be physically "perfect." (Clinically, I was labeled as "orthorexic," which means an obsession with healthy eating, which is ironic since nothing about the way I was eating was healthy.)

Passing out on the high school track was the first of a series of events that eventually lead to me getting help. My drastic change in appearance frightened my parents. For the next year, doctor's appointments and visits to various psychologists became routine. It was during these visits that I first experienced that the effectiveness of any practitioner is truly dependent on their ability to discover and see the underlying cause of a problem without being blinded by bias or a lack of understanding. Most lack the tacit knowledge and deep social intelligence that is shared by great communicators and influencers throughout the world. Instead, they see only the up-front manifestation of the underlying issue and attempt to remedy it with a playbook that is replete with pharmaceutical "treatment options," in/outpatient programs, and labels. These are their go-to tactics, supplied from their piles of studies and textbooks which instructs them on how to treat a "patient" rather than a person. Looking back, their approach served as the genesis for how I would later shape my own coaching style. I would coach from the "inside out" and influence the person inside of the athlete. Many of you understand that some coaches shape their plan and try to fit the athletes to it. Or, in the event that they are forward-thinking, shape their plan to their people but don't alter their coaching style in the same way, thus rendering their plan less effective than it could have been had they truly learned how to get inside their athletes' heads and hearts. This is the difference between "transactional" and "transformational" leadership, a paradigm developed by the presidential biographer James McGregor Burns in 1978 and further developed by Bernard M. Bass. Transformational leaders connect on a very deep and personal level, and they are often more effective for it.

Back to my own story, in which my downward spiral continued to pick up momentum. After being prescribed anti-depressants, I was put into an intensive inpatient program focused on eating disorders. The doctors had diagnosed me with a condition called Anorexia NOS, or "Not Otherwise Specified." This basically meant extreme weight loss that did not include typical eating disorder behaviors such as bingeing, purging, or a fear of being overweight. I was infuriated at this label. I was depressed, not anorexic. Even though I had certainly lost an extreme amount of weight, weight loss was never my goal, but rather a byproduct of my depression, lack of interest in food, and absurd obsession with training. I took their diagnosis as an insult and would blow up in their office whenever they insisted "the disease" had control and that I was "sick." It felt like a bad dream as I wanted them to understand that I was angry and confused at what was going on in my life and was trying to work my way out of it. But whenever I voiced those thoughts, they seemed to fall on deaf ears. I felt trapped. The only outlet that I knew for this kind of inner rage and frustration was training, something I was now prohibited from doing. It was as if I was paralyzed in a bad dream with no way out.

The intensive outpatient facility proved to be ineffective. A typical day involved my dad or mom dropping me off at around 7:30 AM and picking me up after their work day ended around 5:30-6. Despite the daily weigh-ins, rigid food control, group therapy, and hours on end sitting in a room with nothing to do until one of my parents picked me up, I continued to find ways to train by sneaking out and going for runs in the evening, or by telling my parents I was going to hang out with friends on the weekends when in reality I'd go work out wherever and however I could. I was utterly non-compliant with the program. In my mind I didn't belong there and they weren't helping. Pay attention to the last part of that previous sentence: it highlights a key error in my thought process at the time and how I approached my situation. I had adopted an external locus of control and blamed my surroundings and others for not helping me and holding me back. In order to get what I wanted most at the time— which was simply to regain the necessary weight without being subject to their "treatment" strategies and both the embarrassment and anger that I felt by having to be a part of it—all I had to do was play along for a while, gain the weight, and get out of there. But the truth is that I could not relate to the other patients, nor the group therapy discussions, because they were almost entirely centered on a fear of food and body image issues (which, per the above, was not my problem). The staff also tried to convince us that eating low-quality food like snack cakes, milkshakes, or other fat-laden and nutrient-devoid foods was "normal and healthy" eating behavior and was necessary if we were going to be successful at putting the weight back on and achieving a higher level of health. I felt like I was in prison, but little did I know that part of the story was actually still to come. My anger and embarrassment fueled my desire to "beat the system." These emotions cultivated a mental landscape that was nearly barren and grew nothing except doubt and distrust, fertilized by negative interactions with my family and those in the treatment center. I was not receptive to anyone or anything and spent what little energy I had strategizing how to get out or outsmart them.

I never ended up gaining much weight in the program and the situation actually got worse. I had lost over 30 pounds in total and the doctors had noticed that my kidney and liver enzymes were elevated to dangerous levels. My resting heart rate had dropped below 34 beats per minute. The combination of those factors put me at severe risk for a cardiac event and the treatment center staff recommended that I be hospitalized immediately. One day soon after, I awoke to find all three members of my immediate family at the bottom of my staircase. My parents had decided to place me into an even more intense inpatient treatment facility where my activity level and food intake would now be monitored 24/7 with rigid stipulations. I fled. Refusing to be put into the program, I grabbed my car keys and, when they weren't paying attention, I ran out the door and took off. My brother came after me. I proceeded to lead my brother in a high-speed chase through city streets. Looking back, I realize how fortunate I was that neither of us, nor anyone else, was hurt as I blew through stop signs and drove at high speeds through residential areas. At one point, I took such a hard left turn that my brother crashed his car into a bunch of trash cans and ended up in someone's yard. I was 16 years old, angry, and felt like my life was getting out of control. I eventually lost him, but returned home eight hours later. I had nowhere to go. I was out of options. I had to face the music, however loud and disturbing it might have been.

I remember during the intake process feeling like I was being read rule after rule as if I was going to prison. Aside from the 24-hour monitoring, any reading material you brought with you was looked through and closely examined, as were all of your bags and belongings. The room they provided for me and the rest of the patients could be entered at any time by the facility's staff. Once I was in the program, we were not even allowed to go into our rooms without supervision and were restricted to a "day room" area for the majority of the day, except for meals or snacks. The sport science junkies reading this would be happy to know that absolutely everything in this place was objectively measured. I underwent daily blood draws every morning at 5:15, followed by weigh-ins and a shower, but only if the hospital staff felt it was safe. With the state that my vitals were in, they were scared that the initial shock of hot or cold water would send me into cardiac arrest. This is a true story. I was messed up. Under the guidance of a hospital dietician, we filled out weekly menus that followed a format similar to that of the diabetic exchange system—which lists common foods such as a chicken breast, a slice of bread, a tablespoon of peanut butter and a cup of spinach under categories such as "meats," "starches," "fats," and "vegetables"—so that patients didn't focus on calories. All food was measured, and every bit of it had to be consumed without protest. No physical activity whatsoever was allowed unless you had progressed to a certain level in the program, and even then it was limited to stretching and exercises with 3-lb dumbbells and ankle weights while sitting on a stability ball. If you had to use the restroom, a nurse would stand outside the door to ensure you weren't doing anything in it other than going to the bathroom. There was no sense of privacy or really any dignity whatsoever.

Most of my days were spent in the aforementioned day room. It featured a few tables, a desk, a couch, and some chairs. The hospital staff could view through a Plexiglass window while they sat at the main desks. They would tap on it to warn you if you were participating in "unauthorized behavior" of any kind such as fidgeting, chewing gum or even simply standing up (since standing burns more calories than sitting). We could only read approved books or magazines that were not training, diet, or even sports related. Only PG movies were allowed, and if you stood for too long a time, fidgeted, or chewed gum, you were only given two warnings before they either made you drink a meal replacement or at the worst, threatened (yes that word choice is accurate) to utilize intravenous feedings to replace any calories you may have burned through non-exercise activity. The dining room where we gathered to eat our total of six meals throughout the day was another experience. If the day room made you feel like an animal in a zoo, then the dining room made you feel like a lab rat. The underlying tension and aggressions of all of the patients was escalated by the presence of hospital staff seated at both ends of the glass table we ate on. Two nurses in particular seemed to take an odd joy in speaking to all of us in condescending tones and found ways to make life in the hospital even more miserable. One nurse in particular, who I'll refer to as Rita, was the worst of them.

The nurses were there to supervise the meals and to make sure that none of the patients were hiding food, mixing it in odd ways to disguise taste, or partaking in any other number of odd behaviors. But oftentimes, these nurses would accuse patients who had done nothing wrong, or threaten to give them a meal replacement at the first sign of any apprehension. This was anything but effective. It only increased patient anxiety, creating a negative feedback loop in regard to eating. During one of my first days at the facility, Rita accused me of hiding food when in fact the hospital dining staff had forgot to place it on my tray. She was writing up a report that would have further restricted any privileges and ultimately would have cost me more time in the program when someone from downstairs finally came up and admitted the mistake was theirs, not mine.

As I sat in the dining room that day, I remember thinking that I had never witnessed anything as odd as some of the behaviors I observed amongst the other patients while they ate their meals. We all sat side by side and across from one another so there was no way to ignore it, even if you kept your eyes down. Here I was at 16 years old surrounded by people of all ages, many of whom would break down emotionally, cut their food into minuscule pieces, and sit at the table staring at their food for hours on end. At first I figured they were afraid of food or other forms of treatment the hospital was administering. With time, however, and as I got to know many of the other residents, I realized that they all had bigger issues in their life, just as I did. The only difference was that while exercise was my way to deal with depression, food was their control mechanism for whatever it was they were dealing with. One patient's husband had left her for another woman. Another was the middle child of nine siblings and used negative food-related behaviors to keep some form of attention on her as she otherwise felt lost in the shuffle at home. Another man, who was around my age, was a former junior Olympic wrestler who fell into a similar trap that I had after he experienced his first defeat. The memory of his loss had consumed him mentally, and he routinely went overboard on dieting and training as if it could somehow affect the outcome that had been decided long ago. While many of the other patients could leave if they wanted to, since I was a minor, I was forced to remain until medically discharged.

The last bit of our day was reserved for therapy and one-on-one sessions with more psychologists. Once again, nearly all therapy sessions revolved around food-related behaviors and other issues not related to the underlying problems that patients were experiencing. The hospital had its curriculum and seemed never to waiver from it. Any time I said I couldn't relate to an issue we were discussing in therapy, Rita would tell me I was in denial and mark down that I was non-participatory. This had the effect of prolonging my stay in the program due to me showing "little to no sign of progress."

I spent over six months of my life in that hospital, including nearly my entire sophomore year of high school. Every day felt as if I was waking up to a life that wasn't mine and any time I tried telling someone my real story— the things that I believed were the root cause of my issues —it fell on deaf ears. In his book, *Thinking Fast and Slow*, behavioral scientist Daniel Kahneman writes, "To be a good diagnostician, a physician needs to acquire a large set of labels for diseases. Each of which binds an idea of an illness and its symptoms, possible antecedents and causes, possible developments and consequences and possible interventions to cure or mitigate the illness." It was clear that while some staff at the hospital certainly seemed to care, the majority had only mastered the "acquiring a large set of labels" part of Dr. Kahneman's description. Rather than adapting their program's approach to the individual patient, they believed that each patient could fit into a singular, rigid system. This happens in the coaching world, too.

Eventually, I was fortunate enough to meet a psychologist named Katy, whose mastery of thoughtful, non-judgmental listening and close observation eventually provided me a way out. It was our first meeting, and I walked into it expecting to fight the same battle I had fought with all of the others at the hospital. It was already odd enough having to talk to a therapist of any kind in the first place, as the stigma behind therapy creates the image that it is only for criminals, psychopaths, or others who are mentally unstable or weak. I remember our initial discussions had nothing to do with the hospital or my current state of health. No clipboards, no theoretical questions about why I thought I was there, no having me lay on the proverbial couch sharing my deepest, darkest fears or regrets. In other words, no bullshit. Instead, Katy wanted to know what made me tick. She got right down to business and asked me what it was I wanted, and how I thought I could get there. No hypotheticals or strings attached. She got to know the whole me, which undoubtedly helped her to figure out the origin of the behavior that got me into this situation, and what it was that could help get me out. She could sense that although I had initially sought out to forge my own path after seeing the one my friends took (i.e., drugs), I had instead lost my way and was blinded by my own anxiety and anger. But she also knew that if I could channel my energy in the right way, I could get better and move on with my life. Once we worked this out together, the appropriate path could be established. Answering the question about what I stood for in particular was easy. Even though at the time I didn't know exactly how, I knew I wanted to make a difference in the world and that I couldn't do it while I was in the hospital. I was confident that I could gain back the weight I needed to gain, and do so in a much healthier way than the hospital attempted to enforce. But first, I needed to gain the necessary weight to get medically discharged.

Once I did that, I was never looking back.

The Escape

My sessions with Katy progressed, and for once I felt like I had someone inside the hospital who was in my corner, someone who truly understood what underpinned the behavior that had gotten me into this mess in the first place. Thanks to Katy's help, I eventually got to a point within the program where I was afforded time off-campus with supervision. It had been over five months and I hadn't stepped foot outside the 8th floor of the hospital. Despite the fact that I walked outside into the dead of a Minnesota winter, the sting of the cold air might as well have been the warmth of the hot sun on a beach. It felt great. Even so, this wasn't a vacation. It was time for me to get out of the hospital for good. I had a plan. I convinced my mother to take me to a nearby Barnes and Noble bookstore; I only had an hour and needed to act fast. I went straight to the part of the store that had books on sports and fitness and I quickly grabbed two books, *The Sports Nutrition Guidebook* by Nancy Clark, and *Complete Conditioning for Football* by Boyd Epley. You can say whatever you want about these books in light of today's current methods and research, but at the time both served as invaluable resources that helped me get out of that hospital. These books played a role in saving my life. Nancy Clark's book helped me to better understand the difference between "fueling" and fad dieting, the latter of which was often showcased in many of the magazines I had previously read. As for Boyd Epley's book, I figured that if his "HUSKER POWER" program could help the Cornhuskers football team win five National Titles, it certainly could put some weight on a scrawny high-school kid from Nebraska like me. The book placed a premium on following a structured, progressive routine based upon sound principles of physical adaptation rather than what I had always done, which could be defined simply as "as much as possible of everything under the sun." Later in my life, Mark Verstegen's book, *Core Performance*, taught me that rest is not something to looked down upon. Rest could be used as a weapon, another concept that was foreign to me at the time of my youthful train wreck.

I knew that I couldn't take these books back into the hospital as they would be confiscated immediately, so I grabbed the book jackets of two other non-fitness related books of a similar size and used them to disguise the covers. We paid, thanked the cashier, and quickly headed back to the hospital. As I stepped off of the elevator and back onto the 8th floor, I was relieved to see that the nurse on duty was not Rita, but rather a new nurse who had just joined the staff. I took advantage of her rookie stature by briefly flashing the books in the bag, not giving her the chance to open them up and investigate more closely. I read both books in little more than two days. Since I couldn't sneak them into the day room without risking others noticing, I would read them once we had to retire to our rooms in the evening. I kept them stashed under my mattress and would literally have to time my reading around the staff's regular evening visits. Page by page, I started to piece together a plan to get myself back on track once I left the hospital. It was easy to see where I had gone wrong and how I could correct it. The only thing left to do was to gain my parents' trust so that I could actually implement my plan. Thankfully Katy helped me to do just that.

Moving Forward

After what seemed like an eternity, I was finally medically cleared to leave the hospital. I said goodbye to a few of the other patients, Katy, and some of the staff. As I headed toward the elevators for the last time, Rita made one more appearance. At first, I figured she was going to wish me luck. Instead, she simply told me that she didn't agree with the decision that I was cleared to be discharged and she was confident that I would be back. Angry, but not surprised, I stared back at her and simply told her she was right—I would be back; back to speak to and help the patients that she had neither the competence nor the compassion to help herself. As the elevator door closed behind us, so did this chapter of my life. I had a newfound perspective on training, nutrition, and life in general. And perhaps most importantly, I was ignited and eager to use my experience to help others. I regained the weight necessary to restore my body to full health, finished high school, and went on to obtain my undergraduate degree in kinesiology and a Master's degree in exercise science. During my last year of high school, I took up boxing and personal training. In college, I began competing in amateur boxing tournaments and would also train other fighters at my gym in exchange for free training of my own. Not long after I had graduated college, I set my sights on a career in strength and conditioning.

To this day I use my past as a platform to inspire my coaching style. At 16 years old I had come dangerously close to losing my life. I had witnessed the struggles of others up close and personal on that 8th floor of the hospital. I also witnessed countless professionals in a variety of fields who, despite their high level of education, professional accolades, titles or scale of pay, seemed to have no idea as to how to truly help people. Their myopic view of people and what drives or affects them was alarming.

These experiences forever changed me as they brought a tremendous sense of urgency to my life. People and athletes everywhere are looking for help. And as much as we'd like to think the next person in line has it covered or has their shit together, you cannot assume this to be the case. It's up to us as coaches to help them as people first, and athletes second.

Unfortunately, too many "leaders" or "coaches" or "teachers" lose their way, much like Rita did at the hospital, and end up doing more harm than good. Their lack of social and emotional intelligence can spread like a virus.

The antidote is you. Rise up and use your past experiences as a tool to better define the person you are and the professional that you want to become. Keep reminders of past struggle close to you so that you never forget the feeling that compelled you to strive for more and make a difference in the first place. Whether you listen to an old song that played during a pivotal moment in your life, view a picture of the house that you lived in when times were tough, or visit a specific place where it all started, these simple things help us to reconnect with past feelings which, in turn, helps center us so we can stay on track.

A few years ago I asked my neighbor, who happened to be an artist, to paint a picture of a street that I used to run down in college whenever I needed to clear my head. More specifically, I asked her to recreate a specific image of me running down the street in the dark while it was snowing, as this was something I often did during a time when I was beginning to outline the specific steps I'd take to carve my future path. She did a tremendous job capturing the essence of that cold, dark, quiet evening. The picture is hung in my upstairs hallway and is one of the first things I see when I wake up and the last thing I walk by before going to bed, always serving as a reminder of the importance of not being scared to go your own way regardless of the hardships that you may incur as a result of it. Find or create your own artifact from your past and you'll see the role it will continue to play in shaping your coaching identity and strategy in the years to come. Reflecting on these stories and artifacts is a powerful way to improve your self-awareness as coach and act upon your unique strengths and motivations. If nothing comes to mind or you find yourself stuck, worry not. The next section will provide a number of unique insights geared toward helping you spotlight traits or tendencies that may have otherwise remained hidden in the shadows.

Identity & Strategy:
Improving Your Self-Awareness

As coaches, we are often the primary agent in the behavior change of those with whom we work. Everything we hope to do and every change we hope to make begins with our own self-awareness. Whether we are trying to shape or reshape the cultures or organizations that we are a part of, the perceptions of the athletes/clients that we guide, or the athletes/clients themselves at an individual level, we must take a step back and closely reflect upon our own past, the lessons it's afforded us along the way, and how it's shaped who we are today. Knowledge of one's self and how others perceive you allows you to adapt across diverse situations, making you more socially intelligent.

In other words, "self-awareness" is a not just a key term, it's a critical skill.

No matter how you may view your own leadership style or personality, there's a good chance there are particular traits you possess (both good and bad) that you have yet to identify. These traits could significantly affect your success as a coach. Are you the type of coach who identifies with the transformative strain and struggle that the weight-room atmosphere often provides? Or, do you find yourself animated by the dynamic movement that you teach, in which you have an intuitive feel of what must come next in a particular drill or how an athlete could have made a better play had they taken a slightly better angle, cut or transition? It's not about obsessing over about whether you are decidedly one or the other (i.e., in the example above, what some may call a "weight-room coach" versus a "movement coach"). Rather, the real key is to know why you tend lean the way that you do so that you can learn to better leverage and amplify those specific and highly influential traits. A method that I've developed which may prove helpful in fostering this kind of self-awareness is to follow the three stages of what I refer to as **Internal Identification**.

Stages of Internal Identification

Reflection: *Questioning* Who You Are
Inspection: *Examining* Who You Are
Progression: *Owning* Who You Are

Reflection involves digging deep into your past and thinking critically about transformative moments within it. (Much like I did earlier in this chapter.) This sort of reflection is critical as it helps you get to the bottom of your drives and also the origins of those drives. When asked what we do and why we do it, many give superficial answers such as "to help others" or "to make a difference." We answer in this way because it may keep us from having to give the non-CliffsNotes version of what really drove us toward what we do in the first place. If you thought that this book would provide you with a better understanding about the psyche of others without making you do the work of better understanding yourself, you are mistaken. At some point, you are going to have to ask yourself some reflective questions if you want to discover how your past laid the foundation for who you are today.

Do you want to make a difference? Great. Why? Why is it important for you to do so and what experience did you have or witness in the past that set you off on such a path? You want to be one of the best so that you can earn a great living to better provide for you and your family? Outstanding! What does being a great provider actually look like to you? How can you lay out appropriate action steps and breathe life into them if you don't break them down to their most base elemental structure? Push yourself to strip away the superficial and get to the root of everything you do. If you truly want to affect people, you better know how to be in touch with yourself and every single one of your drives and vulnerabilities as a human being. I went through this questioning exercise myself over four years ago during a layover in the Denver airport while traveling home for the holidays. It was a time when I was very conflicted about what I ultimately wanted out of my career. It was incredible how much clarity it drove home for me, helping to better align my actions with my fundamental beliefs and values for what I wanted as a person and a professional. Reflection can never be ignored. Thorough self-reflection isn't only critical to becoming a better coach, but also a better person.

Inspection pertains to you taking the insights excavated from your reflection and examining them more closely. Doing so will help you ensure that you embed these insights into your actions as a coach. For example, I know that my experience in the hospital led me to a vivid realization of the shortness of life and how few people out there seem to care about helping others in general, let alone helping others to overcome struggle. Against this backdrop, it becomes easier to understand my intense coaching style and chronic sense of urgency. I saw firsthand through the passive and detached behavior of the hospital staff that I dealt with how the inability to authentically connect with others can smother someone's chance to make real progress. I also saw how toxic an entire environment can become when a few people working in it bring a shitty and rigid attitude. This taught me the importance of aligning my own values with those of my athletes and clients. I need to meet them where they are so we can work together to achieve their goals. Simply telling someone what to do hardly ever yields positive long-term results. If reflection helps us to reconnect with who we really are, then inspection helps us connect with who we want to become, along with the traits we want a future version of our ideal self to adopt.

Progression is the next natural step after we understand the roots of who we are (reflection) and who we want to become (inspection). Progression is about moving closer to who we want to become. It is perhaps the hardest part of this three-part framework and is far easier said than done. Progression involves actually doing the things we must do to bridge the gap between who we want to be (based on the values and insights surfaced during our reflection and inspection) and who we are. One of the biggest obstacles that stands in the way of many hoping to achieve and progress through this third and final step is called *imposter syndrome*, which we will explore more in the next section. For now, just know that all the reflection and inspection in the world is rather pointless if you don't use what you learned to cross the bridge from where you are today to where you want to be tomorrow. That's what progression is all about.

Imposter Phenomenon

Imagine being operated on by someone who claims to be a trauma surgeon, but who in fact lacks any formal medical training or schooling whatsoever; or finding yourself in a quiet room divulging your deepest secrets to a licensed psychologist who isn't actually licensed to practice and is posing under a fake name. Now extrapolate a bit and imagine that this same person is also masquerading around as a prison warden, a monk, a cancer researcher, and a minister duping everyone he meets nearly everywhere that he goes. How would you feel once you found this out? More importantly, how would you feel if it were you who were asked to serve in these roles (and I don't mean at Halloween costume parties or during you and your spouse's "date nights"). I mean, actually acting as if you serve in these roles even though you may not be trained or licensed to do so, or have any true knowledge in any of these fields. This somewhat absurd scenario was common practice for Ferdinand Waldo Demara Jr., who is most famously known as "The Great Imposter" after pretending to be all of the above, not to mention many other professions, including a civil engineer and lawyer. Demara took on so many unique identities that his likeness served as the inspiration for a 1961 film, The Great Imposter. Crazy as it may seem, his story in some ways resembles the practices of coaches who struggle to find an identity of their own, or who struggle to develop a sense of true self confidence and don't take the time to go through the above stages of identification. Demara claimed that his roleplaying was a medium that he relied upon to search for that very same kind of identity, telling *People* magazine in 1977, "Reality to me is best defined by the Latin adage 'Esse quam videri.' That means to be, rather than to seem. I have learned that now, but in my earlier years I reversed it." In his attempts to do so, he proceeded to take on role after role and task after task, hoping that eventually something would stick and give him the self validation of an expert that he so desperately craved.

Imposter syndrome (which is now becoming more commonly known as *imposter phenomenon* since it is not viewed as a true medical disorder or diagnosis) is a term that researchers and psychologists Pauline Rose Clance and Suzanne Imes coined and is often used when referring to an intense internal feeling of "fakery" and anxiety that otherwise high-achieving and highly competent individuals experience. More specifically, it is marked by an inability to internalize accomplishments and a persistent fear of being exposed as a "fraud" by an individual(s) of true significance. (Clance and Imes, 1978). Clance and Imes detail that those who struggle from imposter syndrome do so despite external evidence of their competence within a domain and remain convinced that they are frauds and do not deserve the success they have achieved. They dismiss any success or skill as luck, timing, or as a result of deceiving others into thinking they are more intelligent and competent than they believe themselves to be. This is the exact opposite of what is known as the Dunning-Kruger effect, which is a cognitive bias that exists where individuals who possess a very low level of ability or true competence perceive themselves to be vastly superior to those around them or in their abilities in general. Some studies suggest that impostor phenomenon may be even more common amongst high-achieving women, which can be especially easy to imagine in coaching given the current level of male dominance of our profession.

So how could ignoring inspection and reflection lead us to feel the way in which those who suffer from imposter phenomenon feel? Simple: If we don't clearly and accurately define our own drives, identity, and desires, it becomes increasingly more likely that we will find it more difficult to narrow down a path of our own—a path that ultimately fulfills us or directs us toward a specialized development of unique skills. We could easily find ourselves stuck between both imposter phenomenon and the Dunning-Kruger effect if we let our own insecurities and anxieties guide us as opposed to practices that lead to enhanced self-realization. As members of a multidisciplinary and research-driven field, we also must avoid getting caught up in the habit of social comparison. Some experts in the field of psychology have shown that feelings of "imposterism" are more pronounced within the realm of science and academia since highly intelligent people tend to spend more time around other highly intelligent people, thus further skewing our own perceptions and magnifying our own insecurities.

Reflection helps you focus and quiet the noise that our minds can generate. If you enjoy speaking on a particular subject but instead begin speaking on topics you may be less passionate about simply because others in the industry seem to be making a name for themselves in doing so, you will likely find yourself wondering how you "measured up" to them. Or, you might end up wondering if you made a mistake when citing research you are unfamiliar with. We have seen this happen with all of the trends that have come and gone (or lingered) in our industry. Every year, another paradigm or practice seems to erupt into mass popularity— thus enticing us to "broaden our scope"— when in fact, sometimes we are best suited to simply wait it out and see if the claims match the hype, which they rarely do.

Imposter phenomenon may strike all of us at times, but through this continual reflection and inspection process, we will perform the critical groundwork necessary to stay on a specific and targeted path towards achieving our goals as leaders, coaches, and communicators. Tom Rath, *New York Times* bestselling author and lead consultant to the research firm Gallup, stated it far more concisely. "The key to human development is building who you already are," he said. Rath is right. To better establish a true identity and strategy of our own, we must understand our past, understand the strengths that were born as a result of our past, and finally, understand how to leverage those strengths in order for us to learn how to best put them to use for the benefit of others. We each have unique and distinct strengths and skills, and should aim to seek out strategies that serve as identifiers and multipliers of those strengths. Remember: It is authenticity, not mimicry, that best serves as the coach's initial linchpin toward establishing a strong connection with others. It is only by cultivating this authenticity that the last step of the three-part "Stages of Internal Identification"—where we close the gap from who we are to who we want to be—is possible.

We must be honest, original, and true to ourselves in order to be strong leaders. There are more tools than ever before to help you continue discovering how to be honest, original, and true to yourself. Now that we've looked at the "Stages of Internal Identification" framework—reflection, inspection, progression—let's look at a few other tools that can help you to better know yourself.

Get to Know Yourself Better: Tools of the Trade

There are a number of online personality assessments that span a wide range of detail and complexity. These assessments can be very helpful in learning more about yourself and how you may be predisposed to deal with others. There are far too many to detail here, so I've picked out a few classics as well as some that you may not be familiar with: **Clifton StrengthsFinders System, the DISC Assessment, The Myers-Briggs Type Indicator (MBTI), Insights Discovery, and the Hogan Personality Inventory**. While by no means a comprehensive list, these assessments are amongst some of the most well-known and are commonly used by businesses worldwide and more recently, even some sporting organizations. *Psychology Today* reports that around 80 percent of Fortune 500 companies use personality tests such as the Myers Briggs Type Indicator (MBTI). The American Society for Training and Development reported that U.S. companies spend $110 billion per year on training programs, with as much as 60 percent of that $110 billion coming from programs that include interpersonal skills assessments!

The goal here is not to get into a debate of superiority or to label which of these methods is the best. They can all be effective in various circumstances. The goal here is to simply provide you with a set of resources that can help you gain additional insight as it pertains to your behavioral/perceptual tendencies so that you can discover some things that you did not recognize previously about yourself or the way that you engage with others. Resources like these need not be perfect in order to be practical; rather, they just need to be seen for what they are: tools that can help you learn more about yourself. It's probably best to adopt Bruce Lee's stance of "absorbing what is useful" while not mistaking any of the findings or suggestions these assessments produce as gospel. Collectively, these are fantastic tools and it would be irresponsible for me not to mention them in a chapter that implores you to seek ways to better understand the core of your character. Even so, just as a performance profile containing information regarding an athlete's physical aptitude does not define him or her as an individual, the results of these various personality profiles do not define you as an individual.

Take a moment to further familiarize yourself with each of the systems. For easy review, I have included brief background and high-level bullet points regarding each assessment. Many of the assessments have different "levels" available for purchase, so if you go on to use any of these, you may note subtle variation from what I outline below. I have also included the website URL for each assessment in the event you would, in fact, like to dive more deeply. Please also note that any criticisms highlighted below are not a reflection of my own views but rather are openly expressed by others who have taken the test themselves, utilized the tools included along with the tests, or have done similar reviews of their own. Of course I do favor some of these tests over others, but my purpose is to help you become familiar with what works best for you and your situation, not to push a particular product or to facilitate a "clean hands" bias on your behalf. (In which you favor something just because someone else said they like it and not because you've experienced it for yourself.) Remember that these are tools that help to spark further discussion and deeper reflection, nothing more. So work to restrain your inner "internet warrior" before taking to your keyboard or social media because the one you favor was not represented to your liking. It is also critical to remember that any test, measure, or "indicator" of a given personality type or attribute will only be as valid or reliable as the actual individual taking the test. The reliability and validity of each is and can be affected by how the tests are presented, administered, evaluated, and debriefed. Use these as a conversation tool or as a form of self-discovery, or don't use them at all—the choice is yours. Just remember that sometimes even an imperfect artifact can end up being of immense value if you put it under the correct light and in the hands of someone who knows what they are looking for. The following pages list some of the most common assessment tools on the market.

Clifton StrengthsFinder

The Clifton StrengthsFinder system (www.strengthsfinder. com/home.aspx) is the culmination of 50-plus years of work performed by Dr. Donald O. Clifton. Clifton's research was inspired by the idea of finding what is right with people as opposed to more classical texts, such as the DSM-IV, which typically categorizes what is wrong with someone. Dr. Clifton has won awards from the American Psychological Association Presidential Commendation and has become known as the "father of strengths-based psychology" by his peers. The StrengthsFinder system is broken down into 34 themes which aim to help users find a common language as it pertains to identifying unique personal attributes and unique strengths and/or talents.

Key Characteristics

- You have 20 seconds to respond to each item presented within the assessment.

- Assessment features 177 pairs of self-descriptive statements such as "I dream about the future" or "People are my greatest ally."

- The goal of the assessment is to help you identify where you align amongst the assessment's 34 themes based on your instinctive responses which, like other deep-seeded drives, are less likely to change over time even though you as an individual will.

- Once you have finished, you will immediately receive your top five "signature themes" in ranked order and you will also get a packet of information which will help you to better understand each theme and its distinctive characteristics.

Criticisms

- Many of the prompts listed are very general and may apply to a large range of people. A characteristic that is more widely known as the "Barnum Effect."

- The test only searches for strengths, not weaknesses. This can be a problem, as oftentimes learning where you are weak is more important than learning where you are strong.

DiSC Assessment Profile

The DiSC assessment (www.discprofile.com) has been around for quite some time. It is the brainchild of Dr.

William Marston, the individual who is responsible for the actual "DiSC" theory itself, which he originally constructed in the late 1920's. His theory is focused on the psycho-social trifecta of 1) how an individual tends to perceive him/herself within a given situation; 2) the resulting emotions associated with that individual's perceptions of the situation; and 3) the likely subsequent behaviors or responses to those emotions. Interestingly, Marston never intended that the DiSC theory be used as an assessment. It was not until his friend, industrial psychologist Walter Vernon Clarke published a body of work known as the Activity Vector Analysis that DiSC took on more of its self-descriptive form. After several permutations, the actual assessment was formally introduced in the 1970's.

The letters stand for "Dominance," Influence," "Steadiness," and "Conscientiousness," which serve as the cornerstone descriptor traits behind Marston's behavior profile. The assessment claims to help improve work productivity, teamwork, and communication, as well as to help people better understand themselves. Additionally, the test claims that it helps people better adapt their behaviors in social situations. It is one of the more recognized profiles that exists on the market today. The DiSC website makes it clear that the goal is to measure your personality and behavioral style and NOT your level of intelligence.

(As a funny aside: I remember first taking the DiSC assessment for a class in 6th grade. Clearly I had a forward thinking teacher, but just imagine the comedy behind this notion for a moment. There I sat, a 12-year-old scrawny twerp, barely knowing how to dress—let alone how to be truly introspective—only to have the computer spit out results and tell me it knew nearly everything about me at a time in my life when I was still trying to decide whether I should buy Sega Genesis or Super Nintendo with the lawn-mowing money I had saved up!)

Key Characteristics

- Focuses primarily on patterns of behavior.

- Either forced choice ("Which word describes you the most/least?") or via a rating scale ("Strongly agree/ disagree.")

- Typically takes 15-20 minutes to complete

- Scoring is done electronically or by hand and produces a profile report that details your unique behavioral style, needs, tendencies, and strategies for effective behavior.

- Each report also includes information about other DiSC styles which helps to better understand other profiles as well (helping you to learn not only more about yourself but also more about others who you work with).

- Offerings (that is, varieties of the assessment) range from more generalized assessments to those that are more focused, depending on environments and context (leadership styles, enhanced relationships in workplace etc.)

Criticisms

- Forced-choice questioning: This kind of question formatting makes survey respondents choose a response based on a definitive opinion or descriptor trait even if it doesn't exactly match what they really feel describes them. That is, there is a risk of false precision.

- Seems to predict energy for solving certain problems but not how successful one would be at actually solving them.

- The DiSC is considered an ipsative test (compares you to yourself) as opposed to a normative one (compares you to the population). This means the assessment measures the relative strength of traits for a single person (themselves) versus how the test taker stacks up against the greater population.

Myers-Briggs Type Indicator (MBTI)

Inspired by Carl Jung's typological theory described in his book, Psychological Type, the Myers–Briggs Type Indicator (MBTI; www.myersbriggs.org) was developed by the mother-daughter pair of Katharine Cook Briggs and Isabel Briggs Myers. Jung had speculated that there are four principal psychological functions by which humans experience the world—sensation, intuition, feeling, and thinking—and that one of these primary functions is dominant for a given person the majority of the time (Kaplan and Saccuzzo 2009). The underlying assumption of the MBTI is that we all have specific preferences as it pertains to the unique way that we construct and give meaning to our experiences, and that these preferences serve as the bedrock for our interests, needs, values, and motivations. Despite the many criticisms of Carl Jung's philosophies and how they have been interpreted by the MBTI, the assessment remains one of the most popular ones and is used by a wide array of organizations today.

Key Characteristics

- Aimed at helping individuals to better understand how they are predisposed to view and interact with the world around them.

- The current North American English version includes 93 forced-choice questions whereas the European English version features 88.

- Typically takes around 30 minutes to complete.

Criticisms

- As with the DiSC, the nature of the "forced choice" questioning format lends itself to only two options, yet when it comes to trying to understand people in all of their incredible complexity, the nature of binary choices becomes difficult to digest.

- Although it is very popular in the business world, many in the scientific community believe that the MBTI is not considered to be a valid or reliable measurement of personality or other psychosocial characteristics. However, as is the case with other psychometric tools, some defend that its poor reliability is due to its use as a job candidate screening tool for "measure of success" in the workplace, neither of which are intended uses.

- A 1991 study conducted by the National Academy of Sciences concluded that the scale had not demonstrated adequate validity and that sufficient evidence does not exist to support the use of the MBTI in career counselling programs. This meta-analysis looked at more than 20 studies of the MBTI.

- Wharton Professor of Psychology Dr. Adam Grant stated his views in a 2013 *Psychology Today* article: "When it comes to accuracy, if you put a horoscope on one end and a heart rate monitor on the other, the MBTI falls about halfway in between." Again, like other tests and as I mentioned in the prelude to this section, these tests are good and informative but far from perfect. Use them as a guide, not as exact measures.

Insights Discovery

The Insights Discovery assessment (www.insights.com) is also based on Jungian philosophies and in a number of ways is quite similar to the Myers-Briggs type indicators. Jung proposed that an individual's personality is created within the interaction of four functions (briefly mentioned above) and two primary attitudes (introversion and extroversion) and that when combined, these elements manifest themselves as eight distinct yet common personality types. Jung believed that individuals are unique due to the differences in how these functions and attitudes interact with one another. These differences are represented in the Insights Discovery 4 Color System: "Fiery Red," "Cool Blue," "Earth Green," and "Sunshine Yellow." These "color energies" (as the folks at Insights label them) are inspired by the "Four Humours" of Hippocrates and exist with the goal of helping you to better understand why you behave in the way you do and why others may behave differently. According to Insights, our preference for one or two of these color energies in particular determines our dominant and preferred style of thinking, communicating, and behaving.

Key Characteristics

- Requires the completion of 25 rounds of 4 multiple choice questions. Results are then compiled into a personal profile.

- The assessment categorizes varying aspects of your personality into the 4 "color energies" mentioned above, which are described in more detail on Insight's website. In total, there are then 72 "types" available based on the possible color mixes.

- At the time of this writing, Insights is registered with the British Psychological Society (BPS) and their testing centre (PTC).

Criticisms

- Despite claims as to "rigorous testing of the validity and reliability of the model," the Jungian foundations and theories that it is based upon are widely criticized by those within the scientific and psychiatric communities. This remains the primary criticism of this test as well as any others that share Jungian influences.

- Full understanding and comprehension of results requires one to be trained or certified through Insights.

- The language used within the color-type categorizations can be overgeneralized and thus may lead to stereotypes. Insights hopes to prevent or at least help manage this type of "user error" by certifying practitioners and also through administering the test via on-site (at Insights) workshops.

- Given the highly introspective nature of the questions as well as its intended applications, it is not recommended Insights is performed on those under the age of 18.

Hogan Assessments

This survey was founded in 1987 by University of Tulsa professors Drs. Joyce and Robert Hogan. Hogan Assessments (www.hoganassessments.com) claims to serve more than half of the Fortune 500 companies in existence today. Hogan Assessments offers four separate assessments that look at everything from how we relate to others when we are at our best and our worst (what Hogan refers to as "the dark side of personality") to our desires and unique reasoning styles. According to their website, Dr. Robert Hogan himself has authored a collective total of more than 300 journal articles, chapters, and books and is a fellow with the American Psychological Association (which is significant given that many of these tools receive criticism for not being considered heavily "scientific in nature" or used by actual psychologists themselves). Additionally, Hogan Assessments claims to be the first assessment to scientifically measure the impact of personality on organizational success. Hogan provides an impressive array of tools that look more deeply into many different qualities as opposed to putting them into a reductionist format that may seem easy to digest at first but ultimately provides less insight as to what may really drive someone when they are at their best (and also at their worst). I familiarized myself with their philosophy and offerings while doing research for this book and the amount of effort they put in to make it easier to access both the domestic and international research they conduct was evident. You can view some of these for yourself by visiting this website: http://www.hoganassessments.co.uk/ research.asp. While this does not give Hogan a "pass" in regard to receiving criticisms like the aforementioned assessments, making this information more easily accessible certainly helps Hogan stand out.

Key Characteristics

- Hogan offers four assessments that measure tactical/strategic reasoning styles, drives, as well as positive and "dark" personality traits.

- All of Hogan's assessments take around 15-20 minutes to complete and are available in multiple languages.

- Subsequent reports generated from the test note the strengths and shortcomings of the test taker within the context of the assessment they took. These reports also provide feedback to assist with the assessment taker's personal and professional development.

- Reports also provide suggestions as to how employers or managers may be able to help others better manage their actions or career choices.

Criticisms

- Unlike StrengthsFinder and the DiSC but similar to Insights Discovery, Hogan only offers its services to employers or organizations and not individual test takers. This can be limiting for those who want to use it for personal reasons. I recommend contacting the folks at Hogan with inquiries as to whether or not you can gain access. Their customer support was great in my experience.

- Also similar to Insights, the results can only be fully interpreted accurately by individuals qualified to do so. What does this mean? You need to find someone who has a "Hogan Certification" or training.

- The tools are specific to job performance and don't necessarily apply to areas outside of the work place of a strength and conditioning coach or other leadership-based professions.

- Given the highly introspective nature of the questions as well as the assessment's intended applications, it is not recommended for those under the age of 18.

What Now?
Bringing Assessment Tools to Life

After you have reviewed the resources above, you need to decide if using them in your particular situation makes sense, and if so, how you are going to use them. Simply purchasing any of these assessments and going through them yourself, or hiring a professional from a given organization to train you and your staff so that you can utilize this within your own team and organization, is not enough. You need to have a follow-up plan and a strategy along with a clear goal of what you are hoping to accomplish.

In addition to taking these assessments to better understand yourself, they can also be useful to help you better understand your athletes. I've actually tweaked a few of the assessments to integrate some ideas that are specific to the environments in which I coach. I have stated before that I think these kinds of tools, along with the development of an appropriate follow-up strategy, are vastly underutilized within the sporting world. This is not a strawman argument simply because there are likely some organizations that have been doing similar things within their own walls for years, if not decades. But these organizations are exceptions to the rule.

These practices need to be more openly discussed, implemented, and developed as the psychological perspective, along with that of successful interaction, is a mainstay within every collaborative and competitive realm. They're key drivers of human performance in every facet.

Nevertheless, you must resist the urge to collect resources or data points just for the sake of having them. Be able to explain both *why* you are collecting this type of personality data and *what* you are going to do with it once you have it. In my current position as a coach, consultant, and business owner, it would be pointless if I decided to walk into a staff meeting and announce that everyone is to take part in one or more of the above assessments if my intention was to briefly glance over the results and check off a box in my "feel good" checklist. Does that really help me get to know my athletes or co-workers and become a better leader for them? Additionally, by giving them a pointless directive rather than discussing with them communally as to how the information that we are going to gather will specifically help us to become better coaches and provide a better service, the chances are very high that some would feel uncomfortable or skeptical about the tool. In turn, this would likely lead them to fill out the information in a more protective and possibly even deceptive manner, yielding answers that are untrue or skewed. This is what not to do. It's much better off to explain, or better yet, create, with your colleagues (or the athletes you coach) the strategy for *why* you are collecting personality information and *what* you'll do with it.

The Value of Assessment: Final Thoughts

As coaches, we commonly discuss the notion of talent and the impact that it has on athletic performance as well as life. Unfortunately, one's talent can go untapped due to inadequate stimulation or development of the qualities that are complementary to it. People don't think critically enough about identifying and exploring their talents—and if they do, they only begin to uncover them at a surface level. Mark Twain expressed this very notion when he described a man who had recently died and met Saint Peter at the Pearly Gates of the afterlife. Knowing the wisdom of Saint Peter, the man asked a question that had piqued his curiosity throughout his life.

The man said, *"Saint Peter, I have been interested in military history for many years. Who was the greatest general of all time?"*

Saint Peter quickly responded, *"Oh that's a simple question. It's that man right over there!"*

The man replied, *"You must be mistaken! I knew that man on earth, and he was just a common laborer."*

"That's right my friend," assured Saint Peter. *"He would have been the greatest general of all time, **if he had been a general**."*

Axioms such as these hit home with me. They even haunt me! Even prior to my time in the hospital, I have always been extremely conscious of the limited time we have on this earth. I've even been anxious about the thought of leaving this life without discovering what I was great at and sharing it with the world, something the author Todd Henry refers to as "dying empty." As fellow coaches, teachers, or leaders reading this book, something tells me that I am certainly preaching to the choir here. This is a common fear many of us feel in our heart and in our bones. The entire reason I devoted so much time to both my personal story (and encouraging you to revisit your own) and the personality assessment tools is because taking stock of your past and your present helps you explore your strengths and ensures that you are able to channel them appropriately. Even if the personality assessments are not perfect, they can nevertheless provide you with bountiful opportunities to see where, how, and why you can be more effective in connecting with others, as well as in other avenues of life.

As we continue to advance down the road of self-discovery and becoming better coaches and communicators, it becomes time to step on the gas and learn how we can take the insights we gleaned from self-reflection and use them to adapt and improve. I've always appreciated Viktor Frankl's quote, *"Between stimulus and response there is a space. In that space is our power to choose our response. In our response lies our growth and our freedom."* In the world of both complex interpersonal and intrapersonal interactions, few axioms could be as timeless. Our personalities, feelings, and ingrained heuristics constantly get in our own way. Self-reflection alone is not enough. We need to learn how to match our unique personal leanings with a strategy if we are to become both more fluent and more influential. In the next section, we'll discuss how to do just that.

Crafting Communication:
How Our Identity Influences Our Strategy

He raised his hand in the air so that it crossed the beam of the projector lamp. "Coach," he asked. "How can we best differentiate our communication strategies from athlete to athlete, especially with the limited time that we have?" I had just finished a presentation on how subtle changes in the way we present things to our athletes can influence their perception and behavior. This conference attendee's question was a fantastic one. Often times, my initial response to these types of questions starts with me asking them something along the lines of, "What would you say is or has been YOUR primary or default communication strategy up to this point?" You would be surprised to learn how often that question is followed by a long pause or look of inward confusion. If they do answer, I often reply by asking why they use that particular strategy and if they believe that it makes sense to use it with that particular athlete or group of athletes (based on things like the athlete's age, training background, and even socioeconomic status). Again, you may be surprised at how many non-responses I get to either question, as the truth is that many simply haven't thought deeply enough about what their unique communication strategy actually is, let alone pursued further education on the topic. This isn't a knock on them or anyone else who struggles with identifying a clear strategy of their own. It is perfectly normal to find yourself lost and needing guidance when on the path of learning how to become a better communicator. The way I see it, at least these coaches have the consciousness to ask in the first place. It shows me they have the awareness they need to improve. Part of the issue is that so many in our profession have been trained to expect a singular and unified "best" answer as if they are researching the optimal load to train at to maximally enhance power development.

I have observed many of the classic default strategies related to coaching communication and they often follow the formulaic approach of:

- *"This is what we are doing!" (Plug any exercise, drill or routine in here.)*
- *"This is HOW you do it." (Followed by way too much information or instruction that makes sense to the coach but not the athlete.)*
- *"Now let's do it!"*
- *"Wait, why aren't they doing it how I said?!"*
- **Rinse and repeat (but stated more loudly and in a more animated fashion).**

One note to consider before you make light of the above approach. At times throughout history (and still in some rare instances today), the word "coach" has been a title and designation that commanded near instant respect. Coaches simply didn't need to explain themselves. Athletes lined up and listened up, otherwise they faced the consequences. Of course, today's culture and today's athlete are much different. They have more information at their disposal as well as more competing demands for their attention and resources. This isn't just a millennial thing, it's a reflection of the egocentric and extensively expressive climate of our society today. For better or worse, people are less accepting than ever before, and more likely to question authority, whether they should be or not.

In particular, the open source nature of information has led to more and more people doing their own research and asking "Why?" This has required all of us in leadership positions to learn how to better connect and present our case whenever we want someone to adhere to a certain behavior. Now more than ever, coaching and great communication must be synonymous. Coaches need to further dissect their own philosophies and tendencies, constantly working to strengthen the relational elements of their overall coaching style. When trying to help, it is not advantageous for us to act without first doing some recon of our own, and learning how to deconstruct a current situation and identify the gap to a desired end result. This also requires an understanding of how certain traits of our own can affect those outcomes and when we may need to become a different version of ourselves during the process.

Strategic Use of Our Own Personality Traits

We now understand that becoming a better communicator first and foremost requires tremendous self-reflection. During the course of this introspective excavation, you are going to uncover a variety of truths that you are going to have to face. Some will no doubt lift you up and give you a tremendous source of strength and confidence, while others you may identify are weaknesses that bring you down. It is important to understand that you should never run away from these discoveries, as neither the positive nor the negative findings truly define you. The most successful coaches, teachers, and leaders integrate both aspects into their strategies. They know their strengths but they also know their weaknesses and develop strategies with both in mind.

Remember that we may fit into archetypes at times, but certainly not into a vacuum. We all possess an array of psychosocial and behavioral qualities as well as tremendous variation in both learning and communication styles. The expression of leadership varies widely in regard to the way that it is carried out. The importance of this distinction cannot be understated. No two leaders are alike. This is the same for those you are trying to lead. Put yourself in their shoes. When learning a new skill or concept, some of you may respond well to an intricate description including even the smallest and most mechanical of details, while others may be more visually inclined, relying on body language or other kinesthetic-oriented communication. Still, there are others who need to know the "why" right out of the gate so that the forthcoming information can be put in the proper context and primed for their own intellectual absorption.

People who need to know the right "why" are typically the folks who were frustrated by math growing up as we were often told as kids that certain rules exist simply because "that's the way it is." This includes me, which explains my inappropriate but somewhat valid urges to walk out of the classroom unexcused and look for a football to throw instead of partaking in the day's problem sets. This is also in part why many who initially struggle with math at the lower levels begin to perform better at it once they begin to take courses where that same math now has a more direct correlation to something they care about. For strength and conditioning coaches, physics may serve as an example, since the discussion of qualities related to both force and velocity pertain to the actual physics that we will experience when training our athletes, as well as the quantitative characteristics associated with load and its effect on adaptive qualities of strength training. A newfound appreciation, understanding, and enthusiasm may also emerge if the student finds a teacher who uses more creative metaphors in order to paint a picture, such as a story problem that uses marbles or money as an example while learning various forms of arithmetic.

As it pertains to our coaching personalities, let's analyze two notable examples that are on opposite ends of the spectrum: the hard-nosed/tough love type, such as legendary former Indiana Hoosiers basketball coach Bobby Knight, and the teacher/nurturer type like John

Wooden, who is widely referred to by many as the greatest coach of all-time, irrespective of sporting domain. Now, of course there are more than two types of personalities, but let's look at these two extreme examples in order to more thoroughly dissect what I mean by different coaching personalities.

When considering these two coaches, to which of the two differing styles do you personally relate? Next, is your response based more upon your own coaching style and behavioral tendencies? Or is it based on the strategy in which you approach the design of your training sessions? How does your response align with the first thing that you say to your group of athletes each day at the start of practice, meetings, workouts or formal competition? How does it relate to your tone of voice? The hard-nosed types, such as Coach Knight, may create more of an authoritarian persona and begin an early morning session discussing the importance of urgency, intensity, toughness and resilience in order to instill a gritty mindset in their athletes. On the other hand, coaches who utilize a more authoritative approach may spend the initial moments preaching patience, persistence, and precision, perhaps followed by an analogy or metaphor to drive home their message.

Which one is better? By now you should know that there is no universal "better." What matters is which is most effective—or ineffective—given the context of the situation as well as the personalities of the individuals involved. For us, as coaches who are dedicated to performance optimization, it will never be as simple as saying those who possess more bright-sided leadership traits are universally better than or more effective than coaches who possess more dark-sided leadership traits. In reality, it is the combination of the two and an understanding of when to draw upon elements of both that will aid your development in becoming a true Conscious Coach. Again, this is why there is no such thing as a "bad" component of your natural tendencies and personalities. It's all about learning about yourself and then strategically deploying various parts of your personality depending on the context.

Given the contrasting names and the accompanying associations, it may be hard to conceptualize how dark-sided traits like Machiavellianism or Narcissism could ever be equally as beneficial or even more beneficial than those of the bright-sided faction like Agreeableness and Emotional Stability. Yet research performed by Judge, Piccolo, and Kosalka (2009) in the field of organizational psychology and leadership, as well as a host of others within the fields of evolutionary theory, evolutionary psychology, behavioral genetics, and socioanalytic theory, have shown that there is also a bright side to the dark traits as well as a dark side to the bright traits of leadership. We can examine this a bit more closely by briefly looking at the traits of emotional stability and narcissism.

Note: For a more thorough review and breakdown of these viewpoints and supported research I strongly recommend reading the referenced articles in totality; this section only highlights a small part of the complexities related to this unique leadership paradox and the science that underpins it.

The Downside of Narcissism

For most, this requires little explanation due to our widespread familiarity with the term and its representation in popular culture amongst athletes, celebrities, and even politicians. To put a more descriptive spin on it, Yale-based researcher Seth Rosenthal and Harvard Professor Todd Pittinsky, who specializes in the area of human psychology and organizational behavior, detail that narcissism is a personality trait that is commonly characterized by arrogance, self-absorption, entitlement, and hostility

(2006). Narcissists also typically exhibit an exaggerated sense of pride, entitlement, and self-love which leads them to employ leadership practices that are laced with not only self-serving bias, but also a lack of concern as to how their decisions affect anyone else but themselves. Narcissistic coaches are oftentimes more concerned with "putting on a show" with highlight reel-style training that provides limited utility or practicality to other coaches within the field. They are often quick to point their finger at their athletes or support coaching staff when athletes are not improving at the rate that they should, as opposed to trying to assess what they themselves could be doing better.

The Upside of Narcissism

Despite the ingrained sense of repulsion that we feel when thinking of the term, there are many elements of narcissism that can lead to effective leadership under certain circumstances. For example, in an archival analysis of U.S. presidential personalities, it was suggested that an elevated sense of self -sufficiency and narcissistic entitlement held positive associations with the highest ratings of both executive performance and charismatic leadership (Deluga,1997). Some could certainly claim that the terms "executive performance" and "charismatic leadership" leave room for interpretation given that there have been countless leaders throughout history that have leveraged these traits to orchestrate orders and outcomes that could be politely described as less than honorable. But then again, we are discussing the notion of "effective" leadership as opposed to purely altruistic leadership. Additionally, in a field study of 300 military cadets, the most highly rated leaders were those who were found to test high in egotism as well as self-esteem, both of which are considered to be positive aspects of narcissism given the notion that leaders like these are more willing to confidently and courageously carry out orders than those without high levels of self-esteem. One could debate that simply carrying out orders is not necessarily a sign of good leadership, which I would certainly not contest, but once again it becomes difficult to refute the fact that leaders within both the military and corporate realms are faced with difficult decisions every day that eventually must be acted upon in a proactive and resolute manner in order for change to occur (Paunonen, Lönnqvist, Verkasalo, Leikas, & Nissinen, 2006).

Lastly, and perhaps most importantly, narcissistic leaders have been found to modify their interpersonal communication in order to preserve the positive impression that they seek to make on others. In other words, they are more likely to be able to successfully and strategically adapt to a given situation (Leary & Kowalski, 1990).

The Upside of Emotional Stability

I have made it a point to once again start the analysis of this particular trait with its good characteristics because of the face-value positive nature of the term. Leadership is an inherently emotional process (Dasborough & Ashkanasy, 2002). We imagine someone with a tremendous sense of emotional stability as the picture of equanimity, a rock that we can lean on during hard times, and an individual of steadfast resolve that we can count on to get the job done. Emotionally stable leaders are calm, steady, and consistent in their emotional expressions and also are not likely to experience a multitude of lingering negative emotions or anxieties that befall the vast majority of us (Judge & LePine, 2007).

Emotional stability is widely regarded as a necessary trait in order for effective leadership to be fully expressed (Northouse, 1997) as it is indicative of the ability to be able to right the ship quickly during times of duress, and to do so without falling prey to the quotidian tendency to allow emotions to trump logic and therefore cloud better judgement.

The Downside Side of Emotional Stability

Despite the many benefits of having a leader who possesses a cool and calm demeanor during times of duress, the reality of true leadership (and coaching in particular), is that people want to be led by those who display a range of emotions as opposed to a coach that is monotone and seems to always show up with the same disposition every day. Oftentimes, someone who shows genuine emotional expressions during times of both joy and hardship is more effective: Someone who celebrates with athletes, grieves with them, can relate to them, and also inspire them. When coaching athletes, too much emotional stability can come across as emotional staleness, as it is the periodic expression of real emotions that serve as a psychological performance enhancer as it pertains to enhancing a leader's credibility with those he/she hopes to influence (Kouzes & Posner, 2003). Leaders who instead rely on the constant projection of over-sterilized thoughts, ideas, and communications that are overly objective in nature often come across as calculating and even detached as opposed to trustworthy and inspiring. Additionally, research conducted in a 2005 article published in the *Journal of Applied Psychology* showed that followers of leaders who fail to openly express either positive or negative emotions reported lower levels of overall job satisfaction, trust, and relationship quality, as well as higher levels of absenteeism and turnover (Farmer & Aguinis, 2005).

Findings and observances related to emotional stability become even more interesting when you consider the notion that in some instances, researchers have even found that some of the most influential and successful leaders of all-time rank high in the trait of psychopathy, which is the opposite of emotional stability!

Former U.S. President Theodore Roosevelt serves as the poster child for what authors and psychologists Todd

Kashdan and Robert Biswas-Diener refer to as the "Teddy Effect." The "Teddy Effect" is a term used by Kashdan and Biswas-Diener to provide clarity as to how a traditionally dark- sided trait—like psychopathy—can actually serve as the foundation for adaptable and effective leadership. Though Roosevelt's emotions were said to have swung widely, he was able to maintain healthy relationships with his family, the soldiers under his watch, and the American public all while serving as one of America's most historically successful and pioneering presidents. Roosevelt is a tremendous example of how those who are genuinely expressive and not scared to share their true personality can leverage the full power of a wide range of traits and emotions while leading others, as opposed to adhering to a model what some may consider to be muffled modesty.

Kashdan and Biswas-Diener make it crystal clear in their book, *The Upside to Your Dark Side*, that they are not glorifying the trait of psychopathy or psychopaths in general. Instead, they are trying to draw attention to the fact that psychologists who refer to the term psychopathy are also "talking about a constellation of traits that include some very positive ones: being charming, being immune to the paralyzing effects of anxiety, and being physically fearless."

The Take-Home Message on Traits

One of the most critical attributes that defines a Conscious Coach is their ability to draw upon the advantageous aspects of both dark and bright-sided personality traits. Coaches of all types must recognize and remember that there is no one "ideal" type of leader. Leadership is contextual.

As Uhl-Bien, Marion, & McKelvey (2007) allude to, leadership conditions can, and often do, change quickly and dramatically. When reflecting on traits, it is useful to keep in mind the adaptational and evolutionary biology-based perspective: a trait that promotes fitness (one's ability to successfully complete a task) at one time may become counterproductive when situations and environments change. British behavioral researcher Daniel Nettle provides a tremendous example when discussing the famed Galapagos Finches. Nettle elucidates that Galapagos finches with small beaks do well when the climate is favorable as they can quickly peck many seeds. However, when drought comes, natural selection favors finches with large beaks, so as to better penetrate the barren soil (Nettle, 2006). This Darwinian example is the inspiration behind the old "survival of the fittest" mantra that is often misinterpreted by many who think that "fittest" refers to physical strength, when in reality it references an organism's ability to be adaptable to its surroundings.

Learn from evolution and be adaptable—not dogmatic. Draw upon a variety of both your dark- and bright-sided traits in order to be the best leader, coach and consultant you can be and so you can flex across different scenarios. One narrative throughout history that will never change is that the most effective leaders are able to shift between both bright-sided and dark-sided emotional states. This sense of wholeness, and being who we really are within the moment, contributes to the growth of a *Conscious Coaching* skill set that helps us engineer the best possible outcomes within a given situation.

So far, we've discussed the critical importance of self-awareness and talked about two powerful ways to gain self-awareness: examining the internal drives born out of your past and completing a personality assessment to gain insight into your current strengths and personality tendencies. We've also discussed that there is no one best

THE LEADERSHIP PARADOX

BRIGHT TRAITS & DARK TRAITS

CONSCIENTIOUSNESS		NARCISSISM	
BRIGHT SIDE	**DARK SIDE**	**BRIGHT SIDE**	**DARK SIDE**
·DELIBERATE	·CAUTIOUS	·EGOTISM	·ARROGANCE
·POLITE	·ANALYTICAL	·SELF-ESTEEM	·ENTITLEMENT
·DISCIPLINED	·PERFECTIONISM	·SELF-SUFFICIENT	·HOSTILITY

EXTROVERSION		HUBRIS	
BRIGHT SIDE	**DARK SIDE**	**BRIGHT SIDE**	**DARK SIDE**
·ASSERTIVE	·BOLDNESS	·SELF-ESTEEM	·EXCESSIVE PRIDE
·ENERGETIC	·AGGRESSIVENESS	·AUTHORITY	·DEFENSIVENESS
·OPTIMISTIC	·HASTY DECISIONS	·INSPIRE CONFIDENCE	
·TALKATIVE		·SELF-SUFFICIENT	

CHARISMA		SOCIAL DOMINANCE	
BRIGHT SIDE	**DARK SIDE**	**BRIGHT SIDE**	**DARK SIDE**
·STIMULATING	·MANIPULATIVE	·AUTHORITY	·STATUS-SEEKING
·INSPIRE CONFIDENCE	·EXPLOITATIVE	·ACHIEVEMENT	·POWER HUNGRY
		·APPEAR COMPETENT	·MANIPULATIVE

INTELLIGENCE		MACHIAVELLIANISM	
BRIGHT SIDE	**DARK SIDE**	**BRIGHT SIDE**	**DARK SIDE**
·SELF-SUFFICIENT	·ATYPICAL	·MOTIVATED TO LEAD	·CUNNING
·LEGITIMACY	·ABSTRACT	·DIVERSE LEADER	·MANIPULATIVE
·LAWFUL BEHAVIOR	·HESITANT	·NAVIGATES POWER	
		·FLEXIBILITY	

trait or right way to lead. Rather, we must take stock of all our traits and be flexible enough to use all of them depending on the context. Now, how can we evaluate our environments to better understand which parts of our personality to draw upon?

How a Variable Landscape Determines Which Traits We Leverage

With the constant flux of both the emotional and physical environments in which we coach, it only makes sense that we touch upon the evolving factors that determine which of our traits to call upon. The manner in which we communicate day to day depends on a multitude of factors ranging from the obvious—such as our mood and the type of people that we come into contact with (and, the quality of our relationships with them, their age, sex and ethnicity or country of origin, etc.)—to the not-so-obvious such as the quality of an athlete's sleep the prior evening, their hormonal fluctuations, the stance of company or culture of the organization that they work for, and the compounding emotional effects of the daily life situations outside of training. When coaching and leading others, you need to see the world with your eyes but think with your listener's mind. Getting on the same wavelength as those around us is akin to that of dialing in the right frequency on a radio. We must tweak the dial ever so slightly in order to avoid the relational static that can bubble up if we aren't tuned into an athlete's needs, wants, and desires. You also need to remember that your athletes' values are not necessarily going to be the same as your values due to differences in perspective, maturity, long-term goals, and historical frames of reference. Each given context, and even each given moment, calls for certain traits that yield specific desired outcomes. Not every coaching situation allows for us to slow-cook the process of building trust and rapport; at times we need to use the microwave, and the best way to do that is to identify the traits within yourself that best match up to those of your audience. Whether it's the act of subtle mimicry with your body language, reflective listening, or even talking in the same manner as your athlete.

Most importantly, you want your athletes to see and adopt your perspective, all while thinking that the idea behind the action was theirs in the first place. Remember, enhanced engagement starts by getting someone's attention, progresses by helping them achieve results, and lasts by gaining their trust. All of these stages and strategies constantly feed into one another.

CHAPTER 3
SEEK TO UNDERSTAND

*"There are three principal means of acquiring knowledge...
observation of nature, reflection, and experimentation. Observation
collects facts; reflection combines them; experimentation verifies the
result of that combination."*
-Denis Diderot

People First, Athletes Second

Now that you have been exposed to different methods regarding how to identify and understand your unique personality and coaching/communication style(s), it's time to further examine those of the athletes we hope to influence, from the inside-out. Athletes are people first, and like most people they have agendas of their own. They are not immune to the desires, drives, and distractions that have been engraved into our human psyche. We are emotionally driven creatures, and emotions will almost always trump logic. If you have ever found yourself losing your temper toward a loved one, friend, or colleague because you had a bad day, lacked sleep, or felt "attacked," then you understand that regardless of how level-headed and rational we fancy ourselves to be, we all give into our emotions at times. In other words, emotions are powerful to begin with and they are easily amplified by our environments. Just think of how the type of music we listen to can change the way we feel or perceive a moment in time and space.

Drives and Human Nature

Emotions, logic, and ingrained behaviors together culminate in the drive of an athlete. What are drives? Drives are internal mechanisms, both conscious and subconscious, that lead to the decisions we make and ultimately the behaviors we engage in. Reading this book is a result of your drive to learn. Asking your boss for a raise is a result of your drive to achieve or acquire additional resources.

This concept of drives was established by Paul Lawrence & Nitin Nohria, professors of organizational behavior at the Harvard Business School, with the creation of their "Four-Drive Theory of Human Nature." In this model, they surmise that human behavior stems from one or more of four primary drives: the drive to learn, the drive to bond, the drive to acquire and the drive to defend. This model was introduced by both Lawrence & Nohria in 2002, and serves as a holistic way to observe and identify the employee motivation beyond the "carrot and stick approach" used by many employers in the past.

While they seem alike, drives are different than motivations. The difference is a subtle yet significant one. Motivation is temporary and non-indelible in nature. A drive is deeper and more lasting. Drives are etched into our nervous system. You could say that drives fuel our motivation to act. The science surrounding drives is the result of recent multi-disciplinary research in fields such as evolutionary psychology, biology and neuroscience.

Where Do Drives Come From?

The body and brain are amazingly complex structures. To describe in intimate detail the biology of drive is beyond the scope of this book. What is critical to understand is that drives link the subconscious parts of our brain found in the limbic system (e.g., hippocampus, amygdala and nucleus accumbens) to conscious areas of the brain such as the prefrontal cortex. The limbic system is primarily involved with emotions and their processing, and despite once being looked at as the "reptilian," olfactory-oriented or even the dormant part of our brain, it has been shown that the limbic system actually plays a significant role in influencing of many of our behaviors through stimulation of the hypothalamus as well as its link to the prefrontal cortex. The interplay between this emotional center of the brain and the prefrontal cortex, or the "thinking brain"— which is in charge of handling higher level processing tasks such as decision making, personality expression, moderating social behavior— shapes what we do, how we do it, and why we do it, as well as how we perceive, remember and interpret events around us. Dr. Robert Sapolsky, Professor of Biological Sciences, Neurology and Neurological Sciences at Stanford University, and colleagues are to be credited with much of the more recent understanding regarding the functions of the limbic system. They've found that the interplay of our emotional brain and thinking brain, along with what our physical body is experiencing in any given moment, combine to influence how we perceive and act in the world around us. Antonio Dimasio, Professor of Neuroscience at USC, has a nice statement regarding the role that drives play in influencing our behavior. "A drive originates in the brain core, permeates other levels of the nervous system," he said, "and emerges as either feelings or non-conscious biases to guide decision making."

One of the most powerful tools that comes from our enhanced understanding of drives and how they influence our behavior is that you cannot artificially manufacture somebody's desire to partake in a particular activity, whether that be training or saving money. You may be able to motivate someone for an acute moment, but to change one's chronic behavior, you need to help them discover what's driving them in the first place and bring that to light. Purpose is a performance-enhancer, and it's our job to help the athletes we coach find theirs. To immerse yourself further in the details regarding the power of drives as well as the nuances of our limbic system, I highly recommend familiarizing yourself with Dr. Sapolsky's work, as well as the book, *Driven: How Human Nature Shapes Our Choices*, written by Harvard Business professors Paul Lawrence and Nitin Nohria.

Conflict

When it comes to understanding the roots of conflict, no one summarized it better than author and psychologist Brenda Shoshanna, who said, "All conflict that we experience within the world, is conflict within our own selves."

Our ability to reason is affected by our emotions, and for that reason, as long as we are dealing directly with people, we can expect conflict to be part of what we encounter within our day-to-day interactions throughout both our lives and our careers. Conflict, at its core, is the result of a multitude of factors such as poor communication, ego, personal insecurities, and social comparisons. You will notice the close interplay that these factors share with one another and should fully appreciate how they can work in concert to wreak havoc on our personal relationships and the efficiency of our day-to-day operations. Coaches often experience conflict not only with the athletes that they coach, but also with administrators, support staff and other coaches—both within their own organization or within the profession more broadly. Part of the reason that conflict is inevitable is due to our egocentric bias. This is fueled by the way our brain chemistry enslaves us to our deep-seeded drives and emotions. Our emotions, meanwhile, are amplified when we are involved with or concentrate on areas that we feel the most passionate about. These areas which we are passionate about also tend to be the very same areas in which we are likely to feel the most threatened, insecure, and competitive when we perceive a competitor or potential threat to be invading that same space. This sense of determining who is friend or foe has such a harmful effect that it is the lone subject of a tremendous book of that very title, Friend or Foe, written by Dr. Adam Galinsky and Maurice Schweitzer, on the topic of social comparisons, competition, and collaboration.

To give you a simple, powerful, and all-too-common example of where emotionally wrought social exchanges and appraisals take place, look no further than social media. It's via this medium where a simple statement of one's opinion about a particular matter that may also be meaningful to others can spark a viral over-reaction amongst hundreds, thousands or even tens of thousands of individuals who, at the drop of an emotional dime, feel the need to express their opinions on something that they themselves are often not even directly affected by. It's an evolutionary desire for us as human beings to feel validated and to have our views acknowledged, so we often state them openly and with little thought as to how the other party may receive the messages we transmit. As briefly discussed in Chapter One, we are different than any other animal on the planet in that we are social animals, often wanting to make sure that everyone knows our concerns, agenda, and sentiments. Some would argue that conflict is considered inevitable within our personal relationships (LaVoi 2007) and is actually perfectly normal.

Our biological proclivity for competition and social comparison goes so far that researchers even have a name for the relative joy we feel when we see others whom we envy, are annoyed by, or perceive as rivals fail, perform poorly, or fall from grace: Schadenfreude. Think of Schadenfreude as a momentary lack of both compassion and empathy, and one that is so pronounced that fMRI brain scans indicate that when someone who we perceive to be even slightly superior to us in any way experiences struggle that the ventral striatum, one of the major reward centers of the brain, lights up, indicating a sense of satisfaction or pleasure (Takahashi, Kato, Matsuura, Mobbs, Suhara and Okubo, 2009).

Conflict, whether you address it head-on or passive-aggressively, will never be avoided. Nor should it be. Despite the emotional and psychological toll that conflict can have on both our personal relationships and team/ individual performances (Rahim, 2002; Carron, Colman, Wheeler and Stevens, 2002; Holt, Black, Tamminen, Mandigo and Fox 2008; Vazou, Ntoumanis and Duda 2005), conflict in and of itself is not something that is entirely bad or corrosive. For example, conflict often leads to conversations that become catalysts for organizational, team, and personal growth by opening up the opportunity for different perspectives and views to be voiced. A lack of conflict creates complacency, and in its absence, we are more likely to continue down a path that may be considered safer at the time, but less rewarding, honest, and efficient in the long run. In other words, conflict keeps us honest.

We learn from negative experiences and talent needs trauma in order to be reach its full potential. I cannot count the number of times that I have had to stand up to one of my athletes in order to defend a culture within the training environment that supported the betterment of the collective instead of an individual. This happens within teams and the private coaching sector alike. On the team side, you may have to deal with a player who believes they're above the nature of the task you are asking them to perform. In the private coaching sector, you will have clients who are paying good money for a service, and at times believe they are the ones who should dictate the nature of that service.

One particular experience that comes to mind was a time when a professional athlete I was about to begin supporting during his off-season training period entered the building with a film crew during our usual morning group training session. He had commented at a prior date that a major news outlet was going to be featuring him and his brother in a documentary and that there would be no major distraction given the relatively small nature of the crew. Now, just to provide additional context, this is not a common occurrence on the private side, nor is it often allowed since it becomes both a distraction to the rest of the group and also an invasion of privacy for anyone else who doesn't want to be captured on film. The closed-off session normally featured anywhere from 15-25 athletes and ran on a strict time frame in order to complete all of the necessary elements of training required over the course of the session. During this time, I work hard to create an environment where the flow of the session is not only streamlined and efficient but also dynamic. If you were to walk through the doors, you would hear music blaring and guys lifting weights, sprinting, and asking questions. It's a community affair, and a locker- room environment. But not on this particular day. About ten minutes prior to the session, six cameramen and their retinue of sound and lighting technicians burst into the room and started setting up right in the middle of the training floor. I walked over to them to introduce myself only to receive a disinterested handshake—no eye contact, and a sharp question that came off more as a demand. "Will this music be going the whole time?" the main producer asked.

"Yes," I replied firmly, informing him that we were happy to have them in house but they had to honor the environment that our other athletes pay for with as little disruption to their experience as possible. He sighed, looked disapprovingly, and walked away. I knew this was going to be an interesting morning. We started the group, the rest of the athletes took one look around, noticing the cameras and boom microphones that now enveloped the room. You could see the frustration in their eyes already, and I felt it too. The session commenced, only for me to see one of the athletes who ended up on film using terrible technique during a training exercise. The camera was on him and I could tell he was trying too hard and not focusing on the correct motion of the exercise. I coached him up, only to receive a brief glance of frustration that I would correct him while on camera. Three minutes went by, then as he came back around for another set, I had to correct him again and a third time, each time I could tell he wasn't having it and wanted me to just leave him be. I looked around and noticed some of the other guys rushing through their session as well and felt as if the situation was getting out of control due to the distraction. I begrudgingly wished the cameras would simply get out of the way as this was normally not an issue with this particular group of athletes. A few moments later, I turned the music off and addressed the group. "Listen," I began. "I understand that this is an unusual day and these cameras can be distracting. I feel it as well. But that does not mean you get to rush through the workout and forget everything we have gone through regarding good technique. Regroup, and let's finish the last part without cutting corners. There are far bigger distractions that are going to occur over the course of your career than having some cameras in your face!" I then turned to one of the producers and kindly asked him to make sure his staff stayed on the perimeter and as far out of the way as possible so that we could do our jobs and maintain the safety of our athletes. I was halfway through the sentence when the athlete the crew was there to film screamed out at me.

"If you have something to say to me, you can address it to my face!" he said. "I know it's me you're talking about with the bad form, so why don't you say it directly?!" I looked at him quizzically wondering how he could interpret my announcement as singling him out. I was frustrated with the state of events from the entire morning. I commented back that I had in fact spoken to him directly when I was coaching him and that my concern was to make sure that everyone got the most out of their training and stayed focused, including him. At this point, adrenaline was starting to course through my veins. Anyone who knows me is aware of how passionate I am and that I can quickly elevate my level beyond that of anyone challenging my intentions if I don't check myself. His anger remained, and he fired back several other comments and it became clear that I had a decision to make: I could either respond or react. In these situations, I find it is best to respond and control your emotions for the sake of the long-term relationship and higher purpose. Throughout my life I haven't always been good at controlling my emotions when challenged, but have made concerted efforts over the last seven years to become a better listener and communicator. I took a breath and focused in on him as he spoke. I knew that doing this would lead me to an appropriate response. My entire staff and the rest of the group were all watching, and I knew from previous experience that if you back down, the athlete will feel as if they can disrespect you again. Conversely, if you react too strongly, you may win the respect of some but also label yourself as someone who doesn't know how to handle conflict with class and clarity. In some situations, a whisper can have a much greater impact than a roar. This was one of those situations. As he spoke, I noticed that his eyes repeatedly darted to the right, where the film crew was standing; the cameras were still rolling and it became clear that he knew it. My comments regarding his technique made him felt threatened and compelled to perform. He felt the need to defend himself in case the the media aired that segment; he didn't want to be embarrassed or made to look bad. Realizing his point of view, I simply repeated that my job is to ensure I am honoring my craft of being the best possible coach I can be, while keeping all the athletes safe.

I flicked the music back on and waited for the cameramen and their crew to start packing up before going over to him. He once again reacted sharply at first, and I put my hand on his shoulder and apologized if addressing the group on camera embarrassed him. I told him that I wanted to make sure the cameramen saw him at his best so that his athleticism and abilities were showcased in their truest form. I told him that I care about being great in my profession as much as he does in his, and if I had ignored his mistakes that I wouldn't have been doing my job. He looked at me and said, "I can respect that and I appreciate it." He then went on to tell me he wasn't aware that many cameras would be there, and that he could sense that the other guys were bothered by it too. He admitted his anxiety increased when everyone gave him a hard time about it. Light was shed on the situation, we shook hands, and parted ways leaving the interaction and relationship in a much better place than it would have been if egos and tempers continued to flare in the face of conflict.

It's not conflict that is the problem many face, but rather a lack of skilled conflict management. The level of competence with which a conflict is both identified and handled can, and often does, directly influence the outcome of the disagreement or misunderstanding (Knowles et al. 2015). People disagree with one another because they perceive their goals and values to be incompatible with someone else they may directly or indirectly interact with or be influenced by. This all comes back to building buy-in and trust: if we don't communicate our values and beliefs as coaches and leaders to our athletes, then the bridge we intend to use to connect with them will be built on an unstable foundation and important questions will be left unanswered. As shown in the example above, if Individual A believes that Individual B is understanding and has a good reason for acting in a certain way, and if individual A feels his or her concerns have been heard, then both parties are likely to be able to move forward amicably. If not, then something within the communicative process went wrong. Or, as you're about to learn, perhaps the type of conflict was incorrectly identified.

Types of Conflict

When I first began researching for this chapter, it quickly became apparent that there are numerous categories in which different types of conflict can be labeled. While these categories are only likely to expand over time and with further research, I did my best to whittle the existing research down to something that is actionable. The two most common types of conflict are task and personal (Jehn and Mannix 2001). *Task conflict* refers to disagreements about a particular task and also to differences in opinions about how to manage or deal with such a task. In coaching, task conflict can also be observed when two coaches have contrasting views on how to teach things like speed mechanics, specific lifts, or how to properly record and interpret data from a training session. The second type, *personal conflict*, refers to interpersonal disagreements between two or more individuals, their contrasting view points, and their perceived incompatibilities. It's important to note that this is just as likely to occur between members of the same or opposing coaching staffs as it is between athletes and their teammates.

In the coaching realm (and countless other realms, too) task conflict is the posterchild for positive conflict. As previously mentioned, task conflict often serves as the catalyst for individual and organizational growth. It compels us to redefine our approaches and to think outside the box in an attempt to make our training and communication practices more robust and adaptable. It's our exercise progression and regression sheet, our drill database, our annual planning template that guides us in so far as where to go and what to do in the event that our "Plan A" is not working or suitable for a particular individual or circumstance. It's even a representation for the motor-learning skill cache that we develop from childhood on which helps us better navigate our environment and move with greater efficiency and fluidity. Watch a baby learning to walk for the first time and you see the physical embodiment of "task conflict." In other words, task conflict and progression can easily go hand-in-hand.

On the contrary, what makes deep-seeded personal conflicts so toxic is generally the stubbornness of the parties involved. People of all ages seem to participate in the relational equivalent to "hyperbolic discounting," in which they would rather sacrifice a greater long-term gain for the short-term satisfaction of being right or gaining the temporary edge. As a coach, it is always your job to stop this in its tracks. As a leader, it is up to you to be the first to step forward and sacrifice for the greater good by seeking common ground and a resolution regardless of who was at fault. A personal conflict should never be the result of our own ego. The energy that is sapped in personal conflict is always better focused on the training necessary to compete or coach at the highest levels. The same is said for athlete-to-athlete conflict management. There will inevitably come a time when you will have to break up an athlete scuffle or mediate a disagreement as the competitive climate of wins, losses, success, and personal disappointment will inevitably invoke specters of sadness, anger and hurt which only serve to amplify our reactions and emotional responses. When I was a graduate assistant, I broke up a scuffle between an offensive and defensive player, only to have one of the athletes turn and take a swing at me since he was so caught up in the moment. In order to best manage these inevitable conflicts, you will need proactive and reactive approaches (that don't involve swinging back) along with other relationship management strategies.

Proactive Conflict Management Strategies

Proactive strategies of conflict management include simple things such as the discussion of expectations both inside and outside of the training environment, as well as a discussion of consequences for not meeting those expectations. This is one of the most common situations that you'll encounter, whether it's athletes showing up late to or missing training sessions, substance-abuse issues, general laziness, or an otherwise disrespectful attitude that can become an infection that spreads throughout the team culture. You as a coach can be guilty of falling into these traps as well. Having a whistle around your neck or alphabet soup credentials behind your name doesn't make you any more infallible than standing in a garage makes you an automobile. Set the correct standards for yourself internally as well and embody what you ask others to represent and your character will have a ripple effect on the culture that you are trying to create.

Reactive Conflict Management Strategies

Reactive strategies are those that are designed to ease conflict after it has already occurred (Knowles et al, 2015). This is the time for debriefs and discussions surrounding why the conflict occurred and what can be done moving forward to ameliorate it and avoid similar situations in the future. It's not the time to infantilize the wrongdoer by pointing your finger and telling them not to do it again. Most athletes will only smile and nod in that moment, but after leaving your office, go right back to the behavior that got them there in the first place—or worse, take their anger and aggression outside the facility walls. Instead, have a conversation with the perceived wrongdoer that revolves around openness, awareness, straightforward communication, and coaching support. Remember the goal is for your athletes to see you as someone they WANT to go to and can relate to, not someone who is an enforcer or just another authority figure. Reactive strategies that are successful in the long-term are characterized by mediation and compromise as opposed to force or avoidance. Be firm, but remember that compromise is always best when the goal is to maintain or improve upon the quality of the relationship.

Again, trust is key here. Athletes are a clever bunch. Some will show you whatever version of themselves they know they need to in order to meet their own agenda or get you off of their back. Don't believe me? Ask your interns or volunteer coaches what goes on and what is said when you aren't looking. One of the most powerful lessons I learned when I first started coaching was how to blend in so that I could observe the way athletes truly interacted during workouts when the head performance coach wasn't around or when they believed they were out of his or her direct line of sight. During my first stint in the team setting I noticed that nearly everyone would be attentive at the start of the session as the coach discussed the details of the day's workout. The athletes would nod in understanding and smile obsequiously, but once the initial address had concluded, many would turn around and complain or make comments as to why they didn't want to do some aspect of the workout. Or some would comment that they didn't understand why something we were doing mattered (and that was the nice stuff). Athletes can also be very sensitive about coaches who play favorites. They'll observe how you interact with other athletes and teammates who may stand out in the weight room, practice environment, or who are higher-status athletes in general to get a feel for how you treat them compared to their peers. This stuff happens every day. Be clear with yourself and have strategies at the ready as opposed to resorting to platitudes, pats on the back or getting comfortable and simply expecting them to adapt to your way of doing things. Conflict management is like playing chess, not checkers. If you don't plan several moves ahead and see the whole board, you'll end up sacrificing the very respect and buy-in that you have been trying to build from the very beginning. Keeping with the chess analogy, let's discuss how to set up the pieces on the board and discuss one of the most powerful moves at your disposal: mastering the first impression.

Perception and First Impressions

To truly "know" someone takes time and a multitude of interactions over the spectrum of many different circumstances. I've always believed that you can rarely say you know someone until you first know what they've been through and what they hope to achieve or attain. This is part of the mystique of first impressions: They seem to tell us so much, even though we really only know so little.

First impressions are a chance to gain trust, respect, and sympathy. They're the canal by which every subsequent interaction we'll have with that individual(s) will likely flow. Careers and relationships have stalled because of poorly managed first impressions, while others have flourished because of solid ones. As a coach, teacher or manager of any kind, we are bound to find ourselves in numerous positions throughout our careers where we will have transferred jobs only to find ourselves in front of a new group of athletes and co-workers who will judge us the minute we walk in the door. Some researchers believe that we only have seven seconds to make an impression, and if we want to make favorable impressions, we must learn to interact with self confidence. Why the gravitas behind the notion of seven seconds? Because of the primacy effect. The primacy effect is a cognitive bias that results in an individual being able to recall information that's been presented first (or early on) much more easily and clearly than information that's presented later. The primacy effect is in play not only when we see someone for the first time, but also with the first handshake, how we react to their clothes, their scent, and especially their body language, eye contact, and other non-verbal forms of communication. These bits of information absorbed early on tell us whether or not someone is trustworthy, useful, attractive or threatening to us.

The Anatomy of Emotional Appraisal

When you consider the strong role our senses play in regard to first impressions, you cannot leave out the interesting role of the amygdala. Being one of the few areas of the brain that is keenly tied into ubiquitous sensory processing, the amygdala is as sensitive to social and emotional stimuli as your superstitious friend is to black cats on Friday the 13th. Earlier, we discussed how the amygdala also plays an integral role in our drives (and thus our behavior). But another fascinating part of the brain that serves as the amygdala's impressionable co-pilot is the posterior cingulate cortex or PCC. Amongst its many roles and functions, the PCC is intensely involved with autobiographical memory (especially successful recall) and also mediates the interactions between emotion and memory. The PCC is also active when we make bets and assign a value to an object such as the latest smartphone or a new set of golf clubs we've purchased.

The core of the message? When you interact with others for the first time you must find authentic ways to make it impactful. We cannot hope to successfully alter their behavior if we fail to capture their short, medium and long-term attention. How you carry yourself, how you speak to your athletes, your physical appearance, and your habits and tendencies will all be audited and assessed closely, whether you like it or not. What you need to do is de-personalize this and realize that your athletes sizing you up is just part of the game from a psychosocial and evolutionary standpoint. If you blew your shot, know that even the worst first impressions will eventually pass. The best thing to do in this situation is to reflect on what you may have missed, or even ask a close friend for constructive criticism as to how you may have come across. Use that information to better yourself going forward. This is the same reason it's so valuable to watch videos of yourself coaching, speaking, and interacting. My guess is that you'd be surprised at some of the gestures, stutters, stammers, or facial expressions you make during key moments. Personally, it is tough for me to listen to podcasts or other media I've been featured in as I tend to be overly critical of myself. This is natural, as are the uncomfortable feelings associated with it. Once the reflection is over, absorb the lessons you learned and move on without trying to overcompensate during the next interaction. Overcompensation always backfires and makes things even more awkward and worse. Poor first impressions can be difficult to shake, but if you're able to break through that barrier and get people to truly understand you, an initial flub or judgement matters less and less in the long term. First impressions are important —and can give you a great running start—but they're not everything.

These principles are also at play when it comes to identifying individuals who may fool us with first impressions or an artificially constructed sense of authority. The "Halo Effect" is a relatively well-known cognitive bias in which the hype surrounding a particular individual influences our own thoughts and observations of them as well. This is not to say that the Halo Effect is necessarily a bad thing, but rather that it can blur our own internal sense of judgment and appraisal due to confounding factors. Imagine that you are at a conference and the host is about to announce the next speaker. You respect the host, and the speaker and the host seem to have a great relationship. The host proceeds to deliver an incredible introduction to honor his friend, and from the minute the speaker arrives on stage, the majority of the crowd is excited to hear the presentation—whether or not they actually know anything about him or believe in anything he is about to say. The speaker gets the benefit of the doubt due to the host's introduction and the fact he was asked to present at the conference in the first place.

Being more aware of these biases and nuances as they pertain to our initial appraisals, judgments, and interactions with others can help us better manage ourselves while also looking at things through the eyes of the audience and not just our own. Whether you are speaking to a group of athletes, staff members, or executives in a boardroom, self-management is critical to managing the perceptions of others. This knowledge will be particularly handy when working with a difficult athlete for the first time. Awareness isn't just important when making first impressions, but also when identifying personality "archetypes."

Archetypes

Successful interactions with others are underpinned by our recognition of their individual drives and desires. Once we understand someone's drives and desires it becomes much easier to align on common goals and a pathway to achieve them. One way to do this is to pair a psychological assessment (discussed earlier) with ongoing observation. Another way—and the two aren't mutually exclusive—is to try and group the individuals with whom you work (both athletes and other coaches) into certain archetypes, or predictable patterns of personality. Although the archetypes I describe below are not exhaustive, and some people certainly fit into more than one, they can help guide your thinking on how to interact with various types of people.

Before we get into the archetypes themselves, a few quick words on how I've structured the forthcoming sections:

Archetype Name

The titles used (and their subsequent overviews and breakdowns) are in no way exhaustive of all athlete archetypes. Rather, they are the ones I commonly see and the ones I think will be of greatest value for you to understand. While I know that some of the terms I use may be contentious to those in the strength and conditioning field, I urge you to read closely as the information underneath each archetype name is what matters most.

Overview & Strengths

This provides a snapshot of the characteristics of each archetype. It will tell you a bit more about their common personality traits and tendencies, as well as patterns of behavior. It will also describe how these tendencies and behaviors can be leveraged for a competitive advantage socially, physically, and psychologically.

Weaknesses

Here we will highlight areas of concern relative to a given archetype's traits and qualities. Understand that almost every trait is a double-edged sword: Bravery and intelligence may seem like enviable qualities, but if one is overconfident in their abilities or overthinks a given situation and is slow to react, even the most noble of qualities can become the equivalent of performance quicksand.

How to Connect

This section tells us more about how we can best interact with athletes that fall under each archetype. What kinds of verbal and nonverbal tendencies do they have? Where are they from and what kind of family structures did they grow up in? Are they trustworthy or are they more reticent? How do they respond to criticism? Learning how to answer questions such as these, as well as knowing why individuals in the various archetypes act in the ways they do, provides useful clues as to how we can connect with our athletes and keep the relationship moving in the right direction. Remember, trust is a first principle of *Conscious Coaching*.

Coaching Clinic

Each archetype breakdown will feature an illustration of a real life, practical example given by a veteran coach or practitioner in the field. They are not only professionals who I respect greatly and are amongst the best at what they do, but are also top-notch individuals who take the time to build lasting relationships with their athletes and others in the field. Great leaders don't just teach the lessons; they share the stories that bring the principles of their teachings to life. These individuals have taken the time to share their experiences in an effort to better connect theory with practice. More importantly, they'll show you that it can be done regardless of how difficult the circumstances seem to be. These micro coaching "clinics" will provide you invaluable insights and showcase methods that some of the best coaches and practitioners I know have used in dealing with a particular archetype. Combining the lessons learned in this section with the other principles mentioned throughout this book will ultimately change your path from one of simple contribution to one of leaving a lasting legacy in the lives of others and within the coaching profession more broadly.

The Technician

Overview & Strengths

The Technician is one of the most cerebral of the athlete archetypes. He or she thrives on their knowledge and performance of movement-related tasks. They have many perfectionistic qualities and take great pride in the fact that they see details others do not in regard to skills or drills performed, and they often make them look easy. They look at these tasks as nothing more than a puzzle to be solved with the body as well as the mind. During a training session, you will often see them not only performing the drill, but doing so with a bit of added flair, style, or nuance as if to announce their mastery over the drill. If a drill or activity gives them trouble, they will break it down incessantly and practice until they are satisfied that they have worked through any inefficiencies. Technicians range from introverted to flamboyant. They often keep their social circle small and can be seen practicing on their own well after the session has ended. Through their understanding of skill and movement, it is not uncommon to witness Technicians working with other athletes as well. Others enjoy working with Technicians since they also want to possess these skills and abilities. More than anything, Technicians seek understanding, knowledge, and mastery.

Weaknesses

Despite their obvious movement-related prowess, athleticism, and body control, it is often the Technician's mind that ends up working against him or her. The rehearsal of drills in controlled environments rarely transfers to the chaotic nature of real-life sport. In controlled environments, there are few if any decisions to be made that are unfamiliar or threatening to the athlete or their psyche. If they make a mistake on a drill, they simply start again, perhaps after receiving a few shouts from the coach or verbal jabs from teammates. The presence of an actual opponent, crowd noise, and real-time consequences have a way of changing their internal dialogue. When in control, they can be unstoppable, but if a situation doesn't go as planned, they begin to overanalyze and feel pressure, leading them to become overcome by emotions derived from imperfections that they are not used to. If this chain is not broken, the Technician can quickly fall into the category of an athlete who has the tools necessary for success, but struggles to put them together in game time/ competitive situations. The Technician is at risk for becoming a champion of training, but not a champion of competition.

How to Connect

Technicians value both information and context for each and every drill. They understand aspects of movement theory and enjoy learning new ways to enhance their skills. Teach them by acknowledging their interests and demonstrating ways in which they can take a better angle or find a more efficient way to do something. Once they have seen that you, too, think with a technical mind, they have an easier time seeing the reason for your authority and are more likely to follow your lead since they no longer perceive you as someone just teaches them to lift weights. It is valuable to first acknowledge something that they already know prior to giving them new information as a means to disarm their ego and make them more receptive to your teaching methods. Every Technician is different in regards to their coachability, but once you have their trust and they relate to your message, they can be some of your most loyal athletes.

Coaching Clinic:
Contribution by Coach Anthony Donskov CSCS

It was the summer of 2013 when our facility first began training elite freestyle wrestlers. At the time, we were providing physical preparation services for three of the top Team USA athletes. It was after a training session late in the week when one of our wrestlers asked if he could bring a friend/teammate to meet me and tour the facility. He was interested in joining the group for training. After asking several probing questions, I was told that he was one of the best heavyweight wrestlers in the word, analyzed the training process like a master chess player, was currently in charge of his own training, retained a small social network, and was persistently looking for small pieces to collectively solve the performance puzzle. In other words, he was a Technician: a master at his craft, with the God-given ability to make the complex look easy, a life-long student with the cerebral depth of a University professor.

It didn't take long after our initial meeting for his personality to reveal itself. It was during our evaluation where several traits of the Technician became salient. In my entire career as a strength and conditioning coach, I have never seen a 275lb man move with such grace and finesse. The size of a small water buffalo, he moved more like a white-tailed deer. If efficiency can be thought of as the cost of output relative to input, he ran like a brand new Mac computer. In addition to his physical attributes, he was always asking why: Why are we doing this? Why is this important to me? Why does this matter? I have never been asked "why?" so many times in such a short period of time. My instinct told me that he craved knowledge, was guarded and protective of his own ideologies, and was constantly analyzing each and every process. In time, this over-analysis was more of a hindrance than it was a performance enhancer. The mind is a powerful muscle, and if it's over-stimulated with constant repetition, the machine soon becomes overloaded and its function is compromised.

My first order of business as a coach was to build trust. Transformational coaches take a vested interest in individual characteristics and qualities such as personality and family life. Dealing with the Technician is no different. It was important for me to know him as a man and not just a wrestler. As strength and conditioning legend and coach Johnny Parker states, "I coach people, not weights. What I've learned in 27 years of doing this is that athletes want somebody who cares and somebody who can help them improve. They won't care how much you know until they know how much you care." In time, our relationship blossomed and trust was established. During this period I answered more "why?" questions than most coaches experience in an entire career: questions regarding training, physiology, sport tactics, psychology and game day preparation. Truth be told, his constant questioning made me a better coach. I never bullshitted him. If I didn't know the answer, I would find it. My second order of business was acknowledging his passion, his craft, and his art form. I did this by accompanying him to several meets and practices to watch the action live, to see how wrestlers prepare, how they skill train, and how all of that affects what we do in the weight room. What I found was that if the Technician is assured of your interest in their respective sport, they will reciprocate this recognition directly into the training process. In other words, showing a real interest in their unique sport/work strengthens buy-in!

After trust was established, we eased into a nice coach-athlete rhythm. We took a cooperative approach to the training process, but that didn't mean there weren't hiccups along the way. The wrestling community is saturated with poor training philosophies: Suffering as a rite of passage, high volume, and too much intensity without enough recovery are, unfortunately, foundational bedrocks of programming for combat sport athletes, and they are flawed and outdated. Our minimal effective dose programming flew directly in opposition of these old regimes. I shared journal articles, research studies and other pertinent information with him. The Technician thrives on comprehension. We wanted him to understand that training was a means to an end, and his end was wrestling. We didn't care about a 500lb bench press; we cared about keeping him healthy and producing context-specific strength. The Technician thrives on cognizance as this brings comfort to an overstimulated mind and further strengthens belief in the training process. Once this belief is established, mental energy can be salvaged and used for other training or non-training endeavors. In other words, if they understand the why, they won't think too much about the how, and will trust you to guide them in the process.

The Technician is a personality type that allows coaches to grow, to learn, to adapt, and to change. I truly believe that the best coaches attain a very high level of emotional intelligence, or the ability to coach multiple personalities with one common goal. It is these coaches who change lives, alter the learning environment, promote love, dedication, discipline—all while doing so in a context specific way. There is no roadmap, no atlas, and no user guide in the coaching profession that is more important than the ability to interact and communicate with people. The Technician is another personality that yearns to be coached!

The Royal

Overview & Strengths

The Royal is an archetype that has an aura of entitlement or superiority to them. They typically have been praised in the past—either during their upbringing, amongst peers, through media, or perhaps a combination of the three—which leads them to possess a sense that they are indomitable or that people should recognize their special talents. One area where these pseudo-narcissistic traits benefit the Royal is via competitive confidence. In the heat of competition, they often both believe in and visualize themselves coming out on top. This self-belief can aid performance during times of struggle in which others may doubt themselves.

Weaknesses

Spend enough time around the Royal and you will notice the pampered nature in their behavior, either through their lack of desire to truly get out of their comfort zone or through the subtle ways they seem to avoid participating in activities in which they lack full confidence. They are ever aware of others' perception of them and they guard their reputation closely by making examples of their strengths and athleticism highly visible, while scarcely sharing any details of past or current weaknesses. Athletes who fit this archetype tend to be difficult to coach unless that relationship has been fostered for a number of years.

How to Connect

Engaging with the Royal requires a bit of finesse and self-control on the part of the coach. It is natural for a coach who is dealing with this particular archetype to want to "harden them up" or humble them in order to bring them back down to earth. Remember, this is an athlete you are responsible for developing, and humility is a trait best learned from first-hand experience. It is not as effective if forced or brought about artificially. For now, play their (i.e., the Royal's) game. Ask them questions since getting them to talk about themselves should be easy and come naturally. The more they talk, generally the better and more relaxed they will feel, which will open them up for subtle influence. When describing an exercise or drill, make it appeal to parts of their current skill set that you know they take great pride in or are recognized for. This continues to make the experience more personal as the Royal is always eager to display his or her prowess. Conversely, if they shy away from a particular task, seek out another athlete who is doing it extremely well. Praise that athlete openly and noticeably, yet authentically at the same time. This will get the Royal's attention. Even if they don't respond immediately, they will come around as long as you remain persistent. This is the principle of social proof at its finest. Social proof states that if someone recognizes another individual participating in a behavior that has a perceived reward or positive outcome (praise in this case) they, too, become more likely to adopt the behavior.

Coaching Clinic:
Contribution by David Joyce BPhty (Hons), MPhty (Sports), MExSC (S&C)

The Royal is an archetype that I expect to become more common as a culture of entitlement becomes increasingly prevalent in society. In my experience, Royals are often athletes who chose their parents well in terms of genetics or financial resources. They are often afforded privileges not available to other kids with whom they grew up; for example, they may have been the biggest or fastest kid in school or accessed the best available coaches or summer training camps. As a consequence, their athletic or technical superiority is often accentuated in comparison to their nearest rivals. This profile is not unlike members of the various royal families around the world who were born into a world of privilege. I hasten to add here, though, that this does not in itself make them a bad person. They may have just got to the front of the queue on the back of talent and/or privileged access to coaching from a young age as opposed to the hard graft of some of their less blessed peers.

The problem Royals face, though, is that once they progress to the big leagues, they are no longer a big fish in a small pond. There are several big fish, often bigger, in a vast ocean, and if the Royal has not developed the grit and self-determination required to succeed in life, let alone sport, they can unravel in the most spectacular fashion.

The Royal's behavior, as with so many less palatable character traits, often masks an inner insecurity; a self-doubt that uses bravado and arrogance to paper over the often gaping chasms in one's self-esteem. They have never had to dig deep into their piggy bank to get something they wanted; it was always just there. If you've always got what you wanted, to be suddenly denied something (whether that something is team selection or a personal-best performance) is likely to be a foreign, mystifying, and deeply upsetting experience.

Often, these athletes have a vast reserve of positive experiences to draw upon, as they steamrolled their less entitled opponents early on in life. But when faced with an equal either physiologically or in terms of wit, are bemused by their royal resources not being able to assure victory. It is for this reason that they hate being shown up in front of others. The prospect of failure is daunting enough, let alone in full gaze of their peers. As such, they often find ways to avoid tasks which stretch their comfort zones, something that once detected is often labeled as a mental weakness.

The Royal needs as much love and understanding as any of the other archetypes outlined here. They often fall prey to coaches unwilling to invest the time and emotional energy required to get to the root of their perceived arrogance. This further isolates them from a group that, in team sports, values uniformity and team ethic so highly, thus creating a vicious cycle where they are less likely to be accepted by their peers.

I once had a footballer playing on a team I was working for. A beast of a man, he was widely considered to be the best young player anywhere in the country. He had always been bigger than any of his schoolmates, and when he arrived at the club, he was a ready-made footballer (at least physically). He was able to bully his way through the system and get to the draft without really tapping all his resources.

Early in his professional career, he sustained an ACL rupture, and then re-tore the ligament again 12 months later. (In between tears, he did play at the top of the league.) When I arrived at the club, he appeared sullen, moody, and busting at the seams with entitlement, something that seemed incongruous with his meager on-field output.

No different from any other archetype, when coaching the Royal, you must first get to know the background, motivations, and fears of the individual. When we were doing some gymnastics work with a group at the tail end of his second rehabilitation/retraining period, he stubbornly refused to participate in a drill that required a flip onto a mat from a trampoline. He sulked and made no secret of his disdain for the drill, saying that it was childish and bore no relevance to him playing football. He stormed out of the session, overturning a rubbish bin on the way. This was petulant and immature behavior, but to call him out on it there and then would have done nothing for him, nor would it have brought the situation to a satisfactory resolution.

I knew this outburst would have actually made him feel both angry and embarrassed, so I waited for him to cool down a bit and then sought him out when he was completing his rehabilitation and strength training. I asked his permission to join in and started lifting with him. This got me on his level and after about 10 minutes, I asked him about the gymnastics class. He replied that he thought that it was "stupid and demeaning." The second word told me all I needed to know. Reading between the lines, what he was saying was that if he couldn't do it, he would have felt demeaned in front of the group.

All Royals like to think of themselves as leaders. Frequently, they were the best player throughout their participation in youth sports and thus thrust into captaincy roles. What I had to do here was appeal to his inner ego and let him know very clearly that should he feel a task was "demeaning" in future, he needed to speak to me in private and I would find an alternative, as opposed to creating a scene in front of the other athletes. I nicely and directly told him that his behavior was not leadership and not one that could be indulged. He could see that I was on his side and that I was giving him an out. Had I berated him in front of the group, or even in private, the chance to hone his behavior would have been lost.

As the lifting session continued, I asked him about the flipping drill and he said that he had never done it before. This was my fault for not explaining to him that he was not expected to execute a Cirque du Soleil maneuver, but even a forward roll in this context was fine. I told him that at the end of the weights session, I'd teach him a foolproof method for mastering a flip, but we'd do it one-on-one, with no one else around. He trusted me, and was not afraid to fail in front of me—it was failure in front of his mates that was the issue.

Within 10 minutes he was doing forward AND backward flips on a trampoline without a crash mat! More importantly, we had established a bond of trust that would form the basis of all future interactions and serve as a template for how to work with him whenever his 'royal' tendencies surfaced and he felt under threat.

Over the course of the year, he was able to re-invent his reputation and even began to model this method of defusing diva-like behavior in others. When someone transitions from student to teacher, that's when you can sit back and smile about how influential your role as a coach is. Your job is not to prepare the path for the athlete, but to prepare the athlete for the path.

The Soldier

Overview & Strengths

The moniker given to this archetype can be both literal and metaphorical. Literal from the standpoint that some of you may have the good fortune to work with servicemen and servicewomen from around the world. I personally cannot say how much of an honor it's been for me to have had those opportunities during my coaching career. Nothing puts life and the nature of our careers into perspective faster than being around individuals who truly serve the highest purpose of all: risking their lives to protect the relative peace and freedom that we enjoy daily. If you have worked with these individuals in the past, you likely require no additional information in this part of the overview.

The metaphorical meaning of this archetype can also fit the athlete who not only does what he or she is instructed to do, but does so with tremendous vim, vigor, and attention to detail. Regardless of the skills or abilities that they may or may not possess, they are in it for the love of the process and are willing to sacrifice whatever it takes in order to achieve the ultimate team goal. The Soldier often possesses a unique equanimity that allows them to push forward through setbacks of any kind and seek out solutions that allow them to continue moving forward in the most efficient and mutually beneficial manner.

Weaknesses

In the realm of competition or in the training environment, the main weakness the Soldier faces is a usually a direct result of one of the things that also makes them great: their indomitable will. They find it within themselves to forge ahead at all costs, even if that cause is their health. As coaches, we have to be connected with these individuals and maintain a watchful eye on their habits. They do not know when to pull back, so we usually must do it for them. In their eyes, rest is not a weapon— it's a weakness. It is our duty to show them that rest enhances their ability to aim at their goals.

How to Connect

The first step toward connecting with the Soldier begins with you letting them know that you recognize and appreciate their drive and won't try to hold them back. You must be respectful but also frank with them in regard to expectations. What the Soldier needs most is clarity. When they know how a "mission" also aligns with their personal goals they become experts at aligning their mental and physical resources. To this point, where your efforts will pay off most is by leveraging their supreme attention to detail and commitment by helping them understand how critical restorative means are to enhancing their long-term performance. The Soldier already has an appetite for work and exertion, so hammering these points home is like telling your OCD, Type-A brother-in-law about a new time management tool—it's well-meaning, but likely not what's holding him back. Soldiers are great at leading by example, but often prefer not to stand out. As a coach, this can almost make you forget about them since you rarely worry about whether or not they're doing what they should be. Avoid this mistake. Just like all athletes, regardless of archetype, the Soldier values interaction. They just don't require babysitting. Invest in building relationships with the Soldier and you will have a rewarding connection with him or her for the rest of your career.

Coaching Clinic:
Contribution by Coach Victor Hall CSCS, FMS 1&2

It's a high compliment when a coach describes an athlete as "coachable." In order to earn that moniker, an athlete must work hard, be attentive to instruction and feedback, take ownership of their training process, and express great gratitude toward those who support him or her. In my experience, the most coachable athletes have been in military environments, in part due to their extensive training and intrinsic value systems, these true soldiers can be a coach's dream. Imagine never having to motivate effort, foster attention with a whistle, or wonder if you're making an impact. While those are critical aspects of coaching, you won't find yourself needing them much with soldiers. Instead, the main challenge will often be to protect them from themselves. I learned this firsthand when I began working with military athletes.

When working as a human performance coach within a military unit, it's common for some of the active duty soldiers to not participate in your training programs. Instead, they're permitted to follow their own regimens— usually formed through prior experience, training preferences, or popular mainstream training systems. This is a freedom they earn over their military careers. There were plenty of instances when I would be in the gym and see these independent training sessions being performed. One Soldier in particular had an impressive physical stature as well as a rare ability to perform the same training session over and over again. He clearly operated from the mindset that "if some is good, more is better." Because he was a high-ranking leader within the unit, and he preferred to train independently, my initial goal was just to build trust with him in hopes of eventually influencing some of his programming choices. I started with simple conversation, asking plenty of questions about his military and physical training background, as well as discussing common experiences like parenting, sports, small-town childhood, etc. It wasn't until we had a strong personal rapport that I took the next step and asked to join in with his workout. Once he saw that I could train side-by-side with him (albeit just for one session), I knew I had enough respect to begin offering advice. At first, advice would come in the form of simple suggestions. I'd mention that a few easy additions to his current regimen could help him address physical imbalances that were contributing to some of his chronic pain issues. Over time, our relationship grew, we trained together more often, and he eventually trusted me with planning all of his physical training programs.

I'm confident that had I taken an all-or-nothing approach, suggesting large sweeping changes to his regimen, that there would have been a different outcome. I knew what he needed was a more moderate approach with healthy doses of rest, but I also recognized that he valued high amounts of effort and wanted to maintain a sense of ownership and control regarding his training.

The Specialist

Overview & Strengths

This archetype makes for one of the most unique athletes to interact with despite the fact that their desires are typically the most obvious. As the name implies, the Specialist seems to only care about playing their sport. It is the part of their deepest core identity. The sport itself is not just a game, it's an escape. They aren't interested in the training: just show them the court, field, oval, diamond, turf or track and get out of the way. Their passion for what they do makes them a true rise-up-to-the-challenge gamer. The game is transcendent for the Specialist. Regardless of whether they are introverted or extraverted, you can expect an amplified version of themselves to be on full display whenever they are playing their respective sport. Due to their love for the game, they closely resemble the Technician in regard to their mastery of the nuances of the game. The movements involved with their sport become intuitive for the high-level version of this archetype, but those at lower levels can suffer due to their non-committal attitude towards performance training. They are focused on the end, but don't always see training as a means to it.

Weaknesses

One of the most dangerous habits the aspiring high-performer can have is a singular focus. This may seem counter-intuitive since we are always told that we need to concentrate more, pick a sport to stick with, remove distractions, etc. The truth is that our minds work best when we are able to relate many seemingly disparate ideas together in order to form a more complex whole. Often, the young or adolescent multisport athlete grows up to be a better-rounded athlete once he or she has found the sport to which they ultimately want to dedicate themselves. The movement cache they can draw upon is much more robust since they have years of practicing a variety of movement skills and techniques.

How to Connect

The phrase "know your audience" has never rang more true than it does when addressing the Specialist. The starting point for all interaction must come from an understanding of what the other person cares about most. This allows you to meet them where they are and craft a stronger message that resonates. The Specialists care about the game in which they compete more than anything else. Use this information to craft everything from the examples and analogies you use while coaching to the topics of discussion when you see them outside of the training environment. Let's use a basketball Specialist as an example. Imagine you are coaching a basketball player who takes a lot of pride in their ability to throw up a mean slam dunk. This shouldn't be too hard to imagine as there is an entire competition dedicated toward this during the NBA season. Now, telling this athlete that hang cleans make them "more explosive" isn't going to connect the dots for them in the way they need it most. In their mind, they may already be very explosive. It's hard for a basketball player that may already have little to no trouble performing a slam dunk to understand that picking up a barbell loaded with weight and lifting it as fast as possible is somehow going to help him perform this skill better. "Just give me a ball and let me go do my thing," is oftentimes a variation of the sentiment going through their head. As performance coaches, we see the connection because of our knowledge of science, physics, transfer of training, and adaptation. The athlete, however, just sees it as another thing they have to do that keeps them from doing what they really want to do: play basketball.

A better message could be to first start by telling them why they are performing the hang clean and how it helps; and not in performance coach terms, but in basketball terms. For example, try saying, "Performing hang cleans can increase your vertical jump, which ultimately means even more explosive dunks and an increased likelihood of 'posterizing' your opponent."

The power of personalization is the primary force at play and will help the athlete see the benefit through their own eyes, thus increasing the likelihood that they will perform the drill with a renewed sense of purpose. We've related a concept to the athlete in a meaningful way, and thus reframed their view of it. We will further discuss the art of relating and re-framing later in the book, but for now, just remember that few athletes (and especially not Specialists) care for a detailed science lesson; they just want to know how what they're doing can make them better at their chosen sport.

Coaching Clinic:
Contribution by Coach Adam Feit MS, CSCS*D, RSCC

The term "specialist" has taken on a new meaning in the world of athletics. As injury rates continue to rise and the requests for specific one-on-one coaches empty the wallets of parents, today's coach has a continuous uphill battle to fight. Instead of encouraging athletes to play multiple sports year round, more and more of sporting society is recommending that our youth take a narrowed lens approach to specific skill development. Getting invitations to camps, clinics and showcases at any time of the year celebrate and convince young athletes of possible future success. Athletes are told to focus on one sport earlier and earlier while parents continue to cater to the demands of club-level coaches, guaranteeing recruiting exposure.

But what happens when the journey is over?

When the lights turn off, people back up their bags and everyone goes home.

Can student-athletes move forward in life after the constant hustle and hard work to be their very best? More specifically, can coaches prepare them for success off the field when the final play has been played?

I've been very fortunate to work with thousands of athletes over my 10-plus years in coaching. From NFL MVP's to middle school walk-ons, I've had the incredible opportunity to fine-tune and develop skills at all levels of sport. I have learned that regardless of the level of playing ability, the Specialists are the ones who not only play the game, they live it. Specialists do not see a game for simply a game. They see it as an opportunity to succeed, to fine-tune their craft and excel in their chosen walk of life. But there comes a point in the road where their career comes to a close and the real game of life starts to appear. It's during this time, we as coaches are needed more than ever.

I have noticed that the assumed difference between person and competitor is gray and complicated. There is no clear separation between the identity of the person and the assumed character of an athlete. Specialists identify themselves as a (sport) player when being introduced to new people, list their sport as their favorite hobby and prioritize practice and competitions over life events. They blend the two identities so dangerously well that it's hard for loved ones to separate the two. And if this process continues year after year, we're left with a ticking time bomb when the question, "Now what?" comes up. It could be a season-ending injury, a trade to a new team or a call for early retirement. Eventually, the Specialist has nothing to specialize in and chaos soon ensues.

I was once the youngest head strength and conditioning coach in Division I football. At the age of 24, I was charged with overseeing the development of 21 varsity sports and over 400 student-athletes. Include managing two weight rooms spread across campus, uncooperative Olympic sport coaches and a football program that hadn't won in 20+ years, you can believe my hands were full.

After an unfortunate (but expected) losing start to the beginning of my first football season as a head strength coach, one of our key players went down. Now, we didn't have much to work with, but this player was the closest thing we had to any type of prospect that might go anywhere in football. This young man grew up in a coaching household, spent equal time studying his playbook alongside the Bible and was everything and everyone you wanted on a football team. He put the C in culture and the E in effort. But a broken defensive play at practice on a cold fall night broke this man's body and his will to keep playing football the rest of his fifth-year season.

As I sat with him while the athletic trainer rigged up something to keep him safe and stable, the feelings of empathy and emotion began to overtake me. I, too, suffered a season-ending injury in high school and knew what it felt like. But despite my personal experience, I couldn't muster any positivity and confidence beyond the typical "It's going to be OK, you're going to be fine" statements. I was paralyzed with the notion that as a young coach, I couldn't display my emotions and feelings to one of "my" players.

I did what I could and simply moved over to keep coaching during practice. Why didn't I do more?

As the season progressed, I checked in with him from time to time at breakfast or in the training room. I made the choice to see him.

I knew he was struggling: Struggling to stay with the team, struggling to go to class, struggling to stay afloat in this dark sea of anxiety, depression and fear. And I lacked the common sense and drive to stay with him because I was so busy with everything else. Football was everything to this young man and to have it ripped out of his soul like a price tag off a cheap pair of jeans only added more insult to this man's future.

If it happened again…

I would do more. I would analyze the situation from three separate lenses—the big picture lens, the detailed lens and the athlete lens. Looking back on my career since then, I know I've grown. I've learned to take a more athlete-centered approach to coaching rather than doing what's best for me as a coach. I've looked at athletics not as "all or nothing" but rather "just something." I now spend time with my athletes as people, not performers. And through the evaluation process, I make sure to touch on the following three questions throughout the course of our relationship to ensure we know what's ahead, just in case.

• What is your identity? (Who are you?)

We often classify ourselves as players, coaches, fathers, mothers, husbands or wives. But what if there was no game to play, no child to parent or spouse to love? Would our identity change? (Hint: It shouldn't.) Identities are the very cornerstones of our existence. They're how we relate to people, express our passions in life and live out our day-to-day obligations and opportunities. An identity is not a title. It's not something that can be fired or hired, recruited or graduated, found or lost. It's who we are on the inside, when everything else has been lost.

• What are your values? (What is important to you?)

For the Specialist, more often than not, the process of attaining sports mastery will reign supreme at the top of this list. It will be easy to see the correlation between the time spent focusing on one area and neglecting time on the others. But we always have time for what we value, specifically at a particular moment in time. Whether it's practicing to become a better player, working late to finish a project or bumming around on a Sunday afternoon, at that very precise moment in time, it's what we value most. When a Specialist devotes his or her entire time to mastering their craft, they leave little room for growth in other areas of life, causing disorder and confusion. Helping a Specialist understand there are various forms of value and wealth in areas outside their sport will help transition them more effectively into the real world.

- **What are your goals? (What do you want to accomplish?)**

The ultimate goal for any Specialist is to succeed at the highest level possible—to stand on the highest podium and enjoy the bountiful fruits of labor. However, many specialists are so singularly goal-driven that they tend to compromise other aspects of their life for the sake of achieving greatness in their activity of sport. We've read it in the papers, seen it on the news and quite possibly experienced it as coaches. But, as John Maxwell reminds us in "The 17 Indisputable Laws of Teamwork," if specialists think they are the entire picture, they will never see the big picture. Goals should not just be SMART (Specific, Measureable, Attainable, Realistic, and Timely). They should be PIE (Purposeful, Impactful, and Enjoyable). Big-picture goals reflect not only what lies at the end of the road, but also the road itself.

While most coaches shy away from the deep questions and open-ended reflections, I encourage you to embrace them. Do it now before it becomes too late and you end up speechless, clutching a young man's hand as he screams in pain. Don't ask what your athletes can do for the team; ask them what they will do when there is no team.

If you find yourself working with a Specialist, here are a few things you can do:

Find out what they enjoy outside the confines of the weight room and field. You'd be surprised how authentic your coaching will become when you know more than their name, number and where they come from.

Help them discover who they are as individuals, not just athletes. Do they have something they can contribute to your session or weight room? Can we involve them in some of the decision making process as a player-leader?

Explore every opportunity to prepare them to be not just great teammates, but also great people. Some of the best players are the best people from the inside-out. Build principles of community, accountability and service into your program. Giving and helping earns more points than getting or receiving.

Ensure they understand that there's a time and a place to embrace the seasons of life. Spend time with the Specialist on his or her personal and professional goals outside lower body fat, a faster 40 and a bigger bench. Most importantly, take the time to help them transition into the real world when their "specialty" is over.

Because even though they may spend years specializing in one particular area, the opportunities for impact carry further in life than a trophy in their hands or medals around their necks.

The Politician

Overview & Strengths

Many coaches can recall an athlete they've worked with that has a mouth that could rival their athletic ability. Meet the Politician, who is often charismatic, humorous, wildly talkative, and who knows all too well what they want and how to get it. The Politician will often try to get your guard down by asking questions that make you believe that they are focused on what needs to be done, only to find ways to slip through the cracks with their behavior (e.g. skipping reps, missing sets, or giving less than full effort). The Politician is generally a confident type, but will find ways to blend in when it suits them not to be noticed. They are nowhere near the same level of a distractive force as The Mouthpiece (more below). The Mouthpiece seeks to always be noticed, whereas the Politician will only do so when it benefits them. Otherwise, the Politician prefers sneaking under the radar believing they are "getting one by."

Weaknesses

People who choose to do certain work only when it suits them to do so often sacrifice development to avoid displeasure. They don't want to be inconvenienced with what they view as something not important to them in the moment, and they generally don't think it will come back to haunt them. This is the social equivalent of a person who rests easy thinking that they aren't ruffling the feathers, while unknowingly making the problem worse in the long term. The Politician must eventually learn to follow and to trust the process—to do things they may not want to do in the moment—if they ever want to develop the strengths necessary to lead.

How to Connect

Politicians value options and the freedom to do as they please. They aren't necessarily against doing the work, they simply want to do it their way, under their terms, and on their own time. The simplest and most effective way to deal with this archetype is by making it clear that you know how to play their game. When they try to kill time by making small talk, entertain their distraction for a moment before letting them know it's time to get back to work. When dealing with a dynamic personality like that of the Politician, it's key to humanize the interaction so they can see multiple sides of you. Show them that they're not the only cunning and adaptable personality in the room. What won't work with the Politician is being overly abrasive or authoritarian in your approach. They may respond to your authority in the moment, but at the very next opportunity, they will undermine your efforts and rebel.

When dealing with the Politician indirectly, present them with an element of choice whenever possible. For example, if performing a squat in the weight room, let them decide which variation of the movement they perform based on options that you have laid out for them (front, back, or safety, for example). This kills two birds with one stone: You are being ethical by allowing the athlete to choose the movement he or she feels best suits his or her body, which gives them a feeling of control. And, because you've given them a say in the matter, they are less likely to bicker with you about performing the movement. Sure, there may be times when a certain variation is non-negotiable based on a specific adaptation you are pursuing or a training modality you are using (bands, chains, eccentrics, contrast training, etc.). In that case, simply give them a choice during another movement category later on during the training session. Remember from Chapter 1: there are countless roads to take toward an adaptation, and as long as we get to our destination in a safe and efficient manner, we are accomplishing our goal. With the Politician in particular, it can be important to release your agenda and perhaps travel down a different road.

Coaching Clinic:
Contribution by Dave Puloka M.Ed., CSCS

Politicians are common throughout the NFL. Every team has them. They tend to be clever and likable. They are usually veteran players so they also tend to be very influential. When they are part of a team that maintains a strong culture of integrity and hard work, these personalities are relatively harmless. However, they can be a cancer on a team that is still in search of an identity. Having coached on teams at both ends of the spectrum, I can tell you it's a lot harder to deal with a Politician in the latter situation—or at least the stakes are higher in this position because you're concerned not only about the Politician himself but also about his young, impressionable teammates. In this situation, you must acknowledge that you're aware of his tactics; otherwise, you do him a disservice in not pushing him to maximize his potential. You also need to confront the Politician's behavior head-on so other teammates don't follow his lead.

Here's what you need to know about a Politician: he doesn't like confrontation and he usually cares about what you think of him. So, if you can sit down for a one-on-one conversation, you should be able to make some headway. He'll also appreciate you not calling him out in front of the team.

In my nine years coaching in the NFL, one particular player stands out in this category. Ironically, he used to talk about running for public office someday and it wouldn't surprise me one bit to see that come true. I coached him for several years so we got to know each other pretty well. He had a HIT (high-intensity training) strength-training background in college, so he had a hard time adjusting to our system and philosophy (which was different from HIT) early on. He thought highly of himself and did not like to be coached up in front of others, especially since he believed he had made it this far on his own. Why fix something that wasn't broken? Except it was indeed broken, he just didn't realize it at the time.

He had a hyperlordotic posture, with stiff hips and ankles. He was great at producing force but very poor at resisting it. Dunking a basketball was easy; it was the landing that caused concern. He would write off our plyometric progressions as being a waste of time and "filler" for an already "tedious" warmup. In the weight room, he struggled with single-leg, hip dominant patterns such as single-leg Romanian deadlifts and instead of working at it he would try to skip it altogether—or, if confronted, he ridiculed the exercise as being stupid and irrelevant. It wasn't that he didn't like the weight room; in fact, he spent extra time in there, albeit doing body building-esque training. John Wooden's quote, "never mistake activity for achievement," was never more applicable.

Despite the fact he was generally a pain in the ass, this athlete had redeeming qualities. He had a good sense of humor and a broad range of interests outside of football. If there was a heated debate in the locker room, there was a good chance he started it. Religion, politics, money, relationships—he had an opinion about everything and advice for anyone willing to listen. My challenge was figuring out how to get him to listen for a change. I knew if I simply got angry with him, he'd tune me out. I wanted him to understand two things: first, the why behind our training philosophy and how it could benefit him; second, how his behavior, specifically his lack of compliance and focus, influenced his teammates. At that point in his career, his injuries had been predominantly orthopedic (broken bones), but given his overall movement profile, it was only a matter of time before he strained a muscle.

Sure enough, he suffered through multiple low back pain-related episodes and hamstring issues later that year. And although he never missed a game, his performance had diminished from the prior season and he was frustrated, especially since he was about to enter into a contract year.

When he reported back for the off-season training program the following March, I saw an opportunity to make my case. Rather than a closed-door office session, I invited him to dinner at a local restaurant I knew he liked. I figured a neutral meeting place and the social atmosphere would do some good. I started off by telling him that I thought he had all the necessary tools to be a great player in this league, that he could be a team leader if he wanted to be and that, whether he liked it or not, a lot of the young guys (we had plenty that year) looked up to him. I also told him I wouldn't have taken the time and effort to meet with him had I not cared. I remember asking him, "What's the difference between your contract and mine?"

"Mine has a few more zeros and commas," he quipped.

"True but mine is also 100 percent guaranteed," I said. "Yours isn't. And it's a lot easier to judge your performance than it is mine. I've got a larger margin for error than you do. If you can't stay healthy, you won't have a job much longer. You'll be written off as injury-prone and that will be that. But there'd have to be a dozen hamstring strains in the same month before my work gets questioned. It might not be fair but that's reality."

"So what's your point?" he asked, defensively.

"My point is my job would be a lot easier if I just let you be and let you go through the motions. You might get hurt, you might not. Either way, I collect a paycheck. But that's not me. I care about you and I care about this team. If you have success, the team has success and vice versa."

"So what do you want me to do?" he asked.

"I want you to swallow your pride, trust in the process and be patient."

He agreed and we shook hands. I suggested that with all those zeros and commas in his pocket he should pick up the tab, at which point he informed me that he never pays at that restaurant because the owner was a big Dolphins fan. Unbelievable.

I wish I could say he was an "A" student that year but he wasn't. I still had to remind him periodically to focus on the task at hand. But nevertheless, his lifting skills had improved a great deal and he stayed healthy the whole season.

He ended up signing a lucrative second contract and, more importantly, his actions piqued the interest of some of his teammates. That set the table for a series of new one-on-one conversations, which, after all, is the essence of coaching.

This philosophy reminds me of a quote from Mike Sherman, with whom I had the pleasure of coaching with for two years. *"Demand the truth. Tell the truth. Live the truth,"* he would say. *"If there is no truth, there is no trust. If there is no trust, there is no relationship. If there is no relationship, there is no value or substance to what you are doing."*

The Novice

Overview & Strengths

At some point, every trainee fits the archetype of the Novice. This is the wide-eyed, sometimes overwhelmed and over-eager athlete who is so raw in regard to their development that you literally have to start from the most basic of fundamentals. Whether it's due to them getting into sports late, not having proper coaching, experiencing a late growth spurt, or simply not having had a coach who took the time to truly educate and instruct them, the Novice requires a ton of instruction and even more patience.

One of the biggest advantages of the Novice's inexperienced background is that they present the greatest opportunity to be molded physically and psychologically. They have few hardwired associations when it comes to training, and performance enhancements will come quickly since they generally haven't yet been exposed to serious training stressors. If handled appropriately, the Novice can undergo a metamorphosis that allows them to take on the positive qualities of archetypes like the Soldier, the Leader, and the Crusader (the latter two of which you'll meet soon).

Weaknesses

Patience is the provenance of improvement for the Novice. Like all early students, they are usually eager to improve or at the very least, hungry to keep up and compete with their more highly-developed peers. Just as a great dish can be ruined if not cooked at the correct temperature or for the appropriate amount of time, the development of the Novice can be irreparably damaged if they try to extend beyond their current competencies or capabilities too often or too soon. The key with the Novice is to remember that patient development is often the most productive kind.

How to Connect

To best connect with the Novice, reconnect with the memories of yourself when you were in this stage. How did it feel when you first began? How did you react when you failed the first time you tried to perform a certain skill or task? What do you know now that you would have told yourself if you could go back in time? These questions serve as critical currency that affords you the ability to gain more insight into the mind of the Novice. Through empathy and recall, you can better tailor your coaching message and meet the Novice where he or she is while also helping them visualize how taking a slow and steady approach will ultimately lead them to the development highway they strive to be on. The image that should be etched in their mind is that of water flowing through a rock-bed—steady and consistent, slowly but surely shaping the landscape around it.

Coaching Clinic:
Contribution by Coach Fred Eaves M.Ed., CSCS, RSCC

One of the greatest blessings of coaching high school athletes is the opportunity be an integral part of their physical, psychological, and emotional development during some of their most formative years. This opportunity is not only an honor but also a privilege that is near and dear to my heart. My high school athletes are novices in every way you can imagine. This is why we use what we like to term as a "slow roast" approach with their development. We do not want to rush anything. Unfortunately, this philosophy is in contrast to almost every signal my athletes receive on a daily basis through all of the different outlets that influence their lives.

The greatest reward at this level is to watch a young athlete buy in to the development process wholeheartedly and, as a result, reach his or her highest potential not only as an athlete but more importantly as a person. In my role at a K-12 prep school, I have the benefit of being able to see our students come into our system as five year olds in kindergarten, and watch them progress into young adulthood. It is really a special thing to be able to connect with my students at such an early age, and it has truly been a game-changer in terms of building long and lasting relationships. I am currently working with kids who were in second grade when I arrived on campus at Battle Ground Academy (BGA).

The young man I am going to use as an example of the Novice is well on his way to achieving his potential in a holistic sense. Potential is very individual, especially athletically. Individual improvement and judging yourself against prior versions of yourself is key in our development process at BGA. This young man is not going to be a Division I athlete when his time at BGA is over, but I do believe he is going to be a first-class person, husband, and father. We strive to develop the person first, and we feel that everything else will fall into place if we are successful in that process.

I first met this young man as an eighth grader in my first year at BGA. The first trip into any high-school facility can be pretty intimidating for a middle-school student. Our culture is extremely positive and welcoming, but it is very different from the environment our students experience in our middle school. This young man walked onto the turf wide-eyed and terrified his first day. I knew right away that I needed to make a connection with him to keep him involved in our program. Paying close attention to the body language and facial expressions of your athletes can pay huge dividends if you use this feedback appropriately.

He was one of the few athletes who was not participating in a spring middle-school sport, and his parents had requested that he join the after-school program earlier than the typical start date. I walked up to him and immediately struck up a conversation inquiring about his day, his sports background, and his interests outside of sports before the session began. One of the first ways I connect with young athletes entering their first training session is to create an initial level of comfort between them and me. I will usually joke around and break the ice if possible. I think it is important to not take yourself too seriously when dealing with high-school athletes. In the end, they are kids that are playing sports to have fun. It is important to understand they are not professionals at anything they do, and we need to keep the environment variable and entertaining within the constraints of what we believe in our program. Everything we do is for our athletes, and there is no room for ego when dealing with kids.

Another way that I like to regularly connect is by making it a point to have at least one brief conversation with each athlete regarding something outside of sports or training. This is an extremely valuable technique when your athletes are new to the training environment or training in general. This may seem like a daunting task considering the volume of kids that we work with each day, but it is really just part of the everyday interaction we have with our athletes. Meaningful daily interactions are vital to relationship building. I was able to use this technique to continually build a stronger relationship with the athlete I am referring to in this coaching clinic. The relationship-building process is always ongoing and can also be very fragile. Both the athlete and coach must be diligent to earn trust and cautious to maintain it. We emphasize the importance of building and maintaining relationships daily with our athletes, and we explain to them that it is a reciprocal process. It is important my athletes know that I am interested in them as people first. I never want my athletes to feel that their value to me revolves only around their athletic careers.

I also want to convey, through all of my actions and language in dealing with my athletes, that I am extremely approachable. I will even poke fun at myself in order to help loosen the environment up a bit. I believe it's important to let your athletes see who you really are. Each coach must get to know his or her athletes on a personal level in order to help the athlete reach his or her true potential. I was able to get this young man to relax through our initial conversation. I inquired about him personally and cracked a few jokes at my own expense. It's amazing what a little self-deprecating humor from an authority figure can do for a shy young man with low self-confidence.

In my initial conversation with the athlete, he remarked how big everything in our facility appeared. Change can be overwhelming for young athletes coming into new programs, and it can also be frustrating and frightening for the athlete early on. Displaying empathy for your athletes is another valuable way in which you can connect. I always try to remember those times in my life when I was faced with a great transition, like when dealing with a new crop of athletes. I can almost still feel the emotion that I felt during those transitional times, and it helps me share in what they are feeling. I told the athlete a story of my first day in high school and how intimidated I felt going into a strange place for the first time to let him know I had walked in his shoes before. I believe we must let our athletes know fear and anxiety are common emotions that we all feel in moments of uncertainty, and it is OK to feel those emotions. How we channel our emotions is what is truly important and teaching this skill becomes a focus for us in dealing with young athletes.

I watched this athlete's comfort level increase every year, and with it, his confidence, as he has consistently mastered technique. He has put in tremendous work and he has experienced progressive and steady improvement in all facets of his training. This athlete has transformed in the four years he has been in our upper-school program. His work ethic is second to none, and he has surpassed most of his goals and expectations. We have had to constantly readjust his goals due to his hard work and excellent attitude each day. I have watched him struggle from the eighth grader who could not hinge correctly, to a junior who is technically one of the best in the school.

It was important to stay patient and be encouraging with him through this process. Patience is vital in dealing with the Novice. These athletes are going to progress quickly when they are able to figure things out, but getting them to that point is not always easy. The training environment is something that is most likely very foreign to them, and it is important that the coach does not take this for granted. Being patient and consistent will serve both parties well. We must model the behavior we expect from our athletes. If we expect patience and consistency from them, we must hold ourselves to the same standard. The neurological adaptations they will experience alone will provide significant improvement. It is important to recognize and celebrate these adaptations in the early stages of dealing with a beginner.

The Novice will have good days and bad days, but we must remain consistent in coaching him or her and make sure he or she remains consistent in their attitude, effort, and attendance. As a coach, the process is what I enjoy the most, and it is important to stress this with your athletes when celebrating their improvements and progress. Athletically, the athlete I've been referring to has been able to transfer all of his hard work and express this improvement on the field of play. It is always satisfying to see an athlete who a sport-specific coach believed would never be able to contribute to the team in an on-field capacity earn varsity playing time.

There are many times in teaching and coaching when it becomes easy to question whether it is all worth it. Long hours, low pay, and low job security are some of the normal perils we deal with in this field. To truly be successful in the industry you have to be service-oriented and selfless. You will spend the majority of your time with the athletes you coach, sometimes more so than your own family. There are also many times that you will not see the fruits of your labor, especially when you are dealing with young athletes. I have had many guys leave our program over the years, and I would say to myself "that guy just doesn't get it." I would be frustrated, feeling that we didn't do enough to reach the athlete or that we could not find a way to connect. As I have matured, I have learned not to come to such conclusions because the maturation process is so fluid and ongoing. Time after time, I have been witness to an athlete who didn't "get it" during his time with us, only to find out that something we said or taught resonated later on and made a difference in his life. I am always reminded of the story of the three stonecutters when working with young athletes: A traveler comes across three stonecutters and asks them what they are doing. The first cutter describes how tough his job is and he is very unhappy. The second cutter replies that he is working to earn a living to provide for his family and he is relatively happy with what he makes. The third stonecutter, with a sparkle in his eye, tells the man, "Can't you see, I am building a cathedral." I subscribe to the idea that we are building "cathedrals" with our athletes. We may never see the finished product, but we are part of building something much greater and more significant than ourselves.

The Leader

Overview & Strengths

Out of all of the archetypes you'll encounter, the Leader is the most recognizable. With their seemingly indomitable will, charismatic nature, and natural desire to improve and succeed, the Leader serves as an invaluable piece to creating a truly high-performance culture. They have an amazing gift: the ability to use their own strengths to bring out the best in others. The Leader is a natural influencer, and through demonstrating traits such as accountability, trustworthiness, integrity, charisma, and a second-to-none work ethic, they make those around them want to get better as well. Yet there is a caveat to be aware of: some athletes have the "leadership gene" deep inside them, but may not yet have the confidence or maturity to know how to express it. It's important to recognize these budding stars. With guidance and perhaps a few words of encouragement (i.e., letting them know that you recognize these traits inside them and want them to assume the role of leader) you can help them cultivate self-belief and hasten the process of their development.

Weaknesses

While it may seem like the Leader simply doesn't have any weaknesses, we know this is not the case. Leaders are often comfortable taking the whole team on their back if necessary. They are the ones who are willing to sacrifice so much to achieve an end goal. They work relentlessly in order to feel like they did everything they could to contribute to a positive outcome. While these are laudable traits, they put the Leader at risk; for they often carry the burden of others or inappropriately take the blame for a loss. They may not show signs of this stress externally (although some certainly wear their heart on their sleeve), but the internal negative self-talk occurring inside the Leader after a loss can be as unremitting as their work ethic in preparing for victory. They will often replay every moment and every action inside their head, wondering what they could have done differently and deconstructing what needs to be done next in order to avoid repeating the same (losing) fate and subsequent feeling.

How to Connect

Depending on your own personality and communication style, connecting with the Leader should be amongst the easiest of all of the archetypes. They will recognize a coach who has a purposeful vision, is honest, strong in their convictions, and dedicated to helping others succeed. Whether you are assuming a new role within a team or organization, or you are simply addressing a new group of athletes that you are responsible for developing, early identification of Leader archetypes is critically important to making your job easier and setting the social dynamics in your relationship with the Leader. When meeting with the Leader, utilize the tactic of gaining power by giving power, in which you let them know that you appreciate what they bring to the table, you support them, and you want them to serve as a galvanizing force for their peers (which they will likely do naturally). In doing so, you are activating their true nature and also elevating their opinion of you, which in turn strengthens your relationship and gains you a powerful ally as you work to build a productive culture in the team/training environment.

Coaching Clinic:
Contribution by Coach Ron McKeefery M.A., MSCCC, CSCS*D

One of the things I love most about working with college athletes is having the opportunity to help them transition from high school to college. In our recruiting efforts, we look at lots of metrics; but one specific trait we look for is leadership. Was the athlete a captain on their high school team? Did they have a positive or negative influence on their teammates? Did they inspire those around them?

The problem with these criteria is that for most (but not all) high school teams, the captain's vote, influence, and inspiration becomes more about their popularity rather than substance. It is not uncommon during January and February recruiting weekends to have the majority of athletes in the room profess to be a captain of their high school team—a leader. They often lead their teams to great success on the gridiron, full of confidence and bravado, only to find themselves unsure of their leadership abilities on Saturdays in September eight months later at the collegiate level, when the speed and stakes of the game have increased.

I have yet to work with a natural-born member of the Leader archetype. However, I have worked with a number of players who have developed into exceptional Leaders. One player in particular that I had the opportunity to work with serves as a shining example.

He showed up his freshman year as a quarterback. He had a successful high school career, captaining his team and leading them to a State Championship. His parents, an interracial married couple, were both educators and phenomenal people. Additionally, he is a man of faith and had grown up around the church.

Most might say he was a natural-born Leader. However, to the one person who truly determines whether or not you are a natural born Leader—yourself—he was not one at all. In his eyes, he was just another scrawny freshman that was sitting at third on the depth chart at his position. He was unsure if he would ever play let alone lead this team.

There were points during this athlete's freshman year where, as a coaching staff, we were disappointed in his ability and lack of leadership. We were left wondering if he would ever meet the standards we set for him. He was aware that people gravitated toward him and that he had leadership ability, but he really couldn't understand why. Doing the right thing, exerting great effort, and being coachable were all things that had been reinforced in his childhood.

Despite his perception of having a very posh life, he had to deal with his own challenges and adversity. As a young boy he had to overcome some racial undertones of being a mixed child, and as a sophomore in college he had to accept that playing quarterback, a position he had played his entire career, was not working out. Up until that point, this athlete never really felt he was a Leader. He had always identified his leadership by the position he played or simply by being in the starting lineup.

John Maxwell, in his book, *5 Levels of Leadership*, outlines the five levels as: Position, Permission, Production, People Development, and Pinnacle. With position, people follow you because they have to, and as a quarterback in high school, he had become accustomed to this. He had also gained permission to lead (from coaches and other players) and he was producing (he was, in fact, talented). Once he got to college, however, he lost those levels of leadership when he moved positions, away from quarterback. I wanted to help him progress from Level 1 (based on his position) to Level 5, pinnacle, which is based on earning the respect of your peers for who you are as a person. At the same time, I had to coach him in the traditional aspects of strength and conditioning.

Most will assume that training leaders is easier. Yet often, it can be more difficult. With this particular athlete, I did four things:

1. **Gain Permission:** As mentioned several times in this book, you have to establish a relationship with your athletes to be able to have an impact. Leaders are an especially informed consumer. They have a set of beliefs and values, and they view themselves and the world around them in a certain way. Consistency and long -term progression is very important. As a great friend of mine would always say: "You spell love T-I-M-E." It is very important to allow a Leader to have input into the process. With these athletes,

there is a paradigm shift that needs to occur. They need to see themselves at a new level. With our player, gaining permission began with sending him motivational quotes and Bible verses (knowing he would take to these things). This led to extended conversations after workouts, and then to heart-to-heart conversations about his position change.

2. **Define "Good":** We had to take what he considered to be "good" and set a new standard. Up until that point in his life, getting a college scholarship was good. We had to show him another level and encourage him that he could get there. Early on, we used testing numbers to show what he would need to do to become a starter. Later, we used the NFL combine statistics for quarterbacks (and then safety when he later moved positions). We also had to show him the impact he could make outside the world of athletics. We did this by challenging him to be more than just another student; to help him see that he could use his celebrity as an athlete to create meaningful change in the world that extended far beyond the playing field. This started by defining how he could use football as a platform to make an impact in the community. In his later years, we dialed in on what it would take for him to become a professional football player.

3. **Harness Peer Pressure For Good:** College is a time when most people discover who they really are. There are so many influences, both good and bad, in that process. Peer pressure is powerful and as coaches we want to tap into that power for good, not evil. With this athlete and others like him, we created a leadership group called "The Commission." We met each week and read the book 21 Irrefutable Laws of Leadership. The guys in the group each took a law and would discuss how it applied to themselves and

the team. By providing an environment to embrace those leadership qualities, it became cool to do the right thing. In other words, we harnessed peer pressure for good.

4. **Hold Accountable:** In team environments, when there are 100-plus athletes, minor infractions by leaders often go unchecked. Yet with each minor infraction, the Leader's ultimate potential gets lowered. Leaders will rise to a challenge if they are expected to hit it. You must set and maintain a high bar, and hold a Leader to the same degree of accountability as everyone else. With this particular athlete, he often felt as if I had his number. He and players on the team would wonder why I was so hard on him. However, by the end of his career, he was beyond grateful for my maintaining such a high bar.

This particular athlete went from a "former quarterback" who struggled to see a Leader in himself to a high NFL draft pick that led not only on his NFL team, but also in the community.

Not every player will become the captain or a Leader on the team. On those January and February recruiting weekends, I tell recruits that strength and conditioning goes beyond sport; that I want them to be the best overall leaders they can be, across all walks of life. Those young 18-year-olds will someday be leading their own families and to do so effectively they will need to draw upon everything they learned as an athlete.

I can think of no better place than the weight room, conditioning field, or gridiron to teach the skills necessary to impact this world in a positive way. In those environments, athletes have the opportunity to set goals, work to achieve them, deal with adversity, persevere, manage success, and collaborate with others.

You may never know who the Leaders of your team will be. Heck, like in this case, they may not even know themselves. However, if you challenge each athlete to become the best version of him or herself that they can be, you will often get exactly what you are looking for.

The Self-Sabotager

Overview & Strengths

Ask coaches or players in any sport if they have ever met an athlete who had the physical gifts necessary to play the sport but couldn't seem to lock down the mental component, and you will likely be treated to stories that could last for hours (if not days). These stories are usually replete with examples of athletes who let moments become monsters by letting their anxieties, self doubts, or tendency to overthink things throw a wrench into both their physical mechanics and psychological mindset. These athletes care a great deal about their performance yet simply cannot shake the doubts or processing errors that occur when the stakes are high and the lights are on. Meet the Self-Sabotager.

One particularly intriguing characteristic of the Self-Sabotager is the variety of ways they can be identified. Some examples of this archetype approach training and practice with diligence, a sound work ethic, a clear respect for the process, and a hunger to get better. Others identified within this archetype can be highly skilled and naturally talented athletes who simply don't take their training or practice seriously enough, overthink, or allow for aspects of their personal life to affect their level of preparation. This overreliance on their innate ability often cannot overcome the incessant infections brought about by poor lifestyle choices, preparation, and overall decision making. In other words, some in this archetype train great and sabotage themselves in the limelight, whereas others have natural gifts but sabotage themselves by not applying them.

Weaknesses

Regardless which type of Self-Sabotager you have in your midst, all in this archetype struggle from the same root problem: paralysis by analysis. Overthinking during athletic competition slows neural impulses that allow for explosive and precise muscular action. This virus spreads as one error is made and thus leads to another. Athletes within this archetype often allow their actions to temporarily become their identity. Once their mindset is infected with self-doubt, anxiety, and frustration, the result is a negative psychological compound interest effect that continues to build, eventually taking them out of competition entirely. It's quite the vicious cycle. Many a Self-Sabotager struggles with fear or anger issues related to these repeated breakdowns, while some deflect their emotions elsewhere, struggling to find a remedy.

How to Connect

Great coaches realize that the Self-Sabotager will only improve by continuing to face the situations that bring about the most anxiety. They know that the opposite of fear is not a lack of fear, but rather a love of learning. This notion serves as a communication on-ramp for the coach who understands the practice of *Conscious Coaching*. It's important for the coach who has identified a Self-Sabotager on his or her team to observe them in a variety situations during practice in order to identify areas of training or skill development in which they do extremely well and brings them confidence. Once these areas are identified, it becomes easier for the coach to put everything into context for said athlete, and they can enact strategies that help alleviate anxiety, like proper visualization practices.

Fighters and their cornermen embody this philosophy. A fighter can hit all of the mitts, bags and dummies they want, but to be great in the ring, eventually they are going to have to stand toe to toe with another fighter and learn what it's like to both see and feel a punch from a true opponent. This is the only way they will learn how to avoid the same punch the next time. Again, as I alluded to above, dealing with fear is about facing fear and learning from the experience. Repetition serves as a convincing argument for the Self-Sabotager. They should strive to immerse themselves in the situations they fear succumbing to the most. From a coaching standpoint, the positive effects of this trial by fire approach is amplified only if the Self-Sabotager is guided along the way. You, as the coach, must help them break down the results of their actions and mistakes so they can see missed opportunities and openings that they can take advantage of next time.

Coaching Clinic:
Contribution by Bryan Mann PhD, CSCS*D, RSCC*D

I have coached several Self-Sabotagers, and I can honestly say I enjoy coaching this archetype. The only thing that gets in their way is themselves. If the Self-Sabotager can step out of his or her own way, they will achieve the greatness that is locked inside of them. Oftentimes there are underlying issues that are beyond a strength coach's realm of practice, but often we are the conduit to get them the help they need.

The first thing I did with a Self-Sabotager I coached was get to know him on a deep and personal level. Once I got to know him, I started to understand the why's and how's of his actions. It turns out the kid was a victim of an alcoholic and abusive father. His father demanded perfection—nothing short of it was ever good enough. As a matter of fact, anything less than perfect would often end in rage from his father.

Any time the sporting situation would tighten, he would always falter. He was not able to perform because he was overwhelmed by the anxiety of potentially disappointing his father. According to the psychologist and founding father of flow states, Mihaly Csikszentmihalyi, to feel flow and reach optimal performance, you must be entirely in the moment. This athlete could not be in the moment because any time the competition got tight, he was not there, but rather a small boy in his father's house about to get beaten.

So how did I reach him? I showed him love, first and foremost. If something went great, I gave him a hug. If something went wrong, I gave him a hug. He had to see and feel that love was not tied to his ability to play the sport. After that, we worked on some other mental skills, such as relaxation and mindfulness. This kid had PTSD (Post-Traumatic Stress Disorder) and needed treatment for it. While he was in counseling, we tried to implement the counseling into his training program in the weight room. We did deep-breathing exercises, we tried to feel as much as we could during an exercise in order to be entirely in the moment. When someone is triggered with PTSD, it's not a cognitive thing, but rather a physiological response. The sympathetic autonomic nervous system is engaged. The response is fight or flight. Any decision the Self-Sabotager makes when this system is engaged is driven by emotion, not conscious and rational thinking. Realizing this, we must try to get the Self-Sabotager to be able to be more mindful and relax in sporting situations. And, to do that, we can practice it in the weight room.

I mentioned relaxation and mindfulness. These exercises were prescribed and guided closely by his psychological provider. I cannot state the following enough: we as strength and conditioning coaches shouldn't cross boundaries, and rather than try to help athletes with underlying psychological problems ourselves, we are better off linking them up with a trained professional in that field. What we did do in the weight room, however, was lots of visualization. Before any heavy lifts, we would go through Cook's model of concentration and visualization. Does the visualization help in the weight room? Yes. But is it absolutely crucial? No. Visualization is a skill, and just like any other skill, you have to practice in order to get better at it. We did it over and over in the weight room and improved that skill so he could use it in his sport, especially when the stakes were high.

Now how did he apply this to his sport? For situations in which he was normally unsuccessful, he would visualize himself being successful time and time again. He repeated this exercise so many times that his anxiety went away. He more or less had hardwired how he would act in pressure situations. Now, instead of overthinking these tight situations (and worse yet, going back to his childhood), he could simply react and be completely present in the moment, in flow, playing to the best of his ability.

We also worked on focus. Visualization and Cook's model helped a lot with that, too. We focused on the things that mattered for his sport, things like the cues he had to read, or the plays that were called, or what was going on around him. There are a lot of things that don't matter in sport (e.g., fans, media, television, and, to an extent, even things like home-field advantage). If you pay attention to those things you will get lost. Of course, there will be some anxiety, because if you compete in sport at a high level you probably have at least 5,000 different distractions to deal with on any given play. But if you can learn how to tune them out and instead focus on what matters, you'll be much better off.

I got this particular athlete to watch a movie called The Peaceful Warrior, and it was probably the best thing I ever did because the messages it contained stuck. There were three questions the guy asked himself to get into the moment in the movie: "Where are you? When are you? And what are you?" The proper response was, "Right here. Right now. And in this moment." In the movie, he explained to a teammate that when he was competing, what his girlfriend thought didn't matter, what his parents thought of his success or failure didn't matter, and the crowd didn't matter, either. All that mattered was that he was right here, right now and in this moment and that way he could compete and succeed. After watching The Peaceful Warrior, any time my athlete started to get away and get a bit squirrelly, so to speak, either I would ask him or he would ask himself: "Where are you? When are you? And what are you?" And, without fail, he would come back into the present moment.

This kind of technique relies upon something called thought stoppage. It's great because no matter how much is going on, you can only think of one thought at a time. It's impossible to think of two thoughts. If his thoughts gravitated toward negative things, all he had to do was return to his mantra of right here, right now, and in this moment. And, just like that, the other thoughts were gone.

Now I wish I could tell you that this athlete went on to compete professionally and had a long and illustrious career, but that's not the case. What he did do, however, was the best that he could with what little talent he had, not to mention against the backdrop of his rough past. I may be in the minority but I think our jobs are more about winning kids with sport than it is winning sport with kids. As a result of our interactions and his participation in sport, this athlete learned how to deal with his demons in a more constructive manner and he lived life with much less fear and anxiety.

Some takeaways from this story: The Self-Sabotager gets stuck worrying about something else, so you must work with him or her to focus on the task at hand. Not everyone can focus easily; it is a skill and it needs to be developed. Coach Self-Sabotagers on strategies like positive self-talk, thought stoppage, and visualization. These three tools can significantly improve their likelihood of success. Lastly, some of these athletes may need counseling, medication, or a combination of both. Not every athlete in this archetype has some sort of underlying trauma, but many do. There is an old saying, "Everyone you meet today is undergoing an incredible struggle, so be kind." They may need help and yelling at them isn't helping.

The Mouthpiece

Overview & Strengths

The Mouthpiece archetype is ever the distracting force and nearly every strength and conditioning coach who has worked in either the team or private setting has encountered one. Their somewhat inexorable determination to be heard or seen at all times makes the Mouthpiece one of the easiest archetypes to identify early on. Depending on the individual, their incessant chatter can range from having undertones of positivity and negativity to being downright useless and delusional.

Despite their obtrusive tendencies, the Mouthpiece can shine in certain environments or situations through heightening the natural energy of the locker room, weight room, practice field, or pre-game environment. Some members of this archetype are masters of elocution in the sense that they often know just what their audience wants to hear, as well as just how to say it so that it provokes maximal peer engagement. In this sense, the Mouthpiece and the Politician are close compatriots.

Weaknesses

Many times, the Mouthpiece struggles to focus. No matter the amount of wind that comes out of their mouth, it rarely points the ship's sails in the right direction. They tend to act is if nothing bothers them or poses a challenge. This initially presents itself as a narcissistic characteristic, but in truth, is usually a guise for insecurity or uncertainty and is often a segue to repeated mental mistakes. Despite the success of loquacious legends of sport such as Muhammad Ali, Floyd Mayweather and Terrell Owens, for the majority of athletes, the perceived value of trash talk isn't supported amongst many within the scientific community. That's because the time and mental effort required for trash talk ultimately serves as a distracting force when the act of simply playing well would be the most intimidating factor.

How to Connect

See situations through the eyes of the Mouthpiece. Even if you're more the introverted and reserved type, or an old-school coach who channels his or her inner Gran Torino persona (see: "Clint Eastwood movies"), you must come to terms with the fact that there are others who are not like you. In order to successfully lead a group of individuals, let alone bring out the best out in someone, you have to first get outside of yourself. As hard as it may be for some old-school coaches to understand, one of the best ways to connect with the seemingly annoying Mouthpiece is to get inside their head. The fact is that with the advent of countless social media outlets and non-stop entertainment-based sports programming continuing to inundate the airwaves, the world seems to never stop talking. As a result, there is now a generation that believes constant self-expression is the new normal. In the United States especially, we are immersed in a culture where being different and loud is often celebrated, even if someone is being different or loud for no good reason. Everywhere today's athletes turn, they hear about their role models or celebrities and have 24/7 access to their thoughts, injuries or personal drama by way of social media, message boards and various online rumor mills. So, they too start to believe that they must make waves as well. After all, trash talk was even present in Biblical times! In Samuel 17:46 it seemed to work for David when he fought Goliath. But as author Malcolm Gladwell has already pointed out, we know that there were numerous other factors at play. David's trash talking was hardly the deciding factor in that showdown.

Even so, we as coaches must compromise and meet the Mouthpiece where they are in order to influence them. Compromise is essential to lasting connections, and to connect with the Mouthpiece you have to win them over by striking a balance between letting them do their thing and reminding them that there's a time when they have to get "off stage." Lastly, today's Mouthpiece would be well served to remind him or herself to not be fooled by the illusions, images, or idolism projected by mediums of popular culture. As coaches, we know that famous examples of this archetype are the exception to the rule rather than the rule itself. The vast majority of Mouthpieces are those you don't hear about because they cannot attain consistent high-level performance. They are too busy talking.

Coaching Clinic:
Contribution by Coach Kyle Holland CSCS

If you're new to coaching, getting in front of a group of people and leading them through a workout can be nerve-racking. It's similar to the anxiety many feel before doing some form of public speaking. When training a group of professional athletes, you can take those nerves and multiply them. And, if there happens to be a Mouthpiece in the group, just sprinkle another layer of discomfort on top of that. How you deal with that individual (i.e., the Mouthpiece) will play a large part in how the training session goes for the entire group, and your ability to deal with the Mouthpiece can also be a big measuring stick for you as a coach to determine if you're ready to coach on a bigger stage. Whether you like it or not, if you have aspirations of coaching for a professional team, this is an archetype you must learn to work with.

At one of my previous jobs, I coached at a private facility that had a fairly steady flow of professional athletes who would travel back to train with us during their respective off-seasons.

The group I worked with was made up largely of NHL players. If you don't know anything about hockey, it's hard to appreciate how grueling their seasons can be on both the mind and body. The sport breeds and attracts a very gritty and tough type of person, and all the time spent with the boys at practice, on the road, and in the locker room often gives rise to a good ol' boy sense of humor that I've always related well to and found to be very funny and refreshing. The Mouthpieces that emerge from this group are really keen on knowing exactly what to say, when to say it, and who to say it to—all with a great combination of edge and wit. They've spent years sharpening their skills in this area, just like the blades on their skates. There is one athlete in particular that sticks out in my mind that fits the archetype of the Mouthpiece perfectly, and I was lucky to have had the opportunity to work with him. With the support of my superiors, I was given the chance to train this person, make many mistakes, and build a relationship for numerous off-seasons in a row. These experiences were priceless and I'm forever grateful. Hopefully you can learn from them no matter what setting or population you are working with.

Before you begin training a Mouthpiece, remember the rule about making assumptions: They make an ass … you've heard it. It's trite but true. Whether the person is only outspoken amongst their teammates or a social media soundbite giant, don't make any assumptions about them as a person or why they make noise. It could be for a number of reasons. Maybe they talk a lot because it motivates them and they're attempting to boost their own self-image. Or maybe it's because they like to see their name in print and they believe any press is good press. Or it could be that their persona is a complete act and their actions are part of a master plan to build their brand and turn that into money (this happens more often than you think). No matter their motivation, the Mouthpiece wants people to pay attention to them. It's natural. Don't sweat it too much or become too disappointed with it. You have a job to do, and if done well, the benefits could range from you getting a better coaching job or possibly finding yourself in the public eye as the coach who was the Mouthpiece's secret weapon.

I shouldn't have to say this but I feel like it should be addressed: Before each training session you MUST be well-groomed, look professional, and be prepared. You don't have to be in better physical condition than the athletes, but you have to at least be in the ballpark. Whatever moniker you want to use, whether it's "dress for the job you want" or "if you want to be the man you have to wear the suit," there's some truth in those statements. You'll be taken more seriously when you present yourself professionally. Don't believe me? Try it. Wear a polo for a few days with your gym shorts and you'll notice a difference. You must also show up early and have the room set up for the workout you're leading that day. How early?

Earlier than the earliest athlete who comes in to stretch or do their pre-workout routine. No one in the group should see you setting up the gym. It should be done before they walk in the doors. Not being organized is a bad look for you as a coach, and when dealing with Mouthpieces, you have to be put together. You cannot give them any ammo to use against you before the session even starts. Start off on the right foot and mitigate the risks of things not going the way you want.

Equally important to being prepared is being yourself. You must be authentic. Don't put on a front or try to coach using someone else's style. I am currently a Tactical Performance Specialist and I coach with the military. The Commander of our unit is a very good leader and one day I asked him if he had any advice on how to influence others. He told me to just focus on being me—a lot of me. He said to be yourself and turn up the volume. It's one of the finer bits of advice anyone has ever given me. People can sense when you're trying to be something you're not and it's awkward. The hyper-socially aware Mouthpiece will generally pick up on it, along with the rest of the team or group, and you'll become one of the Mouthpiece's punchlines. It will be hard to recover from this mistake and you'll have a tough time getting anyone to take you seriously.

If the Mouthpiece chooses to do his or her chirping during a team or group training session, it's your job as the coach to keep it a team or group training session. Don't let the Mouthpiece steal the show. By doing this you'll have the collective strength of the rest of the group behind you and they will generally police themselves. Their support will help aid you in keeping the Mouthpiece in check. But when he or she is bringing a positive energy, feel free to ride that wave. You can't go around ignoring the athlete.

Use all the benefits that the Mouthpiece can bring you but be careful not to go all-in and get out of being who you truly are, or worse yet, give up your control to the Mouthpiece. Give away your control too often, and it will be hard to deny the Mouthpiece whenever they want it again.

The Mouthpiece might also turn negative. Acknowledge this but go about your business as usual. Between drills, try to connect with them quietly on the side and ask, "Hey are you doing alright? I noticed you were a little out of it today. If there is something I can do, let me know." Making a personal connection with them is critical. If they know that you care about them as a person, they will never turn on you or look to undermine you. You'll be on the way to building a solid, lasting rapport that can do wonders for both you and the athlete.

As with any athlete, the more you get to know the Mouthpiece on a personal level, the more you'll find out what makes them tick. Always keep your coaching consistent on a global level with the team or group, but keep making connections locally with the athletes who need that personal touch. If the Mouthpiece ever comes to you with a request or asks for alterations in their workout, keep an open mind and hear them out. Unlike the Politician archetype, I've never found a Mouthpiece that wants to get out of doing work. Mouthpieces are often some of the hardest workers on a team. If their suggestion is reasonable and you have enough autonomy over the training regime to make a change—and it doesn't make it look like you're caving into the superstar in front of the team—then do it. This will further strengthen your personal connection. If you can't accommodate them for whatever reason, be aware that big egos don't like to be told no, or that they can't do something. So be able to justify your reasoning and present them with alternatives that accomplish the same goal. You must maintain your relationship with this person and use the situation to display your knowledge as a coach. If done tactfully and with a good explanation, saying no can actually build the Mouthpiece's trust in you because it shows you care about them and are looking out for their best interests.

There will be times when the Mouthpiece will test you. Athletes spend so much time around strength and conditioning coaches, especially during the off-season, that they will become very comfortable with you.

I once made a big mistake with the particular Mouthpiece mentioned above during a conditioning session. I had been working with him for the previous two off-seasons, so we had built a certain comfort level with each other, but we weren't best buddies. He made a remark to me that I thought crossed the line, and since it happened in front of the entire training group, a response was in order. In hindsight, I probably shouldn't have come at him as strongly as I did, or maybe at all. On that day, however, I went back at him hard. We exchanged words and then it was done. No apologies were offered by either of us. The next day, we both showed up and clocked back in for work. In no way am I condoning that you should get in verbal battles with your athletes. You'll need to assess the situation on your own and hopefully make the right call. But sometimes, you've got to stand up to the athlete.

Lastly, don't abuse the spotlight that comes with training the Mouthpiece (if they happen to be in the public eye). Too many coaches in this field try to make their name as big as their athletes' names. They just can't help themselves. If you focus on doing a great job, credit will land where it's due. People can sense when you're trying to sell them something, and if you're trying to cling onto the successes of your athletes, you'll lose all credibility. On top of all that, you'll alienate your fellow coaches and superiors who have helped you along the way, and they will quickly turn on you, too.

If approached with the right mindset, coaching the Mouthpiece archetype can be very rewarding and a lot of fun. Gaining your athlete's trust takes time, so be patient. We preach consistency with our athletes and we must do the same with ourselves as coaches. Consistently show up with the right attitude and create a great environment for athletes to train hard, and good things will happen.

The Wolverine

Overview & Strengths

For many of you, just reading the name given to this archetype says it all. Not because it is more descriptive than the others, but because the character that the name is inspired by has been so visual for several decades via the superhero faction known as The X-Men. For those of you who grew up watching Saturday morning cartoons or later in life have found yourself drawn into movie theaters to see movies inspired by author Stan Lee's creations, you are likely familiar with this archetype already. For those of you who aren't familiar, Wolverine is a fictional character whose rage, relative introversion, distrust and general rogue tendencies (the genesis of which is embedded in past traumatic experiences) make him who he is: a complex personality who is often hidden or withdrawn. Shrouded in pain, anger, sadness or sometimes all three, this archetype can be one of the trickiest to navigate and is one with whom you must be most patient. Ironically, the inherent strengths of this archetype are often fostered by the same things that bring about their weakness. Their rough background, sense of distrust, often fiery demeanor and predilection for laconic interaction lends them to being someone who typically relies only upon themselves and doesn't feel that they need a large crowd of supporters to push them forward. Their self-sufficiency is often fueled by their inner angst and seems to have a way of maturing them earlier in their life since they've had to face the harsher realities of the world early on. This oftentimes keeps them from being as outwardly rowdy as the Mouthpiece or as internally disruptive as the Manipulator (more soon), but if tempers flare then all bets are off.

Weaknesses

The Wolverine's fear, anger and distrust can get the best of them. Much like the Self-Sabotager struggles with over-thinking or self-doubt, the Wolverine struggles with finding an outlet when their emotions run hot and things get rough. We've seen extreme examples of athletes that share traits of this archetype in the past.

Former World Heavyweight Champion and boxing legend Mike Tyson was notorious for his unpredictable paroxysms and displayed Wolverine-like tendencies in different periods of his life. While under the guidance of coaching legend Cus D'Amato, he flourished. Cus helped Mike discover an outlet and introduced a sense of stability into his life by bringing him into his home, establishing a consistent training routine, and giving Tyson realistic targets to aim for that helped build up his self-esteem. Unfortunately, once Cus died and negative influences entered Mike's life, he experienced a rapid personal and professional downward spiral during the latter part of his career.

If the Wolverine is left to his or her own devices (as is commonly the case since many coaches struggle to interact with this archetype), they run the risk of ruining their own athletic career before it truly gets started. This is not to say that Wolverines cannot be successful without personal or professional guidance or intervention, only that their performance ceiling is likely much higher if they have someone to help them remain emotionally in control.

How To Connect

When it comes to the Wolverine, I am biased. This has always been one of my favorite archetypes to work with and also one of the most rewarding, despite the initial difficulties a Wolverine may present. To this day, some of my closest athlete relationships are with Wolverines I've trained. These relationships took a long time to bud and required hard work from both parties. Remember, you do not truly know someone until you know what they have been through and what they want out of life. Trust and understanding are the macronutrients that best nourish the coach-athlete relationship, and both of these qualities are of the utmost importance when dealing with the Wolverine.

Many coaches tend to approach this archetype incorrectly by falsely perceiving their strong will or presence as a threat to the coach's authority. They believe the Wolverine to be inherently pugnacious and meet them with a head-on approach, aiming to make him or her concede to their coaching directives. Yet this strategy often stalls true progress and heightens tension between the Wolverine and his or her coach. In other words, Wolverines are not bent through your iron will and persistence as a coach. A successful recipe for connecting with the Wolverine archetype requires a unique combination of patient observation, authenticity, empathy, and both indirect and direct communication methods such as mimicry (verbal and non-verbal), careful word choice, and mindful avoidance of pejorative overtones within your interactions. You should never find yourself backing down from their strong-willed persona. Instead, think three steps ahead and think about the long play. The Wolverine isn't used to people interacting with them in this caring and long-term manner. Thus, it is important to continuously remind yourself that forging a relationship with the Wolverine will take time and trust, and will depend upon your ability to relate to this athlete and convince them to see you in a new light as a positive, stable and consistent influence in their life.

Nothing about the Wolverine's personality or upbringing is textbook, so don't expect the wishy-washy advice you often read in leadership books to help here. Be real with them, and even when they disagree with you or rebel, they will ultimately come to respect you.

Lastly, if you find yourself sharing some Wolverine tendencies of your own and find yourself in a confrontation with the Wolverine, resist the natural urge to "fight fire with fire" and instead practice self-control or mindfulness strategies to bring you back into the reality of the moment. It's OK to be passionate, but you must remember the difference between igniting a match and burning a bridge.

Coaching Clinic:
Contribution by Coach Denis Logan MS, CSCS, USAW

break
verb \ ' brāk
: to separate (something) into parts or pieces often in a sudden and forceful or violent way
: to cause (a bone) to separate into two or more pieces
: to open suddenly, especially because of pressure from inside

What does it mean to break a horse? It is another term for training a horse to take a rider. It is a bit of an unfortunate term as it sounds like the animal is being beaten into submission! This is not true and the "breaking" process is undertaken according to the needs and ability of individual animals and is built upon gaining the trust of the animal. It can take anything from a few months to a couple of years and must be done carefully; if a horse is frightened by the process the fears will stay with it for life.

If there were an archetype that I would assign to myself, it would likely be the Wolverine (commonality in the name Logan, as in the X-Men character's name, aside!). Because of this I am constantly looking to spot other Wolverines, while at the same time thinking, "How would I want to be coached?" when I design my strategies to coach fellow Wolverines.

Buck Brannaman, known to many as the real-life Horse Whisperer, once said, "Discipline and punishment are not the same things. They've been made to seem synonymous but they're not. Discipline is giving people meaningful work to do…punishment is breaking them meaninglessly."

"Breaking" a horse is the more common term used for creating a state of obedience in the horse. Buck uses the word "start" instead. The actions of the horse should come through trust, which is accomplished by "being firm in what you do, but gentle in how you do it."

When dealing with the Wolverine, I've found that authenticity and patience are paramount to success in that both authenticity and patience foster trust. Whenever I encounter an athlete of this type, I immediately know that time is the primary companion I will need in order to reach them and remind myself to be patient.

While I generally love the statement, "Middle-class coaches coach through logic, world-class coaches coach through emotion," it turns out that logic is actually the best first step when coaching a Wolverine. Since Wolverines are already highly emotional, engaging their logical/intellectual brain first makes a lot of sense. For me, engaging their intellectual side provides the distance and safety they will need as they continue to try and figure me out. They must decide, at their own pace, whether or not I am worth trusting. They are typically no-nonsense people, but their introverted disposition keeps them from immediately calling them on their bullshit. So, if at the very least I can logically prove that I am capable of helping them achieve their objective goal, this is the perfect first step to begin the process of gaining their trust.

I've had many athletes of this archetype say to me, weeks removed from when I first told them something, "you were right about this," or "you weren't lying about this," or "you said this was going to happen." If you don't know something, you're better off admitting it. Although this may fall short with other types, it won't with the Wolverine. While they want your expertise, what they really want is to trust you—they're just unsure whether or not they should.

By nature, coaches have a tendency to wield their generally insecure, Type-A personalities toward their athletes, utilizing their positions of power as a means of creating outcomes. Preoccupation with obedience before teaching can very easily create disconnection with the Wolverine: They have already established a mistrust of people who occupy positions of power and use that position instead of truly teaching. Be a leader for the Wolverine. They want to be lead, not pushed around. They want to work, not be punished. Clarity of intent and explaining how something will help them achieve their goal is important. The Wolverine generally dislikes "busy work."

Once you've started to generate some trust and you've passed the logic stage, push them. But again, push them with discipline, not punishment. The world they're most accustomed to has punished them for being who they are, so more often than not they will challenge the work you give them if it appears to come from a place of punishment. Most recently, I was working with an athlete that consistently reminded me of this. "I don't do well with punishment work," he said. There has to be a clear meaning to the work being done. If this meaning is there, the Wolverine will put everything they have into the work because they want to succeed. They don't want to be broken any more than they already have been. But they do want to be started.

To create that lasting connection, it has long been my belief that empathy will go further than sympathy. If there is a common entry point, utilize it. If there isn't a common entry point, don't feign that there is. Rather, be authentic and patient, and allow time and the process of creating trust to work its magic.

The Free Spirit

Overview & Strengths

If there is one archetype that can teach us a thing or two regarding a common weakness of our own (as coaches), it's the Free Spirit. Coaches lead a stressful lifestyle. The early mornings, long days, intensive physical and psychological commitment, Type -A personality characteristics and lack of job stability can suck the life out of you if you let it. To top it off, when we do struggle as coaches, we mask it with bravado or try to expunge it from our memory banks by burying ourselves in our work. We often forget that while our pride pushes us to be the best, in reality, it often keeps us from doing so. In many ways, the Free Spirit is the antithesis of us. Regardless of their age, they exude a youthfulness and childlike wonder in regard to how they approach life and sport. Everything they do appears as if they are in a constant state of play. Oddly enough, it's how we as coaches felt when many of us first started in our field. The difference is that the Free Spirit never seems to lose it. When observing the Free Spirit, it is not just that they march to their own beat, but rather it is as if music flows through their veins. Often light on their feet, smiling and energetic, they remind us of a goal that we should all strive to achieve: to die young as late in life as possible, and to enjoy every moment.

Weaknesses

Certain gifts can be both a blessing and a curse. With the Free Spirit's laid back nature and psychological buoyancy comes a tendency to be a bit forgetful and absent-minded at times. You may find yourself frustrated with the Free Spirit's lack of focus and/or patience, something especially true in younger members of this archetype (think: teenagers into early 20's). Be patient, but not passive. If instances of aloofness tend to stockpile, address them early and try to alter the behavior on the spot.

How to Connect

Some confuse the Free Spirit for someone who isn't serious or driven enough to reach a high level. It is a mistake to typecast so quickly. The reality is that a fierce competitor lives within many Free Spirits; it's just that their competitive fire is manifested in a different manner. In their book, Social Psychology in Sport & Exercise, Anne-Marie Knowles, Vaitheny Shanmugam and Ross Lorimer discuss the theory of peer-oriented motivational climates. More specifically, they highlight two distinct dispositional achievement orientations: one centered on task orientation, and the other centered on ego orientation. The authors state that task orientation manifests via perceptions of competence and is evaluated in terms of personal development and also through exercising maximum effort toward the task at hand. Ego orientation, on the other hand, is focused on outperforming others through demonstrations of superiority and via exerting minimal effort to achieve performance or success (Nicholls 1989; Vazou, Ntoumanis, and Duda 2005). To paint a clearer picture of understanding, task-oriented individuals feel more competent if they improve their skill, learn something new, or master a craft, while those who are more ego-oriented feel competent if they demonstrate superiority to others (van de Pol, Kavussanu, and Ring 2012). Through these descriptions, it's easy to see why the competitive nature of the Free Spirit can so easily be misconstrued. They are typically not concerned with asserting dominance in order to feed their ego. Sure, they may want to be the best at a particular sport, game or activity, but the root of their drive to do so is not stitched into the fabric of insecurity or narcissism but rather to a state of competence and satisfaction in performing the act of improvement itself. A large body of social and behavioral psychology evidence has demonstrated that a task-orientated disposition is more closely related to positive outcomes such as increased enjoyment, satisfaction, commitment to skill development, moral functioning, and reduced anxiety (Bortoli, Bertollo, and Robazza 2009; Kavussanu and Roberts 2001; Roberts and Ommundsen 1996; Smith, Smoll, and Cummings 2007). Gamifying drills, competitions, and coaching strategies are great ways to engage the Free Spirit. Still, be careful not to fall into the trap of becoming an entertainer. Instead, simply find ways to unveil the more engaging aspects about a certain drill by showing the Free Spirit how the drill links specifically to the craft they are trying to master, or include events and competitions that require unique problem solving and obstacles within your programming. App developers worldwide have transformed the gaming business by changing our framing of what would normally be considered the simplest of tasks. This works in our industry as well. Even so, that can also get tiresome over the course of the year. So at times, especially in the off-season, try to link drills to other things in life that the Free Spirit enjoys, such as their hobbies (e.g., for a football player who likes surfing, relate a drill to surfing).

Avoid the urge to try overpowering the Free Spirit with a hard-nosed personality. Be direct but don't be dictatorial. Showing that you have a laid back or human side to you can go a long way toward creating better rapport with the Free Spirit. Perhaps more than any other archetype mentioned in this book, the Free Spirit wants to see your relaxed side (which, as I said at the outset of this section, is a challenge for many Type-A coaches).

Coaching Clinic:
Contribution by Coach Matt Gifford CSCS, USAW

Somewhere between San Francisco and New York City, Adam "Magic Man" Mania is freelancing, dabbling in the pool and bringing life to whatever environment surrounds him. At 33 years old, Adam is wildly playful and personifies the idea that "age is just a number." Always dressed rather artistically, Adam shape shifts from athlete to maverick to hipster. He is unforgettable in the swim world for his rocket fast backstroke, Aztec Sun tramp stamp and carefree spirit. If that doesn't paint a clear picture, Adam's "Linkedin Summary" brings poetic justice: "You could say my career path is akin to a blind man's dartboard... and boy was that last shot a doozy! I work in creative advertising and am a former Olympic swimmer in a love affair with my accordion, Moscow mules, Tom Robbins, kebabs, and dressing up for Halloween."

For seven years, I thoroughly enjoyed coaching and riding alongside Adam. I sought to understand him first and foremost. Within reason, I even made it an objective to embrace all his harmless quirks. I became friends with his large network, listened to his band "Hot By Ziggy" and often withstood his infamous bear hug chest compressions (an affectionate version of a defibrillator machine). Quite frankly, I am proud to say I became the best chest compressor in the greater Milwaukee area.

Throughout our training journey together, I aimed to serve him as a travel guide and not a boss. Joseph Campbell famously said, "The privilege of a lifetime is being who you are." When you allow the Free Spirit to live out loud while at the same time taking ownership of their training process, connection is created and "buy-in" begins. Adam taught me much about coaching the Free Spirit and in this process, he helped to set me free.

The highlight of this archetype is the Free Spirit's ability to outwardly inspire their environment. With a unique enthusiasm, charm, and authenticity, the Free Spirit often carries a vibrant yet mystical energy or aura. Whether it is a slick haircut or an aptitude for esoteric conversation and thought, this type of athlete is unmistakable and often easy for a coach to identify. Embodying your own passion and introducing structure eloquently is paramount in establishing the foundation for this relationship. Often, what the Free Spirit appreciates in themselves will be congruently appreciated in you.

Free Spirits crave positive energy, creativity, and innovation. They actually desire a fairly transparent leader to be the yang to their sometimes abstract yin. The charismatic leadership style can often create perfect harmony when implemented appropriately. A Free Spirit with affection for leadership can become an awesome teammate in that they will help their comrades relax, have fun, and enjoy the training process. A relaxed and open environment suits them best and I have found that middle ground needs to be created. Loose and casual conversation is often a must.

I love to accompany the why to everything we do as this archetype looks for big-picture meaning. These athletes crave independence. When trust is built and the situation allows, it is OK to casually turn your back on the Free Spirit and let them be as they create, work, or put in a little extra time to hone their craft. Once the athlete is educated appropriately and has a high training age, including them on decisions regarding set and rep ranges will help this athlete take control of their training process.

Free Spirits love to be guinea pigs and enjoy variety in their training. For that reason, they often respond best to shorter microcycles. Cueing and creating a spark for their imagination allows for further exploration. These athletes love external cues, analogies, and stories. Tell your free-spirited athletes to "broad jump like they are jumping from one end of a falling cliff to another" or encourage them to make the connection with their "inner tiger."

If you cultivate this person correctly, your shared positive results and relationship will explode in a positive manner. However, when overwhelmed, the Free Spirit often implodes. A challenge for this archetype is that sometimes they can be a gamut of emotions. Free Spirits experience epic highs and lows and need to develop coping strategies for when particular moments in time threaten to carry them away. During times of crises, the Free Spirit can become extremely analytical. These situations call for polite bluntness. Goal-setting is a must, as many Free Spirits often struggle with concrete daily targets or long-term agendas.

Conscious Coaching isn't black and white. For that reason, a Free Spirit can either be a coach's dream or their biggest nightmare. Often, our interaction with the ever-so-colorful Free Spirit needs to reside in the grey. This "out there" and eccentric personality can be a rainbow of emotion and that is why a middle-way approach best suits them. Create structure purposefully, give them the why to the what, pick and choose your battles, and remember to have fun while embracing their essence! Whatever you do, do not over-coach them!

The Manipulator

Overview & Strengths

Awareness and recognition of this archetype and the traits that accompany it is critical to preventing headaches as well as entropy of the culture you are attempting to create. The Manipulator has a hidden agenda they will camouflage by appealing to your ego or by catering to your insecurities. They know if they can get you to believe that their goals fall in line with your own, they have you where they want you. Manipulators are also extremely skilled at presenting themselves in a variety of forms and you should expect a degree of difficulty when it comes to identifying a Manipulator. They are constantly shape-shifting their personalities. They are experts in laying low in order to get a read on you before you have the chance to identify them. They are often skilled observers. Below, I have listed several types of Manipulators that you may find yourself encountering at some point of your career. The extensive nature of those with manipulative tendencies make these sub-classifications necessary and are also helpful when it comes to choosing an appropriate strategy for interacting with them. This is by no means a definitive list. It is simply a representation of my own experiences and observations.

Charlatans: Those who utilize a charlatan style of manipulation will find ways to make it appear as if they are the ones who are doing you a favor or have come up with a great idea to somehow improve your own station or situation. This new "friend" will often play the role of a double agent/huckster in that they will often present themselves to be something they are not or as if they possess a helpful bit of knowledge or type of skill set that is best served to help you out, when in reality it likely only serves their own self-interest. For example, an athlete employing this strategy in the training environment may tell another athlete (whom they may perceive as a threat of some kind) that they have recently been getting incredible results by taking a new pre-workout drink prior to their strength-training sessions and that they should try it as well, despite the fact that the supplement was not provided by the school's licensed sports dietician or nutrition staff and not NSF-certified. They know full well that their "victim" may get in trouble or test positive for a banned substance, but will deny any allegation of wrongdoing if caught or questioned. Sound crazy? It's happened. Another example would be telling a teammate that they will cover for them if they are somehow bending team rules or otherwise not following an appropriate code of conduct, when in reality the Charlatan will find a way to indirectly draw attention to the wrongdoing thus getting their counterpart in trouble.

Charismatics: The Charismatic Manipulator is skilled in leveraging the power of elocution and/or an ebullient nature to inspire belief and trust in others. Charismatic manipulation is one of the most commonly observed forms as it is used by politicians, salespeople, and even those within strength and conditioning. On the extreme front, Charismatics in the strength and conditioning realm typically lack a broad understanding of science-based knowledge of performance, but are skilled at motivating others and thus tend to compensate via exaggerated antics, shouting, and other theatrics. One of the most unique traits of Charismatics is that they know how to take an idea or reality that was once perceived as black and white and transform it into a 3D-color image of whatever the audience connects to most. They seek to fill a void by "magically" showing us what we have been missing in our lives or careers, and they have a formula for continuously feeding this fantasy to others. Generally, this formula will include one, many, or all of the following seductive ingredients: the use of humor, wit or charm; an inspiring story of their own or of a great leader in business/history etc.; a notion that they understand what others are going through and how they've gone through it themselves; a desire to help; a willingness to share unique knowledge; and an immediate call to action based upon the urgency of life! These ingredients make them seem more likeable, relatable and trustworthy, all traits that we inherently seek in someone we wish to follow or align ourselves with. The only problem is, often times the Charismatic Manipulator is full of crap!

Charismatic Manipulators can often pull others into trusting them by appearing that they are the life of the party or that they have it all figured out. For example, in student-athletes, at an off-campus party the Charismatic Manipulator may be the one that suggests an idea, steps forward to initiate it, then quickly steps back while others follow the lead and take it to the next level. In the weight room, the Charismatic Manipulator knows exactly when you are looking for them and what you are looking for. Whether it's watching a last set or making sure that they've filled out their training card correctly, the Charismatic Manipulator will do just enough to inspire your trust in them while secretly finding ways to cut corners once they have secured it. This is the type of athlete that is so aware of their surroundings and your tendencies that they will do things at a high level, but not too high as they then know you would expect that from them all the time, which would prevent them from slipping into the background whenever they so choose.

The archetype that the Charismatic Manipulator most closely resembles is the Politician. Thus, you should consider using many of the same strategies when interacting with them. Beware of their chameleon-like abilities to appear as the Leader or the Crusader, for once they have your trust or feel as if they are off your radar, the real danger of what they are capable of can begin to emerge.

Listeners: Listeners can be one of the most dangerous variants of the Manipulator archetype. What makes them so slippery is their ability to veil both their intentions as well as their emotions. People are easily seduced by great Listeners. They make us feel as if what we have to say is important to them and they give us the perception that they want to understand our problems. We are easy targets. Blame our biochemistry, specifically the reward pathway in the brain known as the mesolimbic dopamine system which, under normal conditions, serves as a key detector of rewarding stimulus such as food, sex, and social interactions. In other words, we are literally addicted to sharing information about ourselves. There's science that supports this. In a 2012 study, Harvard psychologists Diana Tamir and Jason Mitchell found that humans devote as much as 30 to 40 percent of their speech to talking about themselves or informing others of their own subjective experiences. They found that people are even willing to sacrifice money in order to talk about themselves.

Listeners prey upon this tendency of human behavior. They are experts at mining for information and holding onto that which is most useful to them in order to leverage it at an opportune time.

An example from my own coaching career featured a Listener who had come into my office and began asking what seemed to be innocuous questions regarding the training program we were on at the time. We were about to finish a particularly difficult absolute strength phase and had one more week left, which was going to be our most intense. He knew this. He asked a few more questions regarding what we would be doing next, as well as how it fit within my philosophy (misdirection) and then finally asked if I had spoken with the head coach of his team lately. We wrapped up the session, he thanked me for the information and headed out. It took me a second at the time, as this athlete had rarely asked about anything related to training in the past (let alone showed any true interest in detail), but I eventually caught onto what he was really asking. At the time, the sport-specific coach was very supportive of strength and conditioning (if you have ever found yourself to be fortunate enough to work with a coach like that, you also understand how good it feels to truly exhale). Periodically, this coach would stop in to see how everyone was doing in the weight room and observe a bit of their training session. I didn't mind as he never questioned anything and enjoyed seeing the kids work hard. What I had learned later is that a number of kids on the team were planning a large party the weekend before. The athlete who oddly came into my office was really asking whether or not the coach would be down to observe their squatting session the following Monday. The athlete would later be upset to learn that prior to his questioning I had not spoken with the coach, but after our meeting I had shot the coach an email letting him know that Monday would be the perfect training session for him to come down and observe!

Regardless of the aforementioned type listed above, Manipulators are insidious in that they are always observing, angling, and waiting for just the right moment to strike so that they can propel themselves into a more favorable situation. They often have a hidden agenda they will camouflage through appealing to your ego or by catering to your insecurities. Whether it is telling their sport-specific coach that their current performance has suffered due to workouts that the strength coach has put them through recently, or telling their strength coach that they are tired due to a long practice that their sport-specific coach ran them through, they will find any way to harness excuses (external locus of control) that are based upon throwing others under the bus in an attempt to paint themselves in a better light. The previous two examples are relatively harmless; yet it is not unheard of to experience Manipulators making up excuses of a far more disconcerting nature like fictitious family emergencies or personal problems since they believe they will not be questioned after providing such a dramatic example.

To manipulate means to control or influence a person or a situation cleverly, unfairly or unscrupulously. It is important to read this definition several times in order to best understand it completely. Even though the Manipulator archetype is largely characterized by selfish intentions and damaging behaviors (both to the individual described as well as to those impacted by them), it is important to realize that they clearly possess strengths as well. If this were not true they would not be able to seduce others so successfully or get them to fall for their ploys. Manipulators are often supremely skilled at reading people and situations. They also possess an uncanny knack for timing and creativity, both of which they use in order to craft their strategies or stories. The irony here is that many of these traits can also be found in the Leader & Crusader archetypes. The distinguishing factor is the intentions behind how these traits used for either the betterment or detriment of others. The Manipulator uses these traits to bring others (and him or herself) down.

Weaknesses

Any success that Manipulators enjoy usually exists within the short term only. They are experts at masking their motives and motivating others by painting a picture that seems to align with another party's goals or desired gains, whether they are as innocuous as wanting to help a teammate or as insidious as taking credit for something they had little true involvement in to improve their position or perception. So, what's their kryptonite? Their big (and often fragile) egos along with their overconfidence in their deceptive methods generally lead them to believe themselves to be more clever than they really are. In the long term, methods that once passed the acid test now become easier to identify by those around them. Those surrounding the Manipulator will eventually become tired of their antics and see the Manipulator for who they really are.

How to Connect

Connecting with the Manipulator requires a soft heart but a firm hand. Remember, your goal is to help someone, not to defeat them. This is useful to keep in the back of your mind in order to keep your emotions in check, especially when the Manipulator tries to undermine your authority or the culture that you are attempting to create. Beating someone at their own game is best illustrated by showing them a better way to achieve their goals, not by matching their tactics or aggressions. If you lose your cool during an interaction or confrontation, you only give the Manipulator more cards to play against you and also show yourself to be someone who is susceptible to their strategies.

One of the best ways to truly connect with the Manipulator is by opening consistent lines of communication between you and other members of the administration or coaching staff regarding the observed manipulative behavior. By sharing a voice of concern and keeping the head sport coach informed of the athlete's behavior (as well as the of the nature of your training sessions), you are able to nip the issue in the bud by establishing a relationship with the coach that is based upon shared information and trust rather than doubt or concern. Let the Manipulator know that you want to understand why he or she feels the need to disguise their intentions or spread false rumors and negativity. Many times, this inveterate behavior was established through the observation (direct or indirect) of others whom they perceive to be successful, or, as a means to create some element of control in their own lives due to a deeply rooted insecurity.

Coaching Clinic:
Contribution by Coach Jennifer Noiles CSCS

I turned the corner into the gym and immediately dropped my water bottle and sprinted toward the 11-year-old who, in a matter of seconds, was going to drop a 90-pound dumbbell on herself. Phew. A very bad situation was averted and a phone call with a very angry parent avoided. I sat the 70-pound athlete on the bench across from me, her size 3 shoes barely touching the floor. With my heart still racing and my armpits sweating, our conversation went like this:

ME: "Sarah, you know the gym rules – no athletes ar……"

ATHLETE: "…are allowed in the gym without their coach. I forgot."

ME: "You could have hurt yourself lifting that dumbbell. Why are you in here?"

ATHLETE: "I wanted to see if I could lift it."

This was a weekly song and dance with Sarah, a rambunctious, incredibly confident and self- assured young soccer player. She reminded me a lot of myself at that age with two exceptions: 1. I was a rule follower; 2. I was a people pleaser.

I wanted to fix this. I had to fix this. How? It was up to me. I figured I would repeat the gym rules every week to the youth group and my staff and I would circulate in and out of the gym before the youth session. I'd have the group meet me on the turf to avoid the distractions in the gym. My thoughts turned to Sarah. There must be something going on in her life to make her act out like this. Something must be wrong. Poor Sarah.

I put my plan into action. The ship ran a little tighter and I had a greater sense of control. The kids responded great! However—surprise, surprise—Sarah's behavior did not change. She became more creative and more "forgetful" of the rules. I increased our little pep talks to once a week. I wanted to understand what was going on in this little girl's life to influence her behavior.

The answer: Nothing! Sarah was happy and healthy. No bullying or strict parent was to blame.

Truth be told, I was the victim of an 11-year-old's manipulation. This was a very hard revelation for me to accept. Sarah was the classic case of selective hearing. She ignored my warnings and my eventual pleas in order to pursue her own wishes. There was nothing going on in Sarah's life to explain her collective behaviors as a defensive strategy. Sarah was on the offensive and was the aggressor. She would do anything to assert, protect, and defend her power and dominance. I failed to see this and consequently my responses were ineffective.

But she was only 11 years old! You might think I am being too harsh on her. She is not a sociopath and she was not deliberately harming someone for pleasure. Society teaches us to be accepting, forgiving, and tolerant of others—give people the benefit of the doubt. These teachings make it difficult to pass judgement and therefore make it almost impossible to view someone's actions as manipulative, especially a mere child. Sarah consumed the energy and focus of the people around her, myself included. This was unfair to the other athletes in the group and unfair to the staff members I pulled in with me.

Sarah is not the only manipulator I have worked with. She did however teach me the most about human nature. Thanks to her I am now less naive. People are going to fight for what they want and what they feel they deserve, and they are going to go about it in a number of ways. Accepting this does not mean you are giving up on society. Accepting this allows you to recognize someone's actions as manipulative and empowers you to act accordingly. In Sarah's case, she needed to be told no firmly and there needed to be consequences for her actions. This would have taken her power away.

Today, Sarah is a successful college sophomore, having received a full soccer scholarship. She is a contributing member of society. We keep in touch and I am pleased to see she is going after what she wants. And me? Thanks to Sarah, I am less likely the victim of manipulation.

The Underdog

Overview & Strengths

An underdog can be defined as an individual or group that is at a disadvantage and is expected to lose in a contest or conflict (American Heritage Dictionary, 2015). While we have a natural tendency to rally behind this archetype, a better understanding of the Underdog requires diving a bit deeper into the science. The cornerstone of many a cinematic masterpiece (Think: Rudy, Rocky, Braveheart 300, The Karate Kid, and 8 Mile), we love underdogs. Observations in social psychology show that people tend to root for the underdogs in life and in sport even if their story doesn't pan out (see the annual "March Madness" office betting brackets for further proof). Some researchers will be quick to point out that this doesn't inherently make sense, since a key tenet of social identity theory (Tajfel & Turner, 1986) holds that people form a positive sense of self in part by identifying with in -groups of higher social value. In other words, we should be more likely to attach to others who often experience success. We learned this in high school, as it typically wasn't the mathletes or xylophone club that had the most attractive groupies. Our tendency to distance ourselves from the Clark Griswolds of the world has been well documented by numerous researchers (Cialdini et al., 1976; End, Dietz-Uhler, Harrick & Jacquemotte, 2002; Snyder, Lassegard & Ford, 1986).

Even so, despite what some of the papers say, the fervor for the feeble is real. In a 2015 article, Eddie Pells of the Associated Press wrote, "About a dozen studies over the past 25 years have shown, in one way or another, that we, as sports fans, are inexorably drawn to the team with the odds stacked against it." Another study, performed by Vandello, Goldschmied, and Richards in 2007, presented people with various hypothetical matches between several pairs of countries who were competing in the Olympic Games, for which the participants had no prior affinity or familiarity with. Across all conditions, the participants unanimously preferred the country perceived as the Underdog to win a given event. In this scenario, the Underdog was the country with the lowest total medal count, and the effects were even more prominent when the disparity between the matched country's medal count was the greatest.

We tend to pull for the success of the darkhorse. But why? It's hard to give a decently accurate overview of an archetype that represents an ideal that we are often drawn to but still don't clearly understand the reasoning behind this attraction. Why would our yearning to see the Underdog succeed be so great that we would even sympathize with something as seemingly absurd as drawings of circles that appear to struggle making it up an incline? (Yes, this happened, see a study by Kim, Eylon, Goethels, Hindle & McGuire conducted in 2008.)

The various hypotheses for why we like Underdogs are too expansive to be discussed in great detail for the purposes of this book, but range from our values and feelings surrounding justice and inequality (Lerner, 2003), to the positive emotional impact from unexpected outcomes (Mellers, Schwartz, Ho & Ritov, 1997; Shepperd & McNulty, 2002), to upward mobility bias, which presents the notion that we expect underdogs to get better over time and take action to improve their performance thus rising in ranking over time (Davidai and Gilovich 2015), to an identification with the "little guy." We tend to see the struggles of an Underdog with a lens that provides a similar level of clarity and magnification as the ones in which we viewed our own early or current struggles. Goethals and Allison (2012) talk about struggle as an inescapable aspect of human experience and a key theme in any hero narrative: "We identify with struggle precisely because we know struggle, both firsthand at the level of personal experience and also at the deeper archetypal level" (p. 213)

Voila! Research has helped us to uncover the more deeply embedded reasoning and theories behind the appeal of the Underdog. Perhaps the most easily digestible and poignant of which is that we root for the Underdog because we identify with them. This is exactly why this archetype tends to be one of strength and conditioning coaches' favorite projects.

Ask nearly any strength and conditioning coach who has been in this profession for more than a decade what one of their personal favorite coaching memories or stories was from their own career and you will likely be treated to a tale that more closely resembles that of "Cinderella Man" than "Richie Rich." Are you really that surprised? You shouldn't be, for talent needs trauma in order to manifest in its most iron clad form.

So now onto the identification aspect: How do we know when we are in the presence of an Underdog archetype? Underdogs can take shape in a couple of different ways: there are those who have been overlooked because of their lack of natural physical ability despite being mental warriors, as well as those who have the physical gifts but lack the mental component/ self-belief necessary to let their true potential shine through. I refer to the former classification as the Blue Collars and the latter as the Sleeping Giants. Of course, there are also those who lack both the physical and mental components but these Underdogs do not make up a large percentage of the competitive landscape past high school because they tend to drop out of athletics if neither their head nor heart is in it. In other words, don't expect to see yet another Rocky movie in which the Italian Stallion takes on Napolean Dynamite.

The strengths of Blue Collars are reflected in their name; they roll their sleeves up and get to work. They are used to either being ignored, overlooked, or viewed as a cog in the machine, but their lack of resources will never supersede their resourcefulness. They will leverage any opportunity to improve and routine is part of their DNA. We need people with this mindset—they keep us pushing and they inspire us to do better by never overlooking the small stuff that others view as trivial. Cultures from all over the world have their own stories, whether true or mythological in origin, that illustrate the power of the Underdog who has the right mindset. With their actions, they are able to transform their reality and the reality of those around them. In my own career, I have witnessed several Blue Collars who walked on to the football team and were full-time students while also working multiple part-time jobs due to their lack of financial resources, yet they still made it happen. They have also been some of my best interns and I'm sure will go on to have tremendous coaching careers due to their ability to understand things at a deeper level.

Underdogs understand reality but will not accept it as others define it for them, and they directly or indirectly teach others do the same. Mentally, they maintain a steel will, and they work on strengthening their physical weapons with the steadiness of a medieval iron worker forging a sword. While their physical gifts are not as refined as their Sleeping Giant counterparts, Blue Collar Underdogs are never to be counted out. If given the proper guidance, they can truly flourish (see the Nebraska Football walk-on program in the 90's).

If the Blue Collars forged a sword made of steel, then the physical weapons of the Sleeping Giants more closely resemble the swords used by the Samurai. To provide modern-day context, these swords were largely considered the strongest in the world and would be able to cut through a machine gun barrel. The physical gifts of the Sleeping Giants are never in question; it is just a matter of whether or not they can put it all together. Many of us have coached athletes who have tremendous potential (sometimes to a scary extent) but whom often do not realize it themselves. Sleeping Giants often feel just like everyone else and fail to realize the magnitude of the gifts they have been given. What makes coaching this archetype fun is the new challenge that it presents for a coach. Our job is not one-sided—we need to strengthen mind and muscle. The linchpin of these individuals is their physical prowess. Help them unleash it with confidence.

Weaknesses

Think back to the first time you lost a race against a friend, sibling, or opponent. How did you feel afterward and what did you do to remedy the disappointment or anger you felt? Did you feel like you had something to prove? Like you could do better? Or maybe you knew you could beat that person if given another chance? Welcome to the world of the Blue Collar Underdog. Many Blue Collar Underdogs feel that if just given the right chance they could overcome the obstacles and opponents that obstruct the life they want to live or the victories they so highly covet. But here is the catch: they have to fight like hell in order to just to keep up with their more gifted peers, let alone surpass them! Blue Collar Underdogs must approach their training and recovery with a steadfast and sustainable approach. The mountains they must climb in order to keep up with their more skilled counterparts are high. Without a resilient and focused mindset, Blue Collar Underdogs will find themselves going from what was an uphill battle to one that is suspended in mid-air without a parachute. They need something to anchor them and keep them moving in a thoughtful manner if they hope to succeed.

Success will vary with the Blue Collar Underdog and depend upon their ability to overcome the grind, their age, their maturity level, environmental influencers and, to a point, their ability to remain patient. Timing is everything to the Blue Collar Underdog and they must stay steady in order to capitalize on the mistakes or oversights of those who are naturally more gifted.

Sleeping Giants are a type of athlete archetype that I didn't become more aware of until I had coached for about five years. By then, I had worked with enough athletes from a variety of sports and backgrounds that I had a clearer idea that Sleeping Giants were common enough to warrant their own archetype. As casual observers, we have all been able to loosely pinpoint athletes who we believe to lack certain traits related to focus or resilience, but oftentimes we assign that identity to someone who hangs their head after making a bad play or a quarterback that repetitively throws multiple interceptions per game despite having tremendous physical ability.

One thing I have learned as a coach is that you cannot accurately identify this type of athlete casually or from afar; instead, you have to be around them when the moments become monsters in their head. You need to be present when you see the doubt in their eyes prior to competition or training so that you can bring them back to that very moment later on when you speak with them and try to find out what lies beneath the doubt. This is also where utilizing the body language reading tips (described in later chapters) will come in handy as you seek to find identifying markers of anxiety or fear. The average person often perceives those who are innately talented to possess a bulletproof mindset and unshakeable confidence in themselves. But as coaches, we know all too well that for these athletes the competitive spotlight can illuminate underlying stains on one's confidence the same way a black light makes stains more visible on fabric.

It's hard for some to fathom how a physically gifted athlete can be considered an Underdog. The reality is that a weak mindset is the ultimate disadvantage when it comes to elite performance. Look for signs such as hesitation or anxiety when it comes to one-on-one competitions or high-pressure situations. Also, pay attention to see who they tend to pair up with when training, as they will tend to follow one of two routes when selecting a training partner:

1. Choose someone who is well beyond their mental and physical abilities to see how they measure up so that they can try and muster some confidence.

2. Choose someone who they know poses no true threat to exposing their lack of mental fortitude, or who will not truly test them physically. Which one they choose depends on just how fragile their psyche may be and what they feel like they have to lose should failure occur.

How to Connect

Underdogs, regardless of whether they are of the Blue Collar or Sleeping Giant variety, need a coach who is consistent and willing to help them along in the development process. Blue Collars often work unnoticed in the background while Sleeping Giants are noticed but not easily understood. You can often bridge both of these gaps and spark a fire by cross-pollinating these athletes with one another in the training environment. By doing so, they each push one another in an area of each of their respective weaknesses. The Blue Collar craves the chance to prove him or herself and the Sleeping Giant needs to wake up and realize that facing adversity and failure will only serve as fertilizer for growth. They need to become more comfortable with the anxiety and fear that often go hand in hand with competition. Fear and anxiety are natural human instincts reminding us that what we are doing matters on a deep internal level or requires that we stretch our natural abilities to meet the demands of the challenge.

It's important to note that these types of athletes may not actively seek you out or ask for your direct guidance. Many within this archetype do not want to be a bother and are used to working through their problems on their own.

Others can seem like they have an impenetrable exterior when in reality they are clamoring for attention. As is the case when trying to identify any of the archetypes within this chapter, you must work slowly and gradually when reading the room and those within it. See how they react when you approach them or when you bring up subjects like competition, playing time, pressure situations, and even comfort zones. Pay attention to their behavior in the weight room. We can all relate to a Blue Collar we've coached that seems to lift as if he or she is possessed, and often stays later just to do extra. Many of us can also recall a Sleeping Giant who gets emotional or upset when exposed and perhaps even acts out during training or at the end of a particular drill or competition. As a coach, resist the urge to step in immediately. Take in the moment and find an appropriate time later on when you can talk to the athlete individually. In doing so, you'll create a better opportunity to get a read on them.

We have all been underdogs at some point in our lives, whether it's applying for our dream job, approaching the girl or guy in school we never thought would go out with us, or in our own athletic and competitive endeavors (and perhaps even in our careers as coaches). When trying to connect with an underdog, take the opportunity to reflect on your own thoughts and behaviors from when you were in that situation. After all, these archetypes don't just describe the personality traits of some of our athletes— they describe aspects of our own personalities as coaches as well.

Coaching Clinic:
Contribution by Coach Daniel Noble M.S.Ed., CSCS

In order maximize what you get out of the Underdog, you first have to be able to understand their mindset. I have always felt coaching was a calling more so than a profession. This may be due to the fact that I was the consummate Underdog. When I was young, I suffered a traumatic brain injury in which I almost lost my life. This led to learning disabilities and insecurities that I have only really began to figure out later in life. The bottom line is that I was never the guy coaches or teachers made time for. I was physically gifted in sports but always struggled when it came to the mental side of the game. In school, all anyone told me was what I couldn't do rather than what I could do. While others in university would be out doing what university kids do, I was running stairs or working out. I lived in my own head and constantly struggled with embracing expectations. I always struggled with certain types of coaches and excelled under others. I never understood why I couldn't be more consistent, and why others seemed to let failures slide off their backs while I wouldn't sleep for days after getting benched. When my playing career came to an end, it really made me look back at the coaches in my life and examine why I am the way I am and how I ended up where I did. Coming out of high school I had one coach/teacher who took me under his wing and, in all honesty, saved me from a very difficult path. He was the one that took the time to show me that although I processed and did things differently, it didn't mean I didn't belong. When everyone else in my life was writing me off, he was showing me where my strengths lied. Although this was a step in the right direction, it was only one of many en route to understanding and accepting my own complexities.

Fast forward to my coaching career: The first time I met JK will be forever etched in my mind. It was my first coaching/teaching job and we were already a month into the school year. We were a sports academy that was in only its second year of operation. We had just 19 student athletes at the time. So, when JK's family brought him to the Hill Academy (where we trained at the time), we never really had a choice but to accept him. His grades were failing and he began to surround himself with people that were taking him down a bad path. His parents, both of whom are incredible people, were going through a difficult divorce and they were at the end of their rope in terms of what to do next with JK. I remember immediately looking across at JK and seeing myself 15 years younger (i.e., angry, frustrated, alone, lacking in self-belief, and feeling like I needed to constantly prove something.) Our school's principal and head teacher at the time wanted nothing to do with JK and said everything they could to keep him out of our school. He had stopped playing sports and was nowhere near the caliber of the athletes we had at the school. Everywhere JK went he was told what he couldn't do—no one told him what he could do. I could relate and immediately went to bat for him. I adamantly argued that this was the spot for him. He needed this and I would take personal responsibility for him. It's crucial that certain types of Underdogs, especially ones coming from unique home situations, see that you have their back. JK was reluctantly accepted into the school on a conditional contact. Most of the administrative staff gave him two months to last.

Key points thus far:
— Understand the mindset of the Underdog.
— Also understand where they are coming from and what put them where they are.
— Build trust through action and have their back.

Enter the Underdog:

JK entered the school year in late October and was not only behind academically, but also physically and socially. Although our school was small at the time, we were loaded with high-level talent. Most of these student athletes went on to receive full scholarships to Division 1 schools where they were captains and All-Americans. So, to say the least, this was not an environment that was easy to step into. JK had to make a choice that he wanted to take on this challenge and improve himself, and he desperately wanted to make this choice. He just needed someone to give him the opportunity. JK's first month was not an easy one. Although he made a choice to be at the Hill, he was hesitant to trust anyone and he stepped into a grueling schedule. We would lift every morning at 8 AM and then have a full day of school followed by a full practice. In most programs, this story typically would have ended early for someone in JK's situation. But in this instance, something different happened. Something awoke inside of JK. Although things were incredibly tough, he was receiving something he hadn't had in a long time: A fresh start, and coaches and teachers that believed and cared about him. People quickly started to take notice of the extra effort JK was putting in. His teammates began to rally around him. Although he would finish last in every sprint and puke during most conditioning tests, his effort was never in question. JK began to fall in love with the weight room as lifting became his equalizer. Effort and attitude reign king in the weight room. Although JK may never have been on the same skill level as some of his peers, the weight room gave him a place where he belonged and was able to build courage. Through relentless work ethic, JK went on to become an important part of his team. JK had literally transformed himself and by the spring was unrecognizable compared to his former self. He had confidence, value, and dreams. That April, JK went on to play for his club team. The coaches who had watched JK grow up were shocked by the person and athlete he had become. JK was a new player. He had swagger and confidence, and rather than expecting to fail, he just performed as if he was prepared—because he was.

Unfortunately, JK was running up field with the ball during a weekend tournament when he received a freak hit that caused his head to snap back, resulting in severe trauma to his brain. JK was essentially lost within an instant. This is the most tragic event of my life. It broke me in a way I didn't know if I could recover from. The hurt I observed in his family and friends is indescribable. It's been 10 years since JK left us and I still have yet to fully process what an impact this young man had on my life. It was if we were somehow kindred spirits. My own mess that I had dealt with my entire life suddenly made sense as I was able to use it to play a small role in this incredible man's life. I apologize if this seems disconnected from the Underdog story. But to me it's important for people to understand that in order to truly reach your athletes, you need to open your life and display strength through vulnerability. Every athlete I coach, I coach as if they were my own child. Each one requires a different path and approach.

Although JK has passed, he lived his life in such an extraordinary manner that his legacy only grew with each day since he left us.

JK wore the number #45, which was my football number. I still remember sitting in the room when the coach asked JK what number he wanted. He looked up at me and told the coach #45 for Noble (which is what the students called me at the time). I still think he may have done it partially as a joke, but in the end, I understood it was his way of saying thank you. The way JK approached each day at the school inspired his team and created an unbreakable bond amongst young men. Each and every one of JK's teammates went on to wear JK's number in college and spread his story. Within a year, the story of JK's life was all over the lacrosse world. Athletes all around the NCAA began to learn of his story and would wear his number out of respect, and as a reminder of how fortunate they are to have the opportunity that they have. There are currently more than 100 athletes, both professional and collegiate, wearing the number 45 across their chests.

Key Points:

— The Underdog has to want it!
— Find out what they need to succeed and provide them with it (environment, people, etc.).
— No preconceived notions: Don't judge people before you meet them. We all need a fresh start.
— Build a bond amongst the Underdog's peers.
— Develop courage daily.
— Create the understanding that if the Underdog has to do more, that's OK.
— Say less and simplify the process.

Breaking down the process:

1. "Seek first to understand, then to be understood." —Stephen Covey

This is the first step with all of my athletes. I believe strongly in having unique individual plans and relationships with each one of them. Some will be more meaningful than others, but at the end of the day I need to do the best I can to understand who they really are. Connect to the person to maximize the connection to the athlete. With JK, it was a connection forged through the common struggle we both shared in growing up. I think what often gets lost in this is the fact that coaches feel they have to put themselves above their athletes, that building bonds and connections break the chain of command and will lead to the inmates running the cell. When I first started coaching I led with fear tactics and shouting. It was all I knew and funny enough, but I seemed to forget how much I hated it as an athlete. I know now to lead out of relationships and heightened expectations for my athletes.

One thing that needs to be clarified is that although we want to focus on an athlete-centered approach, we don't ever want to lower our expectations. What we do want, however, is to allow athletes to take a unique path to meet their high expectations. This is a key step in the process of reaching an Underdog because they are usually coming from a one-size-fits-all situation and have never been given a chance to forge the path that brought out the best in themselves. For JK, he just needed a new environment and opportunity to figure things out; he needed time and to forge bonds amongst his peers and coaches. If I had forced the process with JK then I would have lost him. This is the mistake that happens with most programs across North America and in sporting organizations. We want everyone to get it the same way and under our terms. In 2009, the New Zealand All Blacks identified that they had problems. Athletes struggled with drinking, drugs, and violence. They began to develop individual athlete profiles for each of their athletes, identifying what and who they needed in their life to be successful. Some received life coaches, AA counselors, or speed coaches. The bottom line was that each individual got what he or she needed, not what someone else needed. An individualized approach is the best approach.

2. Underdogs require TIME!

One-on-one time with people can never be replaced. As coaches, we are currently inundated with new technology, software, and equipment. We can know everything about an athlete's body, yet we have no idea what's going on inside their heads. Your athlete needs to know that you care and that you are available. This comes in many different forms but at the end of the day it's about asking the right questions and then actually listening to your athlete's responses. With Underdogs—especially of the Sleeping Giant variety, as Brett touches on earlier in this chapter— much of what is holding them back lies within their own heads and not in their abilities. If they didn't have the talent or the ability then they wouldn't be at a high level in

189

the first place. Often what is holding them back is an issue with consistency, understanding, acceptance of criticism for self-betterment, or a fear of failure.

When working with an Underdog, I like to keep it very simple. Overanalyzing and overcoaching is the worst thing you can do for these athletes. A phrase that I use with many of them is "FIJG," which stands for "F&*K IT, JUST GO!" We use this a simple trigger word as reminder to keep it simple and let your preparation take over. Taking daily steps outside of their comfort zone will build the courage for these athletes to maximize their potential. It's important for us as coaches to recognize the doubt and frustration in our athletes' eyes and to address these emotions with them. This doesn't require a big event and it usually works better in small doses. Constant, clear, and concise communication are critical, as well as using small gestures or triggers to put the athlete back in the moment. Certain Underdogs may have anger or temper issues, yet you cannot match their anger in these scenarios. Doing so will only reinforce the behaviors we are trying to deal with. I let them get mad, work through it, and then work to bring them back to the moment. Always finish what you started. Working through chaos and confusion is a hugely valuable trait for not only people but athletes as well.

Underdogs need to be watched daily; one day they may come in and do everything right and the next day they will hide in the back of a line, avoid exercise, or become a distraction. It is crucial to recognize this early in the session and use your trigger words or a quick pat on the back to let them know they need to get back in the moment and be present and purposeful. Again, this is why it is so important to have clear expectations for all of your athletes.

3. Create room to fail. Also, teach resilience daily.

Oftentimes, Underdogs have had negative experiences with failure and will look to avoid it, whether it was a coach who benched them after one mistake, a parent that was too demanding and only provided love based on results, or a teacher who told them they weren't smart enough because they struggled on a test. Whatever the reason for their fear of failure, it is important to understand it. When I first started coaching I used to bark at athletes if they messed up a drill or knocked over a cone. I thought it was the right thing to do. I wanted to instill a mindset of perfect practice all the time. But then I started thinking about how backward that statement was in and of itself. Practice is supposed to be the time during which we are allowed to make mistakes and take risks. When my athletes screw up, it's an opportunity to teach and an opportunity to repeat and get it right. Again, I am not saying lower your standards. The drill has to be done right and with right level of intensity, but if the athlete doesn't know what they're doing wrong, what is yelling at them going to accomplish?

Underdogs, perhaps more so than anyone, need to know they can take risks and are not going to be chastised as soon as they make a minor mistake. They often need opportunities to master and repeat. Courage and confidence are crucial to their success. If you destroy that you will destroy them. Building courage needs to be done daily and often, whether this comes through opportunities to practice leadership, working through adversity, doing things they are uncomfortable with, or holding them accountable. Each athlete has their own value and holds importance. As coaches, we should always be asking ourselves: *Why are we doing what we are doing? And, is it working?*

4. Coach with a purpose and inspire a passion for the process.

Underdogs are largely why I coach. Anyone can coach a genetic freak. Yes, it's fun, it helps build your career, and maybe someday you will write a book about it. But is that really coaching? For me, it is not. The underdogs force us to adapt, understand, and master our craft. I see real coaches as Jedi knights. They can control a room of 100 jacked athletes with the snap of the fingers. With a single look they can understand what does or does not need to be said. True coaches are few and far between. Anyone can count reps and write training plans. Real coaches want the hard cases, the ones on the outer edge of possible. This is where we find out as coaches what we are really made of.

The Crusader

Overview & Strengths

The Crusader archetype belongs to an athlete who identifies with a higher purpose. With the way they project positive energy to those around them, their unshakeable confidence in even the direst of competitive circumstances, and their ability to use words or actions that evoke the spirit of the inner gladiator within all of us, the Crusader is the defibrillator to the emotionally unconscious.

The Crusader will often serve as a unifying or inspirational force for their team and in many ways reflect similar qualities of the Leader. One could even make the argument that the Crusader archetype should be a sub-classification included within the Leader archetype much as the Underdog is broken down into Blue Collars and Sleeping Giants. Based upon the similarities they share in their desired end goals, you would not be wrong in that line of thinking. When distinguishing the between the Leader and the Crusader, it is helpful to remember that I am not suggesting that Leaders are not Crusaders or vice versa. It's just that my experience and observations have led me to the opinion that Crusaders have such a powerful and unique presence within the team/training-group dynamic that they are deserving of their own archetype. Not all Leaders call upon a spiritual element and not all Crusaders desire to be a leader who resides at the forefront or in the center of the action. Some Crusaders are quite content with working quietly in the background and keeping a low more self-reflective profile.

The greatest strength of the Crusader is their steadfastness. When confronting conflict, they favor an approach that can be described as more intentional than aggressive, for they know that a reactive, thoughtless approach will only play into the dominant emotions of the moment and rarely deliver truly transformative results.

Weaknesses

Crusaders know the true meaning of the term "axial loading" (exercises or movements in which the load produces compressive forces longitudinal to an axis, such as a back squat). That is, they often shoulder the load of those around them while also supporting the weight of their own concerns. They are natural nurturers and teachers, but one lesson they themselves must learn is that helping others is most effective when you empower them to solve their own problems rather than making them reliant on you to help them.

For a Crusader to lead most effectively, they must also know when to get out of the way. This is difficult for the Crusader to do, but if they overload themselves emotionally, they will end up suppressing their skills and sacrificing their ability to serve as the stabilizing entity they desire to be. Thus, it is important to help the Crusader find the right balance of intervention and stepping back.

To that very point, there is a reason why the term "Crusader" often conjures the image of someone who carries sword and shield through dangerous territory to fight for a cause they strongly believe in. Adorned with both a weapon and an instrument for protection, the intelligent Crusader understands that they must take both an offensive and defensive approach by leveraging their skills in order to cut through doubt or fear and inspire others, while also deflecting the emotional arrows that can easily overwhelm or pierce their own armor if they hope to succeed.

How to Connect

Due to their warm and often engaging persona, the Crusader can be relatively easy to connect with. Seek to learn more about their purpose and path so that you can find common links between the culture you are trying to create as a coach and the ideals that they believe in as an athlete. Knowing that they, too, seek to unite people, you will find them to be a powerful ally. Crusaders serve as both an example for others to follow as well as a sounding board for your messages to the team.

To make the most out of your relationship with the Crusader, it is critical that you involve them in the leadership dynamic of the team. Something going on with the team or witnessing atypical athlete behavior that you don't understand? Never be too proud to ask the athlete themselves or their peers, especially the Crusader, what's going on. Crusaders tend to be great listeners and often have an "ear to the street" or an intuitive feel for things that are going on within the team.

Just make sure you communicate that you are seeking information so that you can help or better understand. If an honest and straightforward approach is neglected when interacting within an emotionally charged context, you will likely be seen as intrusive and your counterpart perceived as a "snitch."

Lastly, remember that the Crusader feeds off reflection and interaction with others. While their energy may be more self-sustaining than most, they still seek community, guidance, and meaningful mentor/mentee relationships. Make the time to check in daily and you'll not only get a barometer for the team atmosphere, but also a counterpart who can positively influence the long-term motivational climate of the competitive environment.

Coaching Clinic:
Contribution by Coach Barry Solan BSc (Hons), CSCS

You've likely had a Crusader on every team you've coached, including the team you're coaching now. If you're lucky, you may have more than one of them. These are great people to be around. They have endless energy. They are infectious. They light up the room. They possess a special kind of presence. The team is at ease because they are there. You, as the coach, are at ease because they are. Everyone involved knows that when the pressure builds, both behind the scenes and in competition, the Crusader will know what the solution is, what to say and when to say it, and, more importantly, they will back it up with the required action.

It's also likely that if you have coached in a number of different environments or team settings, you are still in contact with the Crusaders from those places. You may even still touch base with them occasionally to get an insight on something with which they have no connection simply because you know they have the potential to help. At many times in your career you end up wishing you had a team full of Crusaders.

In my experience across several team sports in different cultures and locations, these are the people you want in the changing room, in the team meetings, in the leadership meetings, in the gym, and most importantly, on the field. Across all of these settings, the Crusader stands out.

This individual is always a few steps ahead of everyone else in his or her thought process. The Crusader connects with and influences other people in the organization. The Crusader always acts with the end goal of improving the team, and never for individual reward.

Many times, when discussing several different issues related to the team with a Crusader I once coached, I would think "that outlook and thought process never even occurred to me." His high levels of emotional intelligence and strong understanding of the game made him a very unique individual. He always provided me with an accurate needle of how the team was operating. I left all of our meetings with a better sense of how to coach the team. Often at the first signs of trouble—for example, a player lacking confidence, a disagreement between players, a lack of clarity from coaches, a family or relationship issue outside the team—it was this athlete that others leaned on for advice. They knew they could trust him. He often made me aware of how issues outside the team might be impacting certain players' performances. He never gave me too much information, which would have breached the trust other players placed in him, but always enough to make me revisit how I would proceed. He was so caring about others that often, when I wanted to speak about him, we had to reschedule. Why? Because our time was filled with him trying to help me help others. We both had everyone's best interests at heart. As outlined earlier, the Crusader shares many characteristics of a great Leader, too. His effect on the team helped influence the culture, including the way new and younger players were welcomed and introduced to the team environment, the way he expected experienced players to lead the team, and the way he would speak honestly and have no fear of doing so. He was lighthearted and fun when he needed to be, but also serious and business-like when it was required. Most important, his talk was always backed up by high-performance behaviors and actions.

Physically, the athlete I am referencing is an interesting case right up to the present day. During the early parts of his career he remained very healthy, robust and fit for long competitive periods. However, a series of career-threatening injuries in successive seasons left his body unable to prepare and compete optimally. At the outset of my initial off-season with him, his body had reached the point where he simply couldn't continue in his current physical state. His injury history and poor training and load management throughout the previous seasons had resulted in major soft tissue issues which were impacting his preparation and performance. To the untrained eye, he was still performing but he knew deep down inside that he couldn't continue in this way. There was also a very heavy reliance on both treatment and often medication to get through practice and competition. Many others would never be able perform in these circumstances.

This situation does highlight the one weakness of the Crusader: trying to shoulder much of the load of others at the expense of one's own performance, physically and mentally. This was a cycle that had to be stopped for progress to be made. We agreed that the best approach was to de-load this athlete from pitch-based loading and rebuild his body in the gym. This was an easy sell, as he knew his body would not allow him to continue in its current state. One of our first interactions together was meeting a surgeon and specialist to review his issues and plan a roadmap for his return. In this initial stage, much of the medical information was above my level of knowledge. However, as a coach this was my opportunity to gain his trust and let him know that my support was there. Ben Franklin's words, which have been referenced by many coaches with far more experience than I have, springs to mind. *"No one cares how much you know,"* he said, *"until they know how much you care."*

Our approach began with major integration between the medical and performance staff to really drill down to the core issues affecting his physical performance. As with many Crusaders, this athlete had a great interest in his own physical development and that helped the process greatly. He was acutely aware of the small nuances in his rehab and he provided the performance staff with excellent feedback on both progression and regression in certain areas. The downside to this was that he was full of energy, which needed to be channeled and managed to allow the rehabilitation to take place effectively. This was often a daily battle he often lost, as he sought to progress at a faster rate only to be reminded that improvement would take time. I also felt that he feared missing so much time in the changing room and on the practice field with the team, and that the high standards he helped implement for all those on the team would suffer. Due to his injury history, the rehabilitation process did, in fact, take a while and was at times very frustrating for everyone involved. But he made slow and steady progress. Over a number of months, he progressed through the basics of good training and saw increases in his movement efficiency and strength. This did occur later than expected, delaying a return to field-based technical running mechanics and conditioning work, but once it happened, his rate of progress in training increased rapidly. Interestingly, I believe his rehab process had a twofold effect: 1. He was able to step away from the team for a period, which refreshed his own energy and body to return to previous levels of high performance; and 2. When he came back to the team, he had learned many new things to teach to his mates.

The Skeptic

Overview & Strengths

A Skeptic is defined as "a person inclined to question or doubt accepted opinions" (Oxford English Dictionary, 2015). Within the athletic realm, skeptics often present in two primary ways: naturals and followers. These two types will be broken down further below, but first it is important to understand the universal strengths of the Skeptic. Despite what most think, being described as a skeptic does not mean that one is close-minded, but rather that they take careful consideration before filling their cup with the proverbial Kool-Aid that others tell them will quench their thirst. When discussing this very topic with my good friend and physical therapist Jim Godin, he made the excellent point that a purposeful Skeptic forges ahead while always questioning and reflecting on learnings from their past. The main way that Skeptics differ from other athletes is that their openness and willingness to buy in will require thorough and time-intensive digestion. Jim has worked with servicemen and women in the Armed Forces that are amongst the best at what they do when it comes to employing meticulous yet adaptable strategies in order to achieve challenging objectives. They are trained to dissect every possible scenario and to reject assumptions, so Jim's observations and opinions on this matter are not only well received, but are also founded in regular firsthand experience.

Look for Skeptics to always ask for the why behind what they are being asked to do. If they do not ask this outright, trust me, they are wondering it within their mind. This is a great strength of the Skeptic, even if it annoys you at first. Remember, seeking higher level understanding is part of human nature, they just tend to take it to the next level. They want to learn more and thus typically appreciate more than just the abbreviated version of what you are doing with the team. The Skeptic's deeper interest also gives you the opportunity to truly educate them and makes you work on improving your own lead-in strategies when describing a particular exercise, drill, or technique. This is part of the "3R" method that we will talk about in the next chapter!

Most athletes are willing to give something that seems new to them a shot, but if it leaves them feeling confused, embarrassed, or unconvinced, you are going to be fighting an uphill battle. Just keep in mind that the Skeptic does not always intend to give off a natural abrasiveness during interactions. Much like a coarse square of sandpaper can be used to remove old paint from a door or trim, if the relationship is managed appropriately, the initial friction of your first interaction with the Skeptic can eventually lead to the removal of old biases you both may have, thus making room for an optimized surface upon which new impressions can be formed.

Now, for a further breakdown of the above mentioned sub-classifications of the Skeptic, I will introduce both the Natural and the Follower:

Naturals: Naturals are athletes who have great genetics to become physical specimens but have yet to fully develop. They represent a unique challenge as they do not typically enjoy training and view it as something that may help them but isn't a necessity since they have always been relatively successful without it. Being the weight-room workhorse doesn't matter to Naturals, so when they hear a coach mention that squats and cleans can help improve their running speed, they'll likely think, "Well, I can run faster than guys who lift more than me." This is where coaches like us tend to sigh in frustration. Sure, we (kind of) understand where they are coming from, but it drives us nuts that they don't comprehend the big picture: while they may be great athletes, they could perform at an even higher level or be more resilient to injuries if they paired their innate talent with smart training. And while a rare few can succeed without any training, they are the exception, not the norm. It's like saying that some smokers don't die of cancer or COPD or heart disease, so why not light up a cigarette.

If you have coached a Natural you know that we can throw all of the research and examples we want at them, but the reality is that we have to be creative and unconventional in order to influence their beliefs. They have to want to change for a reason that is meaningful to them. Helping them find that reason is a practice backed by behavioral science research, which shows that people are most convinced by ideas they come up with themselves.

So how do we get this archetype to begin to look at training in a new light? Sometimes, if they are proud, they need to experience a setback or failure in order to learn and be humbled. Other times, it takes a bit of a creative intervention on our part. One method that has been helpful for me in the past is to introduce aspects of training they are likely to enjoy and blend it with other aspects of training that are critical (but they may not do otherwise).

For example, one athlete I worked with in the past didn't like strength training because it made him feel stiff and slow. It didn't matter to him that feeling this way is usually indicative of the initial stages of general adaptation syndrome, since his body was encountering a new stressor. He didn't care about the idea of supercompensation and that if he just saw things through, he would find his body rebounding to even higher levels of performance. He had bad experiences in the weight room in the past and in his mind, weight training made him feel slow and stiff and constrained his natural expression of movement, so that was that. He did, however, tend to gravitate toward more explosive movements such those utilized in jump training (box jumps, broad jumps etc.), plyometrics, and some bodybuilding type movements. The former allowed him to showcase his natural athleticism and the latter appealed to his vanity. It was during this observation that I saw an in. I created what I call a "give and take" program that featured a combination of explosive low/load exercises such as trap-bar jumps, or squat jumps; clean/snatch pull variations that were done from the hang; kettlebell swings and bodyweight exercises (spanning from medicine ball pushups to split squat iso-holds to explosive step-ups to pull-ups); and some bicep curl variants, dips, and "ab work," which were all things he wanted. The program was a hit as he perceived all of the movements to be non-threatening since they didn't create a lot of soreness, didn't require much load, and allowed for us to get a bit more creative. It showed him that strength training doesn't have to be stale.

The cynical coach who reads this may scoff and think that this strategy is catering to an athlete who is soft, and that these movements are worthless when compared to deadlifts, heavy squats or more complex weightlifting variants such as the clean and jerk. Save it. I have mistakenly shared that line of thought in the past as well and what you tend to notice is that those arguments of absolutism generally take place amongst coaches whose backgrounds are comprised of coaching the elite of the elite or a physically homogenous group. While I certainly agree that the bread and butter basics are heavily backed by the science and should be a cornerstone of most programs, the reality is that you have to meet your athletes where they are. As a coach, that means you are sometimes going to have to take the longer road to achieve that end. Social media would have you believe that there are plenty of coaches out there who just bark orders and their athletes do whatever they want, whenever they want, however they want—but, if they really told the truth, odds are that isn't how things started.

If you've yet to have an experience where you had to find a compromise with your athletes, don't worry, it is coming! This should be evident by the stories within the "Coaching Clinics" mentioned thus far. Once I began working with teams and organizations that included a diverse group of athletes of all ages, backgrounds, personalities, limitations, and languages, I quickly learned to drop many of my biases and learned to ask myself, "What is the most effective method within these limitations, and for this group of athletes that I'm working with right now?" and not, "What is the most effective method?" Sure, bodyweight movements or low load ballistic exercises may not offer as much adaptational bang for your buck versus bread-and-butter strength training, but if the athlete isn't engaged in the programming or mentally invested in learning how to do the complex movements correctly in the first place, you aren't going to get much out of any exercise, let alone those that are higher in complexity.

In these situations, when we are dealing with someone who is seemingly against training, we must alter their perception so that we can guide them on the correct path over the long term. If you are truly invested in serving their best interests, there should be no concern, bickering, or bravado. "Training" means something different to everyone. Sometimes, in order to gain an athlete's trust, we must start them with things like bodyweight movements or low-load ballistic exercises (both of which offer tremendous physiological benefits of their own) before gradually moving them toward more traditional strength training. This strategy beats puffing out our chests and patting ourselves on the back for being hardcore as we watch an unengaged athlete meandering through the weight room and barely putting out any effort. Swallow your pride and get the athlete on the path, even if it's not the perfect path.

Followers: Have you ever been approached by an athlete who tries telling you about something revolutionary or different? Perhaps they heard about this training strategy from another school, another team, or an athlete at another level of competition. They ask you, "Why aren't we using this training strategy?" And you give him or her your honest reply, something along the lines of being weary of rumors since they don't provide all the details, that no "magic pill" exists, or that what they heard may not in fact be reality. No matter, your statement falls on deaf ears. Sure enough, eventually you catch this same athlete following in the footsteps of the fad-mongers and donning things like altitude masks, running through speed ladder obstacle courses or, worse yet, participating in some kind of "specificity" training with a former athlete turned "performance" guru outside of team training times (without notifying you, of course). This epitomizes the Follower archetype.

Of course, you could argue that perhaps this is just a confused or hard-working athlete who isn't educated on what they should or shouldn't be doing. Perhaps. But if their intentions are pure, then they should not be hiding their usage of these tools or additional training modalities or coaches—and, they would come to you first, prior to trying any of these things. But they sense you may shoot them down, so they sneak around you and follow the hype.

Followers are often very observant of the world around them, which can be a tremendous strength. The problem is that they tend to let their initial impressions and emotions drive their subsequent behaviors instead of being patient and relying on rational thought. They are easily excited by new ideas, yet typically have trouble coming up with them on their own. They are easy targets for anything that is motivational and inspirational. They want to find that one thing that seems to be missing that could better illuminate their path to success. As coaches, we know the one thing for which they are looking so hard is an attribute, not an accessory. When training to attain mastery of any skill or craft, consistency and patience are the provenances of improvement. Many Followers want to believe that it really can be THAT easy—if only they could find out what someone else who appears to be like them does! Of course, they fail to consider the context and below-the-surface details.

I have encountered many Followers in both the team and private settings. My first experience with them on the team side involved a group of football players discussing what they heard a certain school in the SEC did in the weight room in order to get faster. I watched two of them try to circle the wagons in the locker room to rile up some of their teammates to go tell the head strength coach that they thought the team should be trained differently, and that his old-school approach was part of the reason they were getting beat. They may have been fed up, but apparently not enough to muster up the courage to actually go say something (they never did).

Later that evening, I dialed up one of my buddies who happened to be working at the SEC school they were talking about. I wanted to learn more about what they were doing. Based on the way my athletes described what they had heard, I knew they were likely confused but I wanted to learn straight from the source. I told him what some of our players had said about them "paying more attention to speed in the weight room" and it paying dividends. Naturally, I thought they were discussing the use of velocity-based training (VBT). I was curious as I could certainly see how employing more of those strategies could be useful to a team that was already as strong as ours was at the time. The minute I asked, he started laughing maniacally. "Oh yeah, we train speed alright! The head football coach wants to run a more up-tempo offense so he demands that the guys literally run from one exercise to the next in the weight room. It drives everyone on the strength and conditioning staff here nuts because our guys don't get decent enough rest in between sets to actually lift any appreciable weight! Other than that, I can tell you the only other place we are this fast is on the recruiting trails, since that's where much of our success has come from of late."

This was a prime example of a game of telephone that had gone awry, and how easy it is for players to fall victim to rumors and myths and to view strategies outside of context. Perception is truly reality to many athletes—at least during moments of despair or when they are looking for something that will help take them to the next level.

The Skeptic must accept the notion that there is no shortcut before they stop looking for one. All behavior change begins with an internal drive. Skeptics typically have a strong drive to acquire a new skill or capability, but they don't always have the patience required to put in the work and learn it. Don't force this! Provide skeptics with the information you believe will help them understand more and then give them some distance. One way or another, they will learn that the fastest route comes from stepping in the right direction and staying consistent, as opposed to running to all of them at random.

Weaknesses

While questioning is often very productive in daily life, it can be harmful in a training environment, especially given that results and development often take time to accrue. Sure, just about anything you do will work for about six weeks (as Coach Dan John always says), but after that, there is often a slowdown in progress due to the inherent nature of adaptation. If a Skeptic is constantly questioning the program and not trusting the coach, they not only hurt the relationship, but also shunt their progress every time they try something new or adjust the plan on their own.

Additionally, a Skeptic can erode the buy-in of those around him or her, and thus Skeptics may be especially problematic in the team environment.

How to Connect

Skeptics often don't know what to believe. They want results and they'll explore their options and investigate until they find what they believe to be the performance paradigm that is best for them. There's likely a previous event that rests at the root of this behavior—a vital spark that set them down a particular path of critical consciousness in the first place.

Examples of events that could have influenced a Skeptic's outlook include the following:

Bad personal experiences with training in the past to that led to injury, decreased performance, significant loss of financial resources, or excessive wear and tear on the body.

Negative associations with training or coaching, especially those that relate to perceived psychological harm such as coaches using training as punitive means of building "toughness" or inflicting punishment.

Confusion that can often occur through researching both credible and noncredible sources. Just as noncredible sources can provide poor or incomplete information, the same danger applies for credible sources when an athlete who does not have a background in physiology, biomechanics, biochemistry, or a related field of kinesiology tries to make sense of them. Even credible resources can cause significant harm when misinterpreted.

Spending significant time around a role model, parent, teacher or other agent of influence who shares Skeptical traits or has inculcated them in the athlete. This is different than #2 because in this example the athlete is taught to think in a Skeptical fashion, rather than taking on that trait as a result of a negative experience with a coach who had abused their power or influence over the athlete.

When dealing with Skeptics, keep these considerations in mind and remind yourself to not get frustrated by their questions or what may appear to be a lack of trust and or discipline. This can and will be difficult at times. As strength and conditioning coaches, we are a group that takes pride in our scientific approach and careful planning. When questioned or doubted, we can often find ourselves feeling tested, defensive, or otherwise emotional, all of which lead us down the path of wanting to quickly assert dominance and remind the athlete that we are the experts. If you find yourself trending this way during an interaction with an athlete, remove yourself temporarily and regroup. Trust me, as a naturally aggressive person, this can be hard to do, but it is critical to *Conscious Coaching*. For me, having my own physical outlets helps me blow off steam so that I can remain cool, calm, and collected with my athletes. I'm preaching an essence of mindfulness and reminding you not to fall into emotional traps that are based on ego.

Athletes have a right to be skeptical, too. Put yourself in their shoes. They have no real reason to give us their full trust right off the bat. Sure, we may be employed by an organization and hold a position or title, but that suggests they should trust that the organization has their best interest at heart—which is quite a leap of faith! I'm not being cynical, just realistic.

When trying to build trust or find common ground, remind yourself that part of why the Skeptic may be resistant is because you may be asking them to abandon an idea or value that they strongly hold to be true. You think speed ladders are crap? Great! The research would support that notion and nearly all of us in the industry would agree. But if the athlete perceives them to have helped in some way or finds them particularly engaging, take the time to understand why he or she may feel so strongly about them. Only then will you be able to educate the athlete on why something like speed ladders are not a cornerstone in your program.

Over the course of my career, there have been plenty of training approaches that I once drew a hard line on, only to later go back and realize that my thoughts were likely a bit too absolutist and rigid at times. These days, I consider myself a failure if I don't try to find at least one positive or useful aspect regarding most tools. In some settings, you never know what you will and won't have access to, so you better be comfortable getting people to perform under a wide variety of conditions and eliciting adaptations by whatever means possible. That doesn't mean I always listen to the Skeptics about the latest and greatest technology—I still consider myself a minimalist— but it does mean I am willing to be flexible.

Lastly, if you are questioned on a particular training method within your program, take a moment to think about what the athlete is really asking before you respond. What is the reason behind their concern? Part of the allure of charismatic leaders or speakers is the charm that comes from their ability to realize and act upon their knowledge that they are not the central figure in the narrative, even though they may be behind the podium or on stage. Being the authority on a given subject or the one who talks the most doesn't directly increase the influential role that you have on someone's life—listening and being a mentor does.

Understanding the origins of the Skeptic's behavior and controlling your emotions when questioned are great strategies for connecting with the Skeptic. To succeed in building trust with this archetype, we have to be adaptable not only in our programming and methods but also with our personality.

Coaching Clinic:
Contribution by Mike Berezowski CSCS

In my current work environment, I find the Skeptic to be the overwhelming majority of all the archetypes. I find this to be a challenge, but one we must accept. We have the luxury of capturing the behavior traits of all our athletes through the DiSC personality assessment. What we have found is most of our Skeptics would fall into the "C" or "Conscientious" category. These task-oriented individuals tend to be analytical, cautious, calculating, and want to absorb as much information as possible before coming to a decision. Therefore, it's no surprise that Skeptics would question our programming or philosophy or revert back to training they had done in the past.

An example of this would be when I first started working at my current location. Our athletes are elite tacticians that display sound qualities of General Physical Preparation (GPP) along with incredible resiliency. However, in some instances, their training age doesn't match their chronological age, and for us that often means a lack of relative strength. So, while they're able to express their technical and tactical skills through physical performance and precision, strength deficiencies are exploited, which far too often results in chronic injuries and progression cut short.

One athlete I had the pleasure to work with exemplified how a Skeptic processes change, yet I was able to connect with him (and win him over) through common life experiences along with how I introduced both objective and subjective findings. This guy was a former football player at a high level Division 1 university and quite honestly, one of our better athletes. He could definitely be considered a Natural. Prior to my arrival, these guys had no coach to consult with or guide them in the right direction. This athlete was no different and his training consisted of a combination of his past athletic exposures, outdated methods, and training sessions that completely overemphasized volume. The result was stagnant strength and conditioning gains, a constant state of overtraining, and the occasional soft-tissue injury.

I approached the athlete and welcomed him to sit down and chat. I had no other purpose than to get to know each other. Once he found out the extent of my previous strength and conditioning experience in football, I noticed his demeanor changed. Although we debated what his current needs were for this stage of his career, he respected my reasoning and evidence-based practices. This athlete, like many others at our location, consistently asked the question "Why?" It's our job as coaches and practitioners to defend the why in everything we do. This resonates with the Skeptic and builds the foundation of trust. This was also prevalent when I created his first phase of programming.

There was critical feedback on that first program. Questions like, "Only five sets?" or "Do you think 90 minutes is long enough?" were a sample of his reluctance to accept a different philosophy of training. I assured him we were on the right track and also challenged him to a simple "test-retest." I told him if the methods didn't produce the results we anticipated, he could then reincorporate some aspects of his previous programming into our current methodology. What he found was certain movements and energy systems were not in place and therefore put him in a position of failure (i.e. not attaining reps, distances) and now challenged him to improve upon his weaknesses.

Although this athlete has transitioned into another career path, he still trusts me with his programming to this day. What's more important is that we consider each other friends. Although it's been said before, a genuine care for your athletes will go a long way. With the Skeptic, it is essential to drop your ego, be flexible and adaptable, and have the patience to explain the why behind your what, and do so in a way that the Skeptic is likely to understand.

The Hypochondriac

Overview and Strengths

In sports as well as in life, where the head goes the body often follows. This is especially true for the Hypochondriac. Similar to the anxious characteristics of the Self-Sabotager, the Hypochondriac is an individual who tends to be abnormally aware of their health or current somatic state. This increased sense of alertness can be productive when it comes to quickly detecting small nagging injuries that could easily become much larger issues if not dealt with immediately. In this way, Hypochondriacs can help us become better coaches as their heightened perception and feedback can help us to rethink a particular training approach or adopt a new strategy when first teaching it. The naturally heightened state of anxiety in the Hypochondriac can also prove useful when it comes to them being proactive during their training or preparation for an event. Athletes with this trait separate themselves from the pack in a positive fashion through their scrutiny and genuine caring about every step of their act.

Many coaches are familiar with the athlete that continues to come up to them asking a barrage of questions such as "Does my form look right?" or "Can you take a look at this?" or "My (insert body part here) feels a bit off/tight, why is that?" or "Do you think I'm ready?" These incessant inquiries and requests for validation can be welcome interjections, showing us that the athlete actually cares enough to discover whether or not they are doing something at a high enough level in order to be effective. If managed appropriately, the Hypochondriac can learn what signs and symptoms are truly harbingers toward impending danger, injury, or inadequate preparation, and which are just a normal part of navigating the complex puzzle of the human body and its responses to the journey of the training process.

Weaknesses

One large drawback of the Hypochondriac's mindset is their tendency to overreact. While their mindset is useful for early recognition of potential issues, it is often too sensitive. This leads to dramatic reactions to even minor obstacles. This behavior typically masks an internal weakness or lack of confidence in themselves, so they use minor injuries, inconveniences, or imperfections as a preemptive excuse for failure. Ironically, this is often a self-fulfilling prophecy since obsessive rumination about injuries and the like often leads to failure itself.

True hypochondria is also thought to be linked to obsessive compulsive behaviors in that both include excessive preoccupations, compulsions, and extreme rumination over the mention of even minor issues. This isn't meant to suggest that the Hypochondriac archetype is, in fact, actually afflicted with the medical condition known as hypochondriasis. Remember, it is NOT our place to diagnose or play doctor. But gaining a richer understanding of the various factors underlying the archetypes can help us to better relate to our athletes and lead them to high performance.

How to Connect

The best thing you can do for the Hypochondriac is to help them understand that no ideal state of being exists, especially in the realm athletic performance. Almost all athletes have issues ranging from previous injuries, to haunting memories of past failures, to rejection, to illnesses—some of which are simply due to poor timing or bad luck. Despite their insecurities and concerns, Hypochondriacs don't need to be protected or reassured, since both strategies are nothing more than avoidance disguised. Instead, they need to be immersed in the situations that make them the most uncomfortable or uneasy, and then educated, in real time, within those situations. Listen to the Hypochondriac and try to get to the bottom of what they are concerned about and what they are really trying to tell you about themselves through their questioning. You will likely find that behind all the anxiety is something they truly believe is preventing them from the likelihood of achieving success. Hypochondriacs need to be reminded of their own individual strengths and the advantages that they can leverage, such as a heightened awareness of their bodies and environments, otherwise they will find themselves in a never-ending spiral of doubt and frustration. When you get looped into conversations or questions that begin to trend from reasonable concerns to unnecessary or excessive worry, acknowledge their plight and then redirect the conversation toward a more positive route. People are complex creatures. Our psyches are continually being shaped and our perceptions continuously altered. Many people have fears or anxieties they don't understand. At first, it will take time to help them push these anxieties aside and instead focus on their abilities. Part of coaching is building your athletes up and helping them remove the weeds that can grow inside their own head as a result of negative self-talk.

Want a simpler formula for dealing with this complex archetype? When trying to connect with the Hypochondriac, **acknowledge**, **aim** and **alter**.

- **Acknowledge** their concerns and allow them to be heard.

- **Aim** to learn the true source of their anxiety. Tell them to specify their number one worry.

- **Alter** their perception of the limitation. Don't ignore it, but redirect their thought process by using positive phrasing and imagery. In other words, remind them why they can still achieve success despite their issue.

Coaching Clinic:
Contribution by Coach Brendon Rearick CFSC, LMT

I've had the opportunity to work with many athletes on their road to recovery. They often come to me after being cleared by a doctor while still seeing a physical therapist. My job is to prepare the athlete mentally and physically to endure the demands of their sport. Of the few athletes exhibiting the Hypochondriac personality, one particularly stands out, a 30-year-old amateur soccer player named Peter. Peter had injured his back multiple times throughout his career, and the most recent episode laid him up for weeks.

When Peter initially came to me, I think he may have read more about back injuries than I had. The "knowledge is power" mindset is common among athletes of this archetype. I love when an athlete takes the initiative to educate themselves. Unfortunately, with information so readily available, it can be difficult to filter out the good from the bad.

Many of the people Peter was listening to were using fear-mongering tactics to get their point across. Fearmongering is the deliberate use of fear tactics to achieve a desired outcome. All of this noise had Peter's head spinning in circles, impeding his recovery process. Fear is one of, if not the greatest, hurdle to overcome when returning to play.

Peter's most notable crutch was the idea of "perfect posture." He was convinced that standing all day, never bending over, and never sitting was going to spare his spine so he could be sure to never hurt his back again. This is a recipe for disaster. Mundane tasks such as putting on your socks, picking up a laundry basket, sitting at your desk, and going to the bathroom, should not be cloaked in fear. If he was going to kick a soccer ball and play a sport where he potentially could fall on the ground a lot, we were going to have to re-educate his body, and his brain, to be comfortable moving in all directions.

When people hurt their [insert body part here], they often rely on a compensation strategy and avoid using the injured appendage. This is a part of the natural healing process. The brain is protecting you. The problem comes when you've recovered and you still compensate as if you were hurt. The altered pattern has become etched in your brains neuromuscular pathways. The Hypochondriac tends to be especially conscious of protecting the injured body part. An easy way to conceptualize this idea is someone who always wears a support belt to avoid hurting their back. This is well-intentioned thinking, and could help during an acute flare-up, but done chronically it comes at a significant expense: the natural function of the core musculature declines.

Another great example is always having your ankle taped, braced, or in a high-top shoe. These interventions are useful for game day, but to wear reinforcement during all of your waking hours only creates fear-avoidance. You shouldn't have to keep a "neutral" spine and have a support belt on to tie your shoes. You shouldn't have to tape your ankles to go for a walk. These are band-aids. Once a cut is healed you don't keep wearing the band-aid, do you?

With Peter, we started by introducing small movements of his spine and educating him on the importance of getting his full range of motion back. I explained to Peter that your joints are meant to move. If they don't, you'll have to compensate somewhere else up or down the chain. The education piece of coaching is just as important as a progressive training program. Explaining why they are doing something is critical.

I was also sure to check in between sessions with a simple email or text to see how he was feeling. Knowing that I sincerely cared about him getting better was crucial for building buy-in and confidence.

Like most people with the Hypochondriac archetype, Peter consistently did his rehab exercises, and he did them twice per day. The Hypochondriac will do what it takes to become better, sometimes in excess. One of your functions as a coach is knowing when to reel them in. Keep noticing the small wins they may not be recognizing, then be sure to push the envelope when the time is right. As Brett mentions above, "The Hypochondriac doesn't need to be protected or reassured, they need to be immersed in situations that make them uncomfortable or uneasy and then educated."

After six months of training, Peter was finally able

to feel comfortable in his own skin. He could sit, stand, walk, run, jump, kick, and tie his shoes without a second thought or pain. He stopped worrying about always walking around with perfect posture. There are still some exercises that don't work well with his back, but there are plenty of exercises that don't affect his back at all. He is aware of these activities and movements, and has a personal plan for the days he feels the back barking at him.

Training the Hypochondriac archetype is a blessing, as they're willing to do whatever it takes to get better. Build trust, educate, get them comfortable with being uncomfortable, and reel them in when necessary.

Archetypes Summary

People are dynamic and adaptable, so your ability to read them and adjust to their behavior must be, too. Understand that the Golden Rule of treating others how you would like to be treated is a misnomer, as it assumes that everyone is like you, perceives things in the same manner you do, and is driven by the same things you are. Take heed from George Bernard Shaw, who said, "The reasonable man adapts himself to the world; the unreasonable one persists in trying to adapt the world to himself. Therefore all progress depends on the unreasonable man." The reality is that YOU must treat people the way that THEY want to be treated. The knowledge of how to do that starts with you paying closer attention and not trying to deliver homogenized messaging. Not doing so is like trying to blindly catch a falling knife simply because you think that you understand which way the blade is pointed. It's time to stop looking at the art of strategic communication and building buy-in as a "feel good" or "folksy" skill that is written about by the high-short wearing coaches of yesteryear. Instead, we must begin to understand that it's the most critical tool that you have in your arsenal. Want bleeding edge? Than start by improving this skill set. This chapter helped you identify the various types of athletes you are likely to come across, and gave higher-level insights of how best to connect with them. The next chapter is loaded with more tactical, second-level tools to help you do just that.

CHAPTER 4
CONSTRUCTING CONNECTIONS:
TOOLS, TENETS AND STRATEGIES

"Action is the foundational key to all success."
-Pablo Picasso

I've been in the business of coaching for quite some time. And while I've had many successes, I've had my fair share of failures, too. But rather than sweep these under the rug and try to hide them from myself and others, I think it is far more productive to use them as opportunities for learning. What follows is a list of 13 common coaching roadblocks to avoid. These are important reminders. Post them in a staff office or another area where they are visible so that they have a good chance of becoming a permanent thread in the fabric of the coaching culture you are trying to create.

Roadblocks: 13 Coaching Mistakes to Avoid

1. **Focusing on your agenda only:** The athletes are not there to work for you—they are there to work with you. Remind yourself of this every day before you begin coaching. Address your athletes with conviction, not as if you are seeking complete control. This is especially important if you are working with professional or Olympic-level athletes or those who are paying for your services. Reserve harsher tones for when an athlete misbehaves or is being a distraction to the group. If you attempt to make a show of force too often, it will quickly lose its effect. Be willing to release your agenda. Flexibility is key.

2. **Always wanting to be the "expert":** Do your job and show your athletes that you care. "Excellence is self-evident, and so is bullshit," is one of the best pieces of advice I've ever received. Crude wording? Maybe. But you can't deny its weight. Early on, I loved using big, complex words related to training and physiology. One reason was because I truly found the science fascinating, but the other was a subconscious effort to prove that I was smart. I thought using big words would make athletes take me more seriously, especially given my young age. I was wrong. If anything, it had the opposite effect, making me come off as insecure. Don't fall for this trap.

3. **Wanting to be their friend:** Being relatable is one thing, as is having a great relationship. But while coaching, our role is that of a leader, guide, and mentor—not a casual buddy. Respect and understand the difference. One concrete example of this involved a young volunteer coach, who unbeknownst to the rest of the staff, would often attend parties hosted by one of the professional athletes training at our facility in the off-season. These events would feature famous musicians or DJ's, and might be held at any one of this athlete's many houses, complete with sprawling pools and a host of other celebrities hanging around. Meanwhile, this particular coach had never seen anything like this since he came from a relatively poor background. He was desperate to win the athlete's respect and fit in. This friendship began to spill over into the training environment through their recounting of the previous night's "journeys" in between sets. It didn't take long to see that although the young coach had gained a certain amount of influence with the athlete, he had become a distraction to the

group and the rest of us coaches. He was warned once but he couldn't figure out the necessary line of professionalism and continued to party with the athlete. Shortly afterward, this coach was asked to leave the training environment.

4. **Force Feeding:** Your preferred training methods need to stay true to sound ethics and best practices, but not everyone wants to train the same, nor do they need to. My experience working with combat sport athletes such as boxers and MMA fighters has taught me this more than anything else. Appreciate that progressive overload can occur in many forms. Meet the athlete where they are. Don't want to listen? You'll learn the hard way when you see lackluster effort being applied to your "perfect program," thus nullifying the desired adaptations you thought it would bring you as well as any buy-in that you were hoping to build.

5. **Swimming in Your Own Social Bias:** Regardless of where you are from and where your athletes are from, learning to appreciate all cultures and levels of education and maturation is critical. For example, do you think the music your athletes like is stupid? Lord knows I have certainly been in situations where I felt my IQ contracting with each repeat of a certain song requested by my athletes. But you'd be better served asking them why they like such music in the first place, thus learning more about them versus immediately judging them. And drop the "I control the radio" hard-headed shtick. That may work in some settings, but giving your athletes a level of autonomy is a win-win in most cases and can add to the energy in the environment. The "music" example is just one of many examples within the weight room that include the use of technology (cell-phones, cameras, social media), dress code, language and/or whether or not outside visitors are allowed. There is,

however a point where their preferences can certainly degrade the coaching environment, such as if the music they enjoy is laced with profanity, or so loud that it becomes nearly impossible for them to hear any of your instructions. Other examples include phone usage or social media becoming a distraction, or clothing that features offensive gestures, language or imagery. What is most important here is that the middle ground you choose should be based on the type of organization you own or are a part of, the core demographic that you work with, and how your own personal values blend with those of your core clientele and staff.

6. **Letting their emotions and moods dictate the session:** Nearly every coach who has been in the game for some time knows exactly what I mean by this. The days where your athletes saunter in, have little to no life in their eyes, and are already bitching about how their body feels or what they have to do that day. It starts with body language and often proceeds through the warm-up when you see them paying sparse attention to detail or simply going through the motions. Your response here depends on the setting. Many times, I have completely started the session over, telling the athletes to wake up, and even requiring some to walk out of the weight room and back in again, essentially hitting the restart button on the entire sequence. Other times I've found myself pushing forward almost as if my style of coaching could, in and of itself, "will" them to push forward and squeeze any drops of progress out of the session. As a coach, the worst thing you can do in these situations is default to extremes. If you want to teach them the importance of consistency, you need to reflect that virtue in your own actions. I'm not saying not to demand more

from your athletes or raise your voice. By all means, do so if necessary. Athletes need to learn that a large part of training is about learning how to pull more out of themselves when they don't think doing so is possible. Just make sure that you don't allow the emotional contagion that is affecting them to lead you into reacting as opposed to responding. Being consistent is a hallmark of being a professional. They need to learn that, and you should remember it. In other words, address the issue, but don't let it get too deep under your skin or, worse yet, cause you to become erratic in your own nature.

7. **Secluding yourself from other coaches:** Regardless of the level at which you consider yourself to be, you should always be open to other avenues of influence. That goes for older coaches as well, who, all too often, only interact with other veteran coaches. Sure, veterans may have been through plenty of battles and have years and years of firsthand experience, but you can learn plenty from the young guys who are hungry dreamers as well. I cannot count the number of times that I have heard stories of qualified volunteers or interns who were thoughtlessly turned down from roles simply because of their age. This mentality has got to go. Don't forget that today's aspiring coach may end up being one of tomorrow's most influential. Give everyone a fair shot and judge them based on their skill and perspective instead of their age.

8. **Failing to regularly reflect on your craft:** You need to be your toughest critic. I've always thought of this as having a battle-rap mentality in which you must constantly anticipate attacks from all angles. In addition to self-reflection on what you could be doing better, have another coach ask you to evaluate your training methods, communication strategies,

and overall coaching behavior. This shouldn't be the exception but rather the norm. These discussions raise the bar for everyone and yield great discussions. Another strategy is to imagine you are standing on a podium (either before or after a training session) and being interviewed by a slew of reporters who are firing non-stop questions about your coaching methodology. This exercise helps you to become more concise, focused, and pragmatic with your decisions and subsequent actions. It also helps you ensure you're truly confident in your approach.

9. **Being too "clean cut":** The best coaching often lies in the gray area of what we do and how we do it. The gray area is that unique zone where there are not uniformly set steps or standards that exist in regard to what the best approach or behavior may for a particular situation. It's that ever-critical air between what is most practical and what has been shown to be possible. Operating within this space means that we must maintain ethics while also resisting the urge to always be binary in our actions, appearance, and thought processes. Remember, we are in a field that is always evolving and we are also working with the most complex and the most emotionally complicated creature on the planet: humans! More often than not, we will find ourselves working in scenarios that are far from "best case." We will have to utilize strategies that may be the best fit for our current situation (as it pertains to things like budget limitations, facility spacing, athlete quality etc.), even if they are not the gold standard or what works for our peers within the field. Keep this in mind when viewing another coach's work as it may appear on social media, television or other media outlets. These provide only a snapshot or soundbite as opposed to the full context behind the imagery or

practices you may have seen. Sometimes what looks great is not, and what looks sub-optimal is optimal (for a given situation).

10. **Being a course/certification junkie:** No matter the pretty wrapping that people use to describe their new course, seminar, latest piece of equipment, or data-producing technology, there is only so much information that can be used practically within the coaching realm. Quit thinking that your professional hierarchy is dependent on the number of courses or clinics you attend and instead focus more on refining what's in front of you. In other words, don't mistake exposure for experience. The former is a result of exposing oneself to an influencing event (observing, studying and/or simulating), whereas the latter outcome is a result of direct participation with an influencing event (interacting, directing and/or generating). The future belongs to those of us who are willing to continually get our hands dirty.

11. **Expecting too much, too soon:** We've touched on this already a number of times in the book, but it's worth repeating. Whether this pertains to your interactions and expectations of your athletes or of yourself, sometimes you need to let the song play a few times before you understand the full meaning behind the lyrics. As coaches, we often think that if we are on top of our game then we are going to see wholesale changes quickly. That's not how it works. A great coach may not see the effects of his or her work for many months or even years down the road. Chalk this up to the fact that we are often responsible for making cultural changes within organizations as opposed to just physical changes in the athletes who are a part of them. Culture change takes time and patience.

Our ability to create long-term positive change is commensurate with our ability to observe and absorb as much as we act and express.

12. **Not asking your athlete's opinion:** Many of your greatest insights and breakthroughs will come from ideas that were never yours in the first place. Being blinded by your own perspective and failing to keep a finger on the pulse of those you interact with daily not only negatively affects your ability to READ them, it also negatively affects your ability to LEAD them. Engage your athletes regularly and discuss their view of the program.

13. **Taking things too personally:** We like to think that everything is about us, when in reality, very few, if any, people outside of ourselves wake up wondering how we are doing. My good friend Carl Coward reminds me of this often when he says, "Nobody else wakes up worrying about Brett, I assure you." This isn't pessimistic, it's simply reality. Whether you've forgotten someone's name, sent an email that you shouldn't have, or written a plan that turned out to be crap; learn from it and move on. Refuse to let an action become your identity—you need to understand that experiencing a moment when you have fallen flat on your face or embarrassed yourself does not mean that you are destined to be a lifelong failure in it. Rub some dirt on the wound, continue to expose yourself to challenges, and get back to work. There is medicine in this method.

***

Keep these "do not do's" in mind as you move forward. Now that we've explored a few things that can erode buy-in and trust (and how to overcome them), let's shift to examining some critical tactics for building buy-in and trust.

Trust Tenets

I once read that when the Italian sculptor, painter, architect, and poet Michelangelo was asked how he was able to create the iconic statue of David, he replied, "It is simple, I just remove everything that is not David." This illustrates how I view building trusting coach-athlete relationships. One of the most straightforward yet most important things you can do is to remove the things that serve as barriers and roadblocks to trust and better relationships in the first place (i.e., the items discussed in the prior section). But obviously, that's not enough. You must also build up lasting relationships and support them once they're in place.

Regardless of the situation(s) you find yourself in, adhering to the following tenets will not only help you avoid common interpersonal roadblocks that so many coaches get stuck behind, but also help you build new on-ramps that will help you and your athlete arrive at your destination more efficiently. Take notes as you read. Jot down what you are already doing well, and areas in which you can improve. The act of writing forces tremendous clarity and oftentimes illuminates where your gaps lie. Also, write down a list of 1-3 tactics you will try in the coming days. Remember that simply reading and knowing information isn't enough—you must act on it, too.

Trust Tenet #1: Fundamentals, Not Fluff

Regardless of the sport, perhaps nothing is more powerful for building trust than helping your athletes achieve concrete results. When you work with an athlete, don't try to wow them with the latest and greatest technologies or trendy training approaches. Rather, speak with them about their goals, and have an open and honest conversation about how the program will help them achieve those goals. Don't be scared to tell them that your programming and methods are simple. And, your program, as basic and simple as it may be, will help them achieve those results. Simple does not mean easy, and oftentimes simplicity works. Unfortunately, there are now, more than ever, many goofballs in the strength and conditioning industry spouting nonsense, and even worse, doing it in an enticing way. DO NOT fall prey to these con men and con women. Stick to what you know, and repeat over and over again to your athletes that results are all that matter.

Whether the goal is a higher vertical jump, a decrease in pain, a stronger deadlift, or even helping someone to rebuild lost confidence, performance results are the provenance of lasting buy-in with your athletes, and the hard work that gets them there will never go out of style. Yes, there is truth that the skyrocketing popularity of fads within the industry has made it more difficult for honest, fundamentals-centric performance coaches to compete with the "Neverland" facilities that can spring up, or the internet/social media "trainer of the week."

Depending on the nature of the sport and the time frame of its competitive season, when athletes are away from their teams, they often hop from facility to facility to try out different coaches from across the globe. In the time that I have been working with NFL athletes, it has not been uncommon to witness guys visiting as many as six or more facilities over the course of just a month or two! Athletes partake in this nomadic behavior for a variety of reasons, ranging from where they would like to vacation, where they feel most comfortable, and even simply because they have a friend that is training at a particular location. This presents a large challenge for coaches whose programs rely upon consistency (and almost every good program does).

So, what can you do to enhance the results that your athletes get while also adhering to best practices? Help them understand just how dynamic and challenging "simple" can be. Create programs and practices that are easy to implement but challenge your athletes in ways they are not as accustomed to and that will likely exploit weaknesses created by them not adhering to smart training practices to begin with (e.g., isometrics, eccentrics, different loading modalities and conditioning protocols). Also, educate your athletes as to why they are struggling with these methods in the first place and the reality of what may happen as a result of them not being able to nail basic movements (i.e., lack of a strong foundation causes the tallest skyscrapers to collapse, or in this case, the most explosive athletes to get injured). Lastly, stick to your guns and force yourself to be a better educator and programmer. Phony, hype-filled coaches may be popular in the short-term but all fads eventually fizzle out on their own and sometimes the best thing you can do when everyone else is scrambling for the next best thing is to stay where you are.

Implementing Trust Tenet #1

Focus on actions AND words. Consistency and true results trump fads in the long-term. But to get your athlete's attention, you will still need to present simple methods in a way that the athletes perceive to be the most beneficial choice in regard to their training. Speak to how what they are doing specifically can get them in better shape, help them make more powerful cuts or transitions, and reduce their risk of injury through enhancing their level of strength, power and movement mechanics. Find out the issues that plagued them most in the past and then bridge the gap as to both what you are doing and how you are doing it.

Make "simple" challenging and engaging. Athletes, like everyone else, want to be tested and feel like they know what it is they are working toward specifically with each drill and exercise. Accept the fact that you may have some selling and educating to do and use methods that exploit current weaknesses, asymmetries or different body positions.

Stay the course. When an athlete decides to follow a different path than the one you initially lay out for them, or even decides to work with another coach, it can be tempting to wonder if you need to change up your methods. Sometimes, you may need to, but don't ever discredit yourself and start second-guessing everything due to a couple of isolated occurrences. Curiosity and even a bit of insecurity is natural, but don't ever adopt something just because the "crowd" does.

Trust Tenet #2: Educate and The 3R's

The majority of high-level athletes don't care if our methods are based on the latest science. It may serve as a nice soundbite, but ultimately, they are going to judge what we do and the workouts that we expose them to based on how they feel during and after the workout, and within the competitive arena. They will also key in on what they perceive to be true about the kind of training style we adhere to compared to what their peers or role models are doing. If we want them to care about the things we are asking them to do, we need them to see them in a different light. There is nothing inherently sexy about working on the foundations of good posture, sprinting technique or learning a new exercise and only using an empty bar. If we want to educate them at a higher level, then we need a way to alter their perception from the get go. There's a tool I've used for years that I call The 3R Approach. The 3R's pertain to the words Research, Relate, and Reframe. I first referenced the 3R approach on a "Strength Coach Podcast" segment with host Anthony Renna back in 2011, and it serves as a natural and authentic way for you to build bridges with your athletes through doing the necessary reconnaissance about their lives and views, and in turn, communicating with them in a way that shows mutually aligned values or shared experiences. In essence, it enables you to better show them that you understand what they are looking for, what they perceive and feel, and that you know how to address those concerns. The core of the method is backed by research that shows people tend to listen more intently to those who are similar to them, possess a quality they think would help them, or that they respect (or envy).

RESEARCH: Research means asking open-ended questions and reflectively listening in order to figure out what matters to the athlete on the deepest level. Try to find the reason buried beneath the reason as it pertains to your athletes' internal drives. Be patient, for this takes time. You can't just start bombarding an athlete with personal questions out of nowhere, especially if they just walked into your facility or if you know little to nothing about them. If you have coached for a significant amount of time, you likely already know that at first, many athletes will provide only surface-level motivators rather than sharing their deeply held drives until they know more about you and your intentions. Talk to them about stuff outside of sport, or bring up the name of an athlete you trained in the past that you know they get along with or who plays on the same team. Oftentimes, I've spun their nomadic tendencies of "facility hopping" to my advantage by asking how they liked working with a particular coach I might know or am friends with, and then joke about a unique quirk that coach may have to see if they noticed it too. This usually gets the athlete to open up since they no longer feel as if I am a stranger since I also know someone they've worked with or played with, which gives us an easily accessible conversational tinder to use in future dialogue. What you are looking for during and after these interactions take place is a piece of information that illuminates aspects of their personality along with their true why, which can help you figure out what kind of training program and coaching style they'll be most likely to succeed with. Do not disregard even the smallest morsel of information they give you. You may be the expert as it pertains to physical preparation but you must accept the fact that they are experts in themselves and you need to respect their views and space if you hope to influence them over the long term.

RELATE: It's easy for an inexperienced coach and communicator to go overboard here at first. But baby steps are imperative as you are not trying to become your athlete, instead you are simply trying to create a shared perspective and rapport so they feel more comfortable in your presence and with the interventions you will employ down the road. It's seduction in its most elemental form. Proceed slowly, read their body language as you speak, and don't forget to call upon the value of social proof to aid you in the process. When I'm coaching a group of athletes, I often employ the use of social proof during this stage. I do this by making sure the new athlete sees me spending time with another athlete in the group that I already have a great relationship with. This lowers their initial inhibitions and can reduce the risk of stereotypes clouding their judgement. Once you make an athlete see that you are similar to them and that you share an appreciation for their views, the final R—Reframing—becomes much easier to achieve.

REFRAME: This simply refers to our desire to alter the athlete's frame of reference or internal schema(s) regarding their beliefs toward a given construct. As the name suggests, it speaks to our frame of reference which is often based on a combination of our past experiences, biological wiring, cultural expectations, interests, and moods (Parr, 2015). Reframing comes down to taking a core concept, breaking it down, and helping an athlete understand how it relates to another concept that may be easier for them to related to or understand. Reframing follows the Relating step since relating influences an athlete's more immediate perception of a person, thing, or experience while reframing seeks to etch a newly presented construct into their minds over the long-term so that they begin to connect the dots for themselves. Much like when staring at an optical illusion for the first time, we are trying to help an athlete see an image in their mind that they may have been blind to in the past.

For example, several years ago my wife and I rescued our dog Lola, a pitbull/boxer mix. The dog is as harmless as could be and has a personality that is softer than a cotton ball dropped in a pond. But one of my friends was absolutely terrified of her at first glance. After probing as to why he was so freaked out, he informed me that he had been badly bitten by a stray pit bull in the past and he had never forgotten that memory, thus he strongly associated pit bulls with danger. I gave him some dog treats and had him throw small bits her way, slowly letting her get closer as he was more comfortable. It took some time, treats, and a few belly rubs (once he was finally brave enough to pet her), but eventually he was able to see that pit bulls aren't the universally dangerous breed the media often makes them out to be. His frame of reference has been positively altered. Now when he sees Lola, he practically tackles her to the ground and loves to wrestle with her!

I constantly find myself having to teach athletes across all sports why strength is so essential for them. It may surprise you that many high-level athletes perceive strength training to be something that will leave them stiff, sore, and slow. They don't think it will help them at their sport. Now, let's imagine I call upon the Research aspect within the 3R framework and recall that the athlete I'm speaking with has a deep affinity for cars. I can use this info by choosing to Reframe how we are building a more efficient engine instead of going into nerd-speak overdrive as it pertains to how the body is actually recruiting more motor units, which can then enhance force production and help optimize movement economy, which this athlete is not likely to care about or remember.

There are times, such as the dog example listed above, where reframing needs to be actively introduced, and others where it occurs as a natural part of the teaching/ learning process. When working with fighters, there have been numerous times during which I have demonstrated a movement, whether it be with a barbell or a medicine ball, and had an idea of how I wanted to communicate its value to the fighter(s), only to have them come up with an entirely different (albeit far more effective) way in which they believed that the idea would transfer. Many coaches do not realize that these moments are gold! Anytime this happens, the minute the session ends I run to my office and note the idea in order to better identify why it may have connected and also to use for future reference. When it comes to influence, communication, and persuasion, it is to your benefit to take newfound information and synthesize it in a way that is commensurate with what makes a particular individual tick. Other times, we may find ourselves in a situation where we have to fix previously broken associations. This can happen with athletes that have avoided certain kinds of training due to hearing false rumors about the dangers or detriments associated with them, as well as situations where someone has been injured in the past while performing a given movement. Either way, it is your job as a coach to be patient and help your athletes to see these kinds of things in a new light.

Implementing Trust Tenet #2

See yourself with their eyes. Successful reframing requires us to get inside the athletes' minds at the deepest level and understand how they may perceive the environment. Imagine everything from their standpoint. In their eyes, your training facility may look just like all of the others. Sure, there may be a different logo on the wall, but in their mind the equipment is pretty much the same, so are the smells, and the general feel of the place. Where you have a chance to truly separate yourself is in how you communicate, what you communicate, and whether or not they feel comfortable with you.

Repetition, Repetition, Repetition. Reframing within the "3R" framework isn't just about showing how the goals of your athletes align with your methods. It's also about finding a way to alter their vision of that very modality so that an athlete's vision is changed more permanently. They'll now see it as you see it or at least make progress toward doing so. This is done through repetition. Constantly search for creative ways to remind your athletes of how your respective worlds collide. Training a team of soccer players? Let them know just how similar attacking the landing portion of a plyometric exercise is to dropping your center of mass to take the cut necessary to maneuver around a defender in soccer. Alpine skiers? Let them know just how critical the eccentrically focused lower-body exercises you're currently performing are to setting the stage for ACL injury reduction via enhancing their ability to maintain control and positional strength when traveling down the mountain and turns near breakneck speeds. Trust me, athletes care about this stuff, which is why it's worth repeating. The vast majority of our athletes haven't studied what we have studied and don't see the body's architecture like we do. They have gone through their training in an ordered, not educated, manner. The goal is for them to begin seeing the movement they are performing as something that directly correlates to what they care about most. They should be able to visualize it or at the very least, be nearly sick of you telling them about it. Remember: When you frame something in a way that is personal and purposeful, it becomes more powerful.

Don't push it. There are times when you may encounter coaches who reach too far when trying to reframe a given training method and, no matter how hard they try, it just isn't there. We saw this abused (and subsequently debunked) during the "functional training" era. Your goal is to gain trust and get actual results. Bullshitting your clientele for the sake of novelty or generating gossip will only hinder any future attempts at creating the kind of relationship and reputation that you want. Reframe, but do so authentically.

Trust Tenet #3: Make 'Em Laugh!

Humor is a vastly underrated tool for relationship and trust-building. Comedian, conductor, and pianist Victor Borge famously stated that "laughter is the shortest distance between two people." I have absolutely found this to be true in both my personal relationships as well as my coaching relationships. Despite the popular use and effectiveness of metaphors and analogies for teaching, the use of humor seems to be scary for many strength and conditioning coaches.

Research performed by Dr. Ronald Berk in 1998 shows that college professors are also reluctant to use humor as a teaching tool for a variety of reasons. These reasons include a lack of confidence in their ability to use humor effectively and a self-righteousness around the seriousness of teaching. Perhaps this is also the belief of many coaches who have adopted the arms-folded posture and seemingly permanent scowl that's meant to convey a focused and fiery persona. The image of a blowhard, Type-A, or militant-style leader has become all too common at all levels of strength and conditioning coaching, from veterans to assistants to interns. Somewhere along the line, someone was apparently led to believe that in order to successfully lead young athletes, you need to take a strict, authoritarian approach and ensure that the environment builds discipline and mental toughness, whatever that's supposed to mean. It's unfortunate this mindset has taken hold because humor can be an incredibly powerful tool. Humor can enhance engagement, rapport, and learning regardless of the setting in which you find yourself.

Dr. Berk calls the use of humor in education and rapport-building an "instructional defibrillator." And he does so for good reason. A 40-year review of the research regarding the use of humor in the classroom shows that the use of appropriate and non-disparaging humor helps improve group cohesion, increases positive connections between the student and the instructor (and between the student and the environment), and also aids in the retention of the course material to which it (the humor) is connected. (Banas, Dunbar, Rodriguez and Liu, 2011). This is a critical piece of information since we know that true learning does not take place unless the student actually remembers and understands a concept for him or herself. Compare this to the use of leadership or teaching styles that are anchored in fear or power, which may motivate in the short term but rarely optimize long-term performance.

So, what kind of humorous material tends to resonate best? The research shows that humorous material should be comprised of three components: a commonly understood/relatable situation, a buildup of anticipation, suspense, or tension (comedic timing), and an unexpected twist, response or punchline (Berk, 1998). It should not aim to make fun of someone, demean someone, or cross personal boundaries.

For those of you who need another reason to turn down your inner alpha persona, it may be of interest to note the various physiological and psychological benefits that are associated with humor, especially those related to stress management and circulatory function—both of which play a critical role in influencing performance-related adaptations. When laughter occurs, respiratory exchange processes are enhanced, blood pressure is reduced, and the body produces endorphins which act not only as mood enhancers, but also as a natural pain killer (Berk, 1998). Psychological enhancements include reduced anxiety and stress as well as increased self-esteem and self-efficacy, both of which are invaluable in a dynamic learning environment and as a competitor.

In short: Understand that one of the best ways to build trust, rapport and educate others also happens to be one of the best ways to improve your health and the health of your athletes. Laugh it up!

Implementing Trust Tenet #3

Learn from comedy legend Jerry Seinfeld. Humor is all around us, which is what makes the comedic genre of "observational humor" one of the most popular types of comedy. Whether you are trying to teach a young athlete about the importance of good posture, or thinking of a funny way to describe the action of the hips when performing a medicine ball granny toss during training, relating to a humorous example your athletes can understand is a surefire way to make them laugh and help them learn. Regarding the hip example with the granny toss, a good friend of mine who coached with the Dallas Cowboys (and was from the Deep South) would always tell his athletes to "pop the peanut out of your belly button" since when you extend your hips forcefully while jumping out of a loaded "hinge" position your torso will be at a more vertical angle. He loved food analogies and they were equal parts contagious and ridiculous (which is what made them memorable). The posture example was always easy, as anytime I'd look at a "Little Timmy," the perpetually slouched high school or middle-school kid, I'd ask him how he would stand if the prettiest girl in school walked right in front of him. Right away, he'd shoot up straight with his body in proper alignment (or at least as close to it as his gangly body could achieve).

Timing is everything. Nothing is worse than witnessing someone trying too hard to make another person laugh or telling a joke that falls awkwardly on deaf ears. Start with subtle jokes that you can organically weave into the conversation or coaching session. Later on, once you have a pulse for the group's humor heartbeat, you can start adding them in more frequently if appropriate.

Remember, humor is just a tool, not your trade, so think twice before adding a story or quip and make sure what you're about to say actually adds to the session in a creative way rather than serving as a distraction.

Shine a spotlight on others. The best improv comedians understand that the secret of being a great comedian is to make the other person look good as opposed to trying to hit all the one-liners and classic moments themselves. Shine a spotlight so others can showcase the best of who they are. The funniest moments in improv occur when cast members focus on others within the show and create space for something new and natural to happen. Bring your athletes into the fun! Whether it is classic locker-room banter while they are competing on the platform or having a policy that athletes who arrive late for a training session have to sing or dance in front of the group (the enigmatic Coach Rett Larson is well known for doing this with his athletes in China), there are always ways to constructively lighten the mood by poking fun at yourself or giving those around you a hard time.

Trust Tenet #4: Be Authentic

Authenticity is a linchpin for all great coaches, and it comes in many forms depending on the values and communication style of the coach. Three universals of authenticity, regardless of one's unique coaching style, are consistency, clarity and level of directness when dealing with athletes. The realm of sport is chaotic enough. The last thing that athletes need is a coach who fluctuates between the extremes of hot and cold. There is an old military saying documented in the book Why Men Fight by Bertrand Russell that drives this notion home: "Battle morale comes from unity more than all else, and it will rise or fall in the measure that unity is felt by the ranks." The unity that Russell was referring to starts at the top and manifests itself with the level of virtue of the words that are spoken by the commander in charge. What is he saying and does he or she actually mean it? Speech itself is just the vital spark that ignites the desire to work together in the first place. Speech galvanizes and directs. It is at the core of the urge to motivate others to get something done. And when the time comes for it to get done, we are better off banding together in order to do it. Maintaining a sense of the universals mentioned above at all times—in both our words and our actions—goes a long way toward maintaining a sense of unity with those around us.

In the realm of human performance, there seems to be an endless list of credentials one can accrue. There always seems to be yet another degree that could be attained or a certification that could be possessed. Why do we feel the need to hoard these things or add letters to our email signature? Sure, some of these have a purpose and are required to practice within a given scope, but accrual for the sake of accrual is pointless and won't do a thing to enhance your ability to build trust in the long term. Be proud of your accomplishments, but let sincerity and your passion for helping others be your most valued credentials. Even though these qualities can't be displayed on a piece of paper, they will be the things that are most visible on a daily basis to your athlete. When it comes to long-term trust, nothing trumps authenticity.

Coaches and leaders who are authentic exhibit greater influence when it comes to building buy-in and getting results. It is no coincidence that the words influence and influenza (the flu) share a similar etymology as it pertains to the belief that each flowed from the stars and affected the beliefs, actions, or health of man in a way that seemed to spread like wildfire. People want to be led by others who "walk the walk" and embody the values which they preach. Great coaches and athletes have an "animal instinct" and can always sniff out a fraud. Don't pretend to be something you're not. The consequences are never worth any perceived short-term gain. Witnessing others do this at times throughout the years is what led me to create what I call the "4 Horseman Syndrome." A coach that is afflicted by 4 Horseman Syndrome typically displays the following traits:

1. Hasn't experienced or overcome a personal struggle, loss, injury or hardship.

2. Doesn't actually train him/herself in any purposeful or consistent manner, and exhibits health behavior(s) that are otherwise contradictory to those they preach to their athletes on a daily basis.

3. Is fueled by ego and insecurity.

4. Heavily criticizes others within the same industry that they claim to care so much about.

There are other counterproductive traits to be sure, including someone who is focused on creating more followers instead of leaders within his staff or organization. There's also the coach who incessantly feels the need to keep secrets or deceive those that he or she perceives to be a threat to their current role or style of leadership. Even so, the four traits listed above are often the most damaging.

Implementing Trust Tenet #4

Lead from the front. As a coach, you set the tone. Your actions and the example that you set are a powerful catalyst for those you hope to gain trust from and lead. You do not need to be a freak athlete yourself, nor do you need to set records in the weight room, but you do need to set a consistent and visible example through actively demonstrating the personal, physical, and professional values you hope to inculcate in those around you. Perform an internal analysis of yourself and your staff at least three times per year (you can use some of the tools discussed in Chapter 2) and act on the results. Everything from your body language to your professional appearance should be assessed.

Lose the bravado. Oftentimes, we believe that we need to be Superman and that we cannot show any weakness. We've all heard stories of the coaches who wake up at 3 AM and do the same workout their athletes are going to do later in the day before anyone else has even gotten to the facility. As you read earlier in the book I went through my extremist phase too, and even continued some aspects of it—in particular, burning the midnight oil to train after coaching when I was a graduate-assistant coach. Eventually, however, every good coach grows up and realizes that they could be a bit more productive with their time and within their relationships. Left unchecked, virtues can become vices, and being a strength coach means far more than just being a training junkie. Roy Disney always said, "When your values are clear to you, making decisions becomes easier." Take heed in that. If you are reading this book, I would venture to guess that you have values beyond increasing your deadlift max.

Trust your path. So many coaches end up losing their way because they try to emulate someone else. Your coaching style should be a reflection of you and you alone. No doubt, you will learn things from others, and success leaves clues so it is not wrong to adopt traits from those who came before you. But if you want to leave your own coaching legacy, you must embrace your own unique gifts and abilities. People are insecure by nature and even those who seem the most confident often have doubts. Never be afraid of criticism and do not let detractors intimidate you by making you think that you need to fall in line in order to be successful. Have confidence but be willing to change; accept the fact that you will never be a finished product and that your style will evolve over time. It should concern you if you find yourself trying to adopt a false persona for the sake of impressing someone else or trying to gain respect. Your legacy is most likely to last when the shoes you lace up while doing so are your own. Wear them proudly.

Trust Tenet #5: Empathy

Empathy can be summed up best via a quote and some sage advice by Zen Master Tanouye Roshi, who once said, "Become the other person and go from there." Empathy is the capacity to understand or feel what another person is experiencing from within the other person's frame of reference. In other words, empathy is about being able to spend some time in someone else's shoes. (Bellet and Maloney, 1991). We touched on empathy earlier in the chapter when discussing the "3R's" and now it is time to further examine this trust tenet. I consider this to be the most powerful tool second only to authenticity in helping you build better relationships and buy-in with your athletes. That statement may make some of you scoff, but hear me out. People can feign empathy. It happens to folks every time they step into a car dealership and every time they talk to a customer service representative on the telephone. The all too common phrase "this call will be monitored to ensure quality service" is all the proof you need that others will pretend to care about your problems just to save their own ass or help their own bottom line. Is that the case with everyone we interact within those enterprises? Of course not, but it happens and it exists. You must first be truly genuine if you want to enhance the signal strength and bandwidth of empathy and its sister trait compassion.

You have to make a choice to put the other person first if you want a relationship to truly last. A lack of both empathy and patience became a significant emotional obstacle of mine during the first six years of my coaching career. I always saw training as a way to push my body beyond my perceived limit and associated anything to do with training to be a positive driver towards success. But noticed that not everyone I worked with attacked it with the same fervor. It drove me nuts, feeling as if these people didn't understand that all they had to do was to wake up, be consistent, and approach each session with a focused intensity in order to achieve their goals. Yet day in and day out I saw so many athletes not doing so. I couldn't empathize with that type of behavior or mindset and it would frustrate me. Of course, this intense sense of urgency on my end, which led to my lack of empathy for the way that others seemed to approach their goals, was also due to my realization of just how short life is after being in the hospital for so long in my teens. It was due to my lack of empathy that I thought I could revive them using the electricity from inside of me. I was sorely mistaken. Some took to it immediately and saw the transformative power that a sense of urgency in training can have on their life while others, despite being enthralled and/or temporarily amused with my ability to seemingly convert the air between us into ammonia smelling salts, went with it for a while but eventually fizzled out and reverted back into their old habits. I attempted to revive them by trying to inject immense focus on my end into the smallest actions performed during their sessions: from the way they foam rolled, to how they went through each individual dynamic stretch within their warm-up, to the effort they put into each and every rep within their workout. It worked—at times. If someone seemed unresponsive I perceived it was a lack of their commitment to meet my own focus. I'd go sit in my office after a session and feel dejected as if I failed at helping someone, not knowing that I really just needed to do a better job of matching the right type of battery to the specific power source.

Another part of empathy and compassion involves the use of emotional payments when communicating. An emotional payment is when another individual (in this instance, a coach) actively and openly recognizes or validates the thoughts, concerns and contributions of another in order to let the them know they appreciate and understand them.

Most people have a lot to say even if they don't outwardly express it. All of us walk around with countless opinions, concerns, insecurities, questions and idle thoughts, all of which have a direct impact on our emotional state, which in turn can affect our level of effort or engagement toward a task. World-class negotiators use emotional payments when dealing with crisis situations, high-stakes corporate mergers, the negotiation of higher salaries and even, as is the case with politicians, to win over the hearts of the masses when lobbying for public office. We like emotional payments because they make us feel supported and acknowledged, both of which we instinctively crave as human beings. When someone acknowledges an issue that we view as important, it's as if they are saying that they want us to be a part of a larger decision, or at the very least, that we had some small part in influencing a particular outcome. This strategic use of acknowledgement on your end goes a long way toward granting the access you need to gain trust, motivate, and influence someone.

Implementing Trust Tenet #5

Give ground to gain ground. As coaches, we want to compose rather than control. Don't forget that humility is the essence of connectedness and if we want to build trust we need to make sure that we aren't afraid to humanize our interactions with our athletes. Don't be afraid to show all sides of yourself to your athletes. Being real will gain you much more respect than trying to put on a show and constantly psyching yourself up to get into coach mode prior to a session. Invoke the spirit of reciprocity by volunteering appropriate personal information about yourself when asked. After all, can you really expect them to do so on their behalf if they don't know anything about you?

Don't fear criticism or bite-back. Just because someone doesn't appear to be on board with your message doesn't make them a detractor. Take a moment and ask them what in particular they have an issue with and get busy finding a middle ground.

Emotional payments accepted. Our emotions, feelings and concerns need to be validated. Letting your athletes know that you understand what their hesitations or fears may be ahead of time lets them know that you have taken their viewpoint under consideration and at the very least have done your homework in regard to trying to see their point of view.

Trust Tenet #6: Delivery & Persuasion

Effective communication breaks the complex into simpler or more memorable terms. In doing so, we produce a sense of cognitive ease and more deeply embed into an athlete's mind the constructs we are teaching. This is precisely why analogies and metaphors are so powerful —they make complex constructs more simple, salient and, swallowable to the listener. Over the years, I have referred to the use of this method as "talking in color" due to the way it tends to paint an image in the listener's mind. Advertisers, coaches, public speakers, and media moguls have been taking part in a similar construct for decades by varying their use of what is known in social psychology as "routes of persuasion." In 1981, Petty and Cacioppo 1981 suggested there are two routes of persuasion: central or peripheral. The effectiveness of these routes, depends, in large part, on the involvement and engagement of the audience. To further distinguish between the two, central routes of persuasion are based on facts, statistics and arguments. The central route tends to work best when the receiver of the information is highly engaged in the message being conveyed or is involved in some way. Conversely, peripheral routes of persuasion focus on seducing your subconscious with music, scents, idyllic settings or attractive models. Peripheral routes are evident when the receiver of the information decides whether or not to agree with the message itself based on cues that have little or nothing to do with the actual strength or clarity of the message in general. Instead, they are influenced by the perceived attractiveness or credibility of the source, their level of relatability to them, the speaker's vocal tone and the surrounding environment.

Which route to persuasion is effective? It depends. Central routes tend to work best for those like us within the strength and conditioning community, due in large part to our science-based background and our desire for objectively measuring performance outcomes related to a particular variable. Peripheral routes tend to be most effective with individuals who simply want a Cliffs Notes version and don't necessarily want to apply a high level of critical thought when engaging with the message. In other words, the peripheral route may be appropriate for the majority of the general public who have a relatively short attention span and tight time frame, or for high level athletes that simply want to get into their training and don't want to relive their high school or college physiology course. Peripheral means of persuasion also tend to be more effective when the listener is not as educated on the topic and simply wants to know how it applies in a simple and straightforward manner.

Here's an example from beyond the world of sports:

The infamous "Got Milk?" campaign was first created in 1993 with the goal of increasing dairy consumption. In case your memory or lifespan doesn't go back that far, these campaigns often featured a celebrity, sports star, popular cartoon or video game character, or other relatively well-known public figure, sporting a milk mustache or unable to complete a task until they had been refueled with a drink of milk. One of their most popular commercials featured two kids playing the original Super Mario Bros. video game. Eventually, the kids gave up due to their inability to get Mario to successfully jump high enough to reach a platform in one of the levels. Instead of making it onto the platform, poor Mario repetitively smashes into the side of it again and again. When Mario sees the little kids walking away frustrated, he springs through the television set and catapults himself off a number of toys sprawled across the living room floor and into their refrigerator, where you then see him guzzling a gallon of milk while growing larger by the moment. Full-grown Mario, now inexorable in stature, goes back into the game and with his giant-size proportions, is able to climb with a single step onto the platform that previously gave him so much trouble. The commercial, clearly targeting young, growing kids as a primary demographic, closes with the voice-over talent stating, "Want to grow? The calcium in milk helps bones grow." Now, let's imagine for a moment that this commercial featured the exact same vocal talent, but used more of a central route of persuasion. In this case, instead of featuring Super Mario, the actor shows the kids a poster or diagram detailing laboratory results of independent studies that highlight calcium's effects on bone growth and how the amount of calcium in an 8-ounce glass of milk compares to other nutritious foods containing calcium. It ends with the same slogan as before, "Want to grow? The calcium in milk helps bones grow." Which version of this ad do you believe that kids will relate to most? Without saying a word, Mario is able to transmit the idea to kids everywhere that if milk can make a hero like him strong, it can do the same for you. No numbers, charts or fancy graphs needed — just powerful visuals and symbolism that becomes personal. This is a prime example of peripheral influence.

Implementing Trust Tenet #6

Make appropriate associations. With many of our athletes, the use of metaphors, analogies, icons and examples related to their specific desires and interests are psychological and relational adhesives. Coaches should largely rely on these tools and other peripheral examples when delivering their message. Our brain prefers to think in associations—educate by relating to the things your athletes care most about.

Get creative. Find creative ways to label your workouts or individual exercises your athletes will perform in order to showcase or highlight what goal that particular movement is focusing on. Training basketball players? Color code the exercises that are aimed at helping them improve their vertical, torso strength, knee health or shoulder mobility differently from one another so that they're more in tune with what each exercise does for them. As coaches, we know that many of these exercises address far more than just one area, but small considerations like these often go a long way with our athletes.

Coordinate common interests. Central and peripheral routes of persuasion only work if the individual cares about what's being discussed in the first place. Using the example above, speaking to an exercise's ability to improve one's vertical jump matters very little if we are working with a Paralympic athlete who is a lower body amputee instead of a basketball player. Sound like a drastic example? This is precisely the situation I faced at the age of 25, when I temporarily transitioned from primarily working with collegiate athletes to working with members of the United States military who were severely injured or disabled upon their return from duty overseas. Being able to successfully "talk in color" requires you to diversify your own experiences and to understand what is most important or relevant to the athlete first and foremost, as opposed to simply relying on generic external cues or motivators.

Trust Tenet # 7: Autonomy

Autonomy is a cornerstone of human motivation. As a performance coach, it is neither advantageous nor your job to micromanage or try to control every situation. As a matter of fact, if you study history you would be hard pressed to find examples of tyrannical leaders who were not eventually plotted against, overthrown or worse. However, history and government aren't the only examples. Even companies in the world of baking learned a hard lesson about the value of autonomy when it came to engaging their customers.

In the book, *Finding Betty Crocker: The Secret Life of America's First Lady of Food*, author Susan Marks details a period during the 1940s and '50s when three of the largest brands in baking and home cooking competed ferociously in an attempt to become the head of the cake-mix market empire. She details that Pillsbury started the war in 1948 when it released its first chocolate cake mix, only to have Duncan Hines follow suit three years later by unleashing a triple-flavor mix that captured half of the cake-mix market at the time. The surprising lesson was that despite the convenience, none of these products turned cake mix into a household necessity. Consumers could easily peruse the aisles without running into a zombie-like hoard of customers lining up to buy the cake mixes. Meanwhile, the baking companies simply couldn't seem to figure out why, especially considering that a similar product in Betty Crocker's Bisquick was a sensational hit.

The answer to their conundrum wasn't packaging, marketing jingles, or even the flavors—it was eggs. Confused? It helps to know that most cake mixes during that time contained only powdered eggs. In an effort to maximize consumer convenience, the recipe was created so that all one had to do was just add water and BOOM, cake for everyone! The problem was that despite their well-meaning intentions, this "insta-cake" didn't appeal to the overwhelming majority of consumers. Since there was nothing distinctive for the home chef to add, the process was too easy and no sense of accomplishment or creative contribution was provided, and thus no satisfaction or long-term engagement was had by the home chef.

Eventually, General Mills got the hint and decided to remove the dried eggs, and followed it up by highlighting their new approach in their updated marketing slogan: "Betty Crocker Cake Mixes bring you that Special Homemade Goodness Because You Add The Eggs Yourself." The campaign worked so well that by 1951 consumers had purchased nearly a billion pounds of cake mix, with the vast majority of it coming from none other than Betty Crocker, who went on to dominate Duncan Hines and Pillsbury. Soon after, the "add your own eggs" practice became the standard and has now even given way to several other variations that allow for more consumer contributions.

Implementing Trust Tenet #7

Lay the foundation. Athlete-centered participation and contribution can have a tremendous impact on their level of engagement. Create the skeleton or framework for your plan to keep them on track, "nudge" them in the right direction, then give them some breathing room.

Don't be afraid to ask. Too many head strength and conditioning coaches create training recipes that only they like to "eat." Autonomy can also apply to giving your staff more input into what you do and when you do it. A Conscious Coach isn't afraid to ask, as opposed to just telling. The more you're able to capture the attention of your audience, the more likely they are going to reciprocate by following your instructions or guidance when you need them to the most. You need this, as detailed feedback as to what they do or do not respond to is a critical linchpin to achieving long-term collaborative success.

CHAPTER 5
APPLYING *CONSCIOUS COACHING* TO OUR CRAFT & LIVES

"Live your beliefs and you can change the world around you."
-Henry David Thoreau

The quality of our communication and the quality of our relationships are directly related, and when the quality of our relationships is high, so too is the quality of our lives.

In this book, we have discussed many of the relational attributes associated with the practice of *Conscious Coaching* and becoming a Conscious Coach. But most of our focus has been on interacting with other athletes. What about how we interact with other coaches, both established and aspiring? It's not just about what a Conscious Coach does (and how they do it) amongst those they are trying to lead, but also about how they behave amongst others within the field and those who will follow in their footsteps.

Let us also never forget the legacy that matters most of all: our family. The ripple effect of our actions and the way in which we communicate permeates every inch of the legacy we will leave behind. Being a Conscious Coach is not simply a matter of learning how to best manage all of the variables that we face on a day-to-day basis when dealing with our athletes, it's a matter of learning how to optimize ourselves as people and professionals, period.

The quality of our legacy is largely dependent upon the three key performance indicators (KPI's) listed below:

1. Our ability to manage our own **ego** while striving to become one of the best at what we do.

2. Our willingness and ability to successfully **mentor** those who will lead the next generation of athletes and coaches.

3. Finding ways that we can **provide** for our families, and not become passive observers within our own lives while we are changing the lives of those around us.

Lock in these three KPIs, write them on a whiteboard, into the notes section of your phone, or on a sticky note on your computer. They are the things that challenge our growth, the things that we can most easily forget about, and the things that we often times can tend to sacrifice or neglect.

These KPIs all play varying roles within our personal evolution and the shaping of our legacy. Let's now dive a little deeper into each KPI. We'll start with ego, as it can often be considered a core cause of harmful misdirection.

Managing Ego & Your Emotions

Tempers often run hot in the coaching field. We are a group of passionate individuals who tend to share our feelings and emotions more than most. We've become conditioned to state and defend our views, amongst each other and our athletes, and even in the media. Unfortunately, operating from a basis of defense, along with strong emotion, often leads to bickering and debating that is useless and destructive. We look at each other and think: "What's the point, and why is he or she so fired up?" The answer, more often than not, is because of our ego.

Ego is a powerful disruptor and seasoned illusionist. It lies at the heart of each and every insecurity and is threaded within the strands of our DNA. Ego can blind us with our own biases, strip away our enthusiasm, deteriorate our identity, and ruin our relationships. We can try our best to control it, but the fact remains that we can never fully get rid of it. Yes, even a Conscious Coach has an ego— they just understand the difference between when it is useful and harmful. Conscious Coaches are able to identify when they may be traveling down an emotional path that will ultimately take them further away from their primary long-term goal. They know that taking a moment to reflect upon lessons learned from past mistakes and successes is the key to strategically responding to momentary adverse circumstances.

When we are able to better manage our ego, we are better able to manage every situation around us and find better solutions to a given problem, thus enhancing our contributions to those we serve, and the industry that we are part of (which I'll attempt to define below).

While one definition of "industry" can allude to economic or commercial activities (of which there is certainly nothing wrong if we hope to be able to provide for ourselves and our family, but more on that later in the chapter), other definitions such as those found in Merriam-Webster allude to "industry" meaning *the habit of working hard and steadily or a group of businesses that provide a product or a service.* I'm not sure about you, but anything that includes the terms service and hard work in describing the jobs that we all perform daily seems pretty accurate to me. The hallmark of a strong industry— and we want ours to be just that—is one that provides a lasting utility to others, or the world in general, through the professions that exist within it. Timeless crafts may certainly appear different at various points as they adapt to both the cultural norms and infrastructure of a given era, but they remain true to their original purpose. Take some of the longest lasting professions in the world— e.g., carpentry, plumbing, trading, teaching—and you will note that the base of these anachronistic professions are skill sets that have been refined and passed down for generations. Yet none of this can be done with effectiveness if we let our ego divorce us from our better judgment. Author Ryan Holiday is correct that within all we do, "ego is the enemy."

Mentorship

A seasoned craftsman relishes the day when the student becomes the teacher. It is a time when their apprentice's ability surpasses that of their own. It is a moment of pride as the elder craftsmen takes comfort knowing that someone is now able to take his place and look after the next generation of those within the community. The act of mentoring, in the early days, was showcased by local apprentices coming into a foundry day after day to aid the town blacksmith in any way imaginable. They carefully watched the craftsman melt, bend, twist and forge steel or iron into weapons or tools that were used for the betterment or protection of the community. There was a great deal of pride displayed in their work. And, more importantly, there was a great deal of pride in the process of learning the work.

A quote that will stick with me forever highlights the importance of honoring the process. It came from the book, *The 50th Law*, by author Robert Greene. It appeared in the introduction of Chapter 8, "Respect the Process—Mastery."

"The fools in life want things fast and easy – money, success, attention. Boredom is their great enemy and fear. Whatever they manage to get slips through their hands as fast as it comes in. You, on the other hand, want to outlast your rivals. You are building the foundation for something that can continue to expand. To make this happen, you will have to serve an apprenticeship. You must learn early on to endure the

hours of practice and drudgery, knowing that in the end all of that time will translate into a higher pleasure—mastery of a craft and of yourself. Your goal is to reach the ultimate skill level—an intuitive feel for what must come next."

The core of the message? Commitment is not convenient. This is true for both the mentor and the apprentice. True mentoring requires sacrificing an immense amount of time, energy and effort on the part of everyone involved. Some of this may come easy during certain parts of your career, when you may not find yourself with many outside responsibilities or other commitments. Eventually, however, you will need to build in mentorship on top of work, travel, personal, and family commitments. It's also not easy because of the emotional toll that mentoring can take.

I cannot spell out the number of interns and volunteers that I have poured countless hours into only to watch them quit or fall into the habit of wanting to be spoon-fed rather than doing the work for themselves. Much of that was actually on me as I would often immediately provide them with as many resources as I could. Or, I would find myself helping them too much or too early on with tasks that I would assign and were originally intended to make them struggle, think more critically about and seek the answers to on their own. Early on, I was eager to give to others what I felt I had never received. When I started my career, and within the first four or five years of practicing, I never had what one would consider a "true mentor"— someone who showed me the ropes, told me what to read, and guided me as to how I could best write programs or interact with others. There were more people who seemed to want to box me out than there were who wanted to count me in and see me succeed. Some even made threats or went out of their way to keep me from getting a position. I am not special in this regard, as these stories are all too common. I would later learn that these actions were more of a reflection of the insecurities of those around me than on my own abilities.

I used to perceive my lack of formal hand-in-hand education and guidance as a weakness and a drawback in my professional development, but later learned that it served as one of my greatest assets. The lack of formal guidance made me figure things out for myself. I learned to scour every resource that I could, and when I was a volunteer, I would take notes on whatever training I observed. If a coach wasn't willing to give me the time of day to answer a question I had, I would go home and research the method, try it for myself, and piece together why it was (or wasn't) a beneficial.

I also later learned that despite me thinking that I had no mentors, they were in fact all around me. Anyone that did something or communicated in a way that was detrimental or counterproductive became a mentor because they taught me what not to do. A well-spoken person I saw at a conference who had immaculate delivery and enunciation became a mentor. The authors of every book, editorial, puff-piece or research article that I read became mentors. I quickly learned that these "situational mentors" will teach you just about everything you want to know if you can just shut up, pay attention and continue to get your hands dirty.

Once the decision to mentor has been made and you've found a mentee that has shown a high level of commitment and respect for the process, there are still some steps to take. For you to be considered a great mentor, you first need to understand why it is important to you to be considered as such. What legacy do you personally want to leave? Like many of the other topics discussed in this book, this decision and internal "mission statement" will help provide clarity and wisdom for the lessons you want to impart on those who you mentor. This mission statement is so important because it doesn't stop with those you mentor, but will live on and touch many more athletes via the people that your mentors eventually mentor.

Mentorship is more important than the trophies, merits, awards and recognition, all of which mean next to nothing for anyone (except for your own ego) if you don't tell the stories and share the lessons that led you to success. That is how you can move the industry forward and create a legacy that you will be proud of. Rote memorization of facts will never replace the true wisdom obtained by the sharing of stories and real-life coaching situations. Whether it's sharing how you were able to create a great training environment despite a lack of resources in a job that you had just taken, or how you had to go about building buy-in with 23 highly skeptical and sleep deprived Special Forces Operators within a two-week span—it's these kinds of "fireside chats" that often have the most impact and impart the most knowledge on a young coach.

The notion of mentoring is one of the main reasons this book was written. Young coaches are eager to amass tons of information yet they lack the perspective to bring it to life or make it meaningful. That's why I tried to do everything I could to not only give lots of facts (which I did) but also include numerous deep dives on the application of those facts. In other words, I wrote a book that didn't stop at concepts but went on to discuss how the concepts could be brought to life. If I did my job well, there should be more Conscious Coaches in the future as a result.

For the Conscious Coach, the act of mentoring should be considered as a privilege, not a burden.

As a closing thought for young coaches, be sure to appreciate the notion that you first have to experience what you want to express. Regardless of your level of introspection and maturity, you will not find yourself to be an effective guide to others if you have not put yourself in the thick of difficult situations and followed through with commitments.

Finally, remember that mentoring is a two-way street. Find creative ways to give back to your mentors. In doing so, you will plant the seeds of growth for a stronger relationship and enhanced learning down the road. Separate yourself by sending hand-written notes, going out of your way to make something in your mentors' lives a bit easier for them, and most importantly, show a sense of respect and appreciation for the amount of time, effort and emotional energy it takes on their behalf to guide and teach you. The smallest acts of reciprocity can make the biggest difference within your own life and also your career.

Providing for You & Your Family: Life & Career Advancement

As we near the end of this journey, I have a confession I want to make: It's long been my desire to eventually retire and be considered amongst the best at what I do by both my own standards as well as those of my peers. At the same time, I also want to have built up a high level of financial security and freedom for my family.

There, I said it!

Why the relief? Because it's a bad thing for us as coaches to make money and expand our horizons, right? Unfortunately, this is a common line of thinking within the current climate of performance coaching. The word "success" has nearly become synonymous with "sellout," and different factions of coaches within the industry often spend more time competing as opposed to collaborating.

Yes, ego rears its ugly head again. It now seems that as soon as a coach starts making a name for him or herself, or when rumors start spreading about someone within the field being thought of as being at the vanguard for something they are doing, the critics line up in an effort to do their best to try and prove such person wrong or cast them as a fraud. This type of modern day witch-hunting behavior has proliferated insidiously with social media where it has become almost effortless for critics to judge, mistake, or misinterpret a post (which is essentially just a snapshot in time) and make it out to be some sort of complete and validated statement of one's full beliefs and/ or stance on a matter. Chalk it up to the well-known yet faulty heuristic of "what you see is all there is." People in other professions can accomplish "big things" and live great lives, but not us coaches. We have to choose: Either stay off the grid and in the trenches (where few ever know your name except for practitioners who herald themselves as the equivalent of underground warlords), or open your own business where you can create a sense of freedom, autonomy, and maybe even a financial structure that can help you both do better work and spend more time with your family.

What turn did I miss where everything has to be so black and white? What's wrong with coaches in the team setting that would rather ditch the antiquated "first in, last out" mantra for one of "work smart, get out" so that they can get their job done effectively and spend even just a fraction of the time with their own children that they do with everyone else's?

Similarly, what's the issue with the "private sector coach" who happens to enjoy coaching a mix of athletes from different sports or perhaps even some general population clients, while also presenting at clinics and creating a brand for themselves so that they can keep their doors open and more financial security for their family? Aren't we all chasing the same thing? We should all be focused on living the best lives that we can, while we can. It makes little sense to blindly "fall in line" with the expectations of others, especially if those expectations are based on a defunct philosophy that says you need to run yourself and your health and your family into the ground in order to be successful. Let's call a spade a spade: that's B.S!

Conscious Coaches keep their dedication to their families and their own health as they traverse the various roads of their professional career. It's time that we realize that just because the nature of our work is blue-collar does not mean that we shouldn't aspire to living a quality of life that is a level above. There is honesty in hard-work, but the real labor should be shown in the life that we strive to build for our family.

Moving Forward

Conscious Coaching is a movement, a mindset, and, when it comes to guiding your actions as a leader, it's a roadmap. Just as the act of simplification can provide immense clarity in times of confusion or chaos, the principles behind *Conscious Coaching* provide a framework, viewpoint, and perhaps even a playbook that will help you to better understand which methods of focused observation and communication will best complement the associated no-nonsense training approaches that we should all be employing. It also helps us to better choose the "right gear for the right hill" as it pertains to the most appropriate strategies to use over the long term, given the unique characteristics of the individual(s) that we are working with, as well as the particular circumstances we may find ourselves in.

As a professional, adopting a *Conscious Coaching* perspective will help you see things as they truly are, as opposed to how your natural level of bias detects them. This is critical for successfully managing long-term behaviors, perceptions, and relationships. With time, observation, and ample practice, this perspective is born within you, and you will become a filter to the contaminating fads and trends that come and go, along with their concomitant hucksters doing their best to sell them to the masses or the media. *Conscious Coaching* will enhance the level of relational influence that you have in your athletes' lives from the inside out, while also helping you coach them more effectively on the training floor. For it is through this influence, this act of "building buy-in," where lasting relationships are built, communication is optimized, behavior is favorably altered, and legacies are ultimately left. Know yourself. Know your athletes. Build buy-in. You'll not only create better athletes in the process, but you'll create better people, too.

APPENDIX

3+1Cs Framework for Relationship Building

Relationships have been studied as long as social psychology has been a recognized field, but it is only since the 21st century that sport psychology has seen the development of sport-specific models such as the "3+1Cs," proposed by Dr. Sophia Jowett in 2007. Dr. Jowett's research has been integral in demonstrating how the manner in which coaches and athletes interact with one another can impact the quality and effectiveness of their training sessions (Jowett and Poczwardowski, 2007).

The "3+1Cs" model is comprised by four constructs:

- Closeness
- Complementarity
- Commitment
- Co-Orientation

A brief summary of each of the C's within Jowett's model is provided below, but for a more full-scale view on each I highly recommend reading the source text as it serves as a wealth of knowledge on the topic. It was also highly influential in helping me crystalize many of the concepts discussed in this book.

Closeness

The construct of closeness focuses on the affective qualities of the coach-athlete relationship and describes how both perceive the emotional elements of their partnership and daily interaction (Jowett 2006). It may be helpful to think of emotions as inner feelings and how both the coach and the athlete display or express those inner feelings during training sessions or during conversation. I recall working with a coach earlier in my career who believed that athletes should never be able to tell what you are thinking or feeling—that a coach should be stoic. He believed that separating his emotional self from the interaction made him appear more stable within his athletes' eyes—and thus a stronger leader—when in fact it often did just the opposite. The athletes never knew what he was thinking and ultimately few were able to relate to him or felt as if they could openly communicate with him. This barrier led to a feeling of unease around some athletes, which served to rot any chance of long-term success due to a lack of trust. Many of the players simply never felt motivated to do anything beyond what was asked of them.

Complementarity

The construct of complementarity represents the behavioral qualities of the coach-athlete relationship. More specifically, it describes how the coach and the athlete perceive the cooperative nature of their interactions, such as mutual effort or responsiveness during training as well as the type of interaction that the coach and the athlete perceive as cooperative and useful (Jowett 2005). It may be helpful to think of behaviors as expressed actions, perhaps based on inner feelings. This also alludes to displays of how both the coach and athlete are able to reach a level of compromise within their interactions. Working with fighters has taught me more about the concept of complementarity perhaps more than with any other type of athlete. I constantly find myself having to find the balance between having fighters perform something exactly as I want them to within their program, and substituting out certain efforts because they may not be in the fighter's best interest (depending on what they did that day with their striking, Brazilian Jiu-Jitsu, or wrestling coach). These fighters are awarding me with a significant level of trust by allowing me to serve as part of their fight team. In turn, they feel that I have their best interests in mind because they see me adjusting their plan in real-time to ensure that we are not adding stress to strain. This give and take manifests itself emotionally in a unique way due to the deeply personal nature of individual sport, and the level of vulnerability that fighters readily expose themselves to. They are often more in tune with their inner feelings than many team-based athletes are, and because they know themselves well, they in turn can read others extremely well. This makes it even more important for the coach to find the balance between control and compromise.

Commitment

The construct of commitment is centered upon the cognitive qualities of the coach-athlete relationship. It expresses how the coach and the athlete perceive the long-term direction of their relationship, their place within it, and their dedication to it (Jowett and Ntoumanis 2004). An ironclad example here is a relationship that I shared with a former NFL player who was once banned for an entire year due to behavioral issues. At the time of his ban, it seemed as if the entire world had turned its back on him. The press maligned and sought to embarrass him daily with the release of "facts" that were not even related to the incident in question. Those on social media did what those on social media do best by peppering him with insults and derogatory labels. Even people that he considered his friends failed to dial the phone and give him a supportive call, which is exactly what he needed and exactly what I decided to do. Times like these are when any coach worth his or her salt knows that it's time to double down by re-stating your commitment to the relationship over the long term and letting your athletes know that your support for them is unwavering. We continued to work together for that entire painful season as he watched his friends and former teammates play the sport he loved most and had now been exiled from. A year later, he was picked up by another NFL franchise and not only received a Pro Bowl invitation, but also came back with such focus and determination that he was lauded by the media that wanted nothing to do with him the year before.

Co-orientation

The construct of co-orientation is defined by the interaction and concurrence of the previous constructs—closeness, complementary and commitment—in the coach-athlete relationship. Put more succinctly, it describes how the coach and the athlete ultimately perceive both themselves and each other from a sense of achieving a degree of common ground (Jowett 2005). Co-orientation is achieved when the three previous constructs come together. It is the fabric of an authentic and cooperative relationship. And both the coach and the athlete know that it has been achieved when each feels they are personally and professionally respected by the other and that their goals are understood.

One of the take home points from the 3+1C construct is that the overall quality and effectiveness of the relationship between coach and athlete depends on how they understand one another and can therefore adapt and react appropriately. While the cumulative amount of time you (the coach) spend with an athlete over the entire course of the relationship is also critical, if you and the athlete are clicking on each of the aforementioned "C's," the actual time spent together during each individual interaction becomes less important since you are able to extract more value out of even the shortest interaction. (Knowles, Shanmugam, Lorimer 2015).

As a coach who has worked in both team settings and the private coaching sector, this is something with which I identify closely. In the team setting, athletes are part of a school or professional sporting organization which, generally speaking, provides coaches and athletes with more opportunities and time to get to know one another and interact over a longer period of time. This time may be cut short due to things such as free-agency, eligibility, lack of quality play during practice, training camps, matches, games etc., but for the most part, the athlete's purpose is aligned with yours through the values and goals of the organization in which they are a part of. And, your relationship with them plays out over a somewhat consistent time period revolving around the competitive season.

Comparatively, in the private coaching sector, an athlete may be with a coach for as little as one hour during a drop-in to check the place out, one day during a travel layover, one week for a "touch-up," one month for a short training block, or, in the extremely rare instance, one year or more, which typically only occurs if an athlete is recovering from a significant injury, is currently not signed with a team (free-agency), or is facing some kind of suspension or other punishment. On the team side, they are stuck with you; on the private side, they don't have to work with you, so you learn quickly that you better not only build trust quickly, but also show them specifically how you can help them and have their best interests at heart without resorting to gimmicks.

When coaching in the private sector, I have always tried to approach this by doing my homework on the athlete(s) prior to meeting them. This allows me to prime the initial interaction, which is also bolstered by taking the time to ask them (in a respectful but straightforward manner) why they decided to walk through the doors in the first place. I then follow that up by volunteering information as to what my approach is, why I believe in it, and how I am always looking to better adapt and refine that approach based on their goals and needs. Remember, when doing this you have to cut the jargon. It's more important that they see your commitment to them, especially before you ask them to commit to your process. Within the first session or first week of working together, I put my money where my mouth is by explaining every detail of the program as it pertains to addressing both of our concerns. I also make it a point to figure out their communication preferences and also address why I communicate the way I do. This is a start, and just touches upon how I've had to use aspects of the 3 + 1 C's model over the course of my career. The finer details of these tactics and strategies are discussed more in depth in the later chapters.

Just remember, we aren't always going to get an athlete's best or most honest answers, and every interaction is not going to be successful. As a matter of fact, some might be outright painful at times. But the important thing is that we flex our relational muscle to show our athletes that we have their best interest at heart and that we are striving toward co-orientation.

BIBLIOGRAPHY

Banas, J.A., Dunbar, N., Rodriguez, D., and Liu, S. (2011). A Review of humor in education settings: Four decades of research. *Communication Education*, 60 (1), 115-144.

Bellet, Paul, S., and Maloney, M.J., (1991). The importance of empathy as an interviewing skill in medicine. *Journal of the American Medical Association*, 226 (13): 1831-1832.

Berk, R.A., (1998). *Professors are from Mars, Students are From Snickers*. Madison, WI: Mendota Press.

Bortoli, L., Bertollo, M., and Robazza, C. (2009). Dispositional goal orientations, motivational climate, and psychobiosocial states in youth sport. *Personality and Individual Differences* 47, 18-24.

Burke, K.L. (2005). But coach doesn't understand: Dealing with team communication quagmires. In M. Andersen (ed.), *Sport Psychology in Practice*. Champaign, IL., Human Kinetics

Carron, A.V., Colman, M.M., Wheeler, J., and Stevens, D. (2002). Cohesion and performance in sport: A meta-analysis. *Journal of Sport and Exercise Psychology* 24 (2), 168-188.

Cialdini, R. B., Borden, R. J., Thorne, A., Walker, M. R., Freeman, S., & Sloan, L. R. (1976). Basking in reflected glory: Three (football) studies. *Journal of Personality and Social Psychology*, 34, 366-375

Clance, Pauline Rose; Imes, Suzanne A. (1978). The imposter phenomenon in high achieving women: Dynamics and therapeutic intervention. (PDF). *Psychotherapy: Theory, Research & Practice*. 15 (3): 241–247.

Dasborough, M. T. and Ashkanasy, N. M. (2002): "Emotion and attribution of intentionality in leader-member relationships," *The Leadership Quarterly*, Vol. 13, pp. 615–634.

Davidai, S., and Gilovich, T. (2015) What Goes Up Apparently Needn't Come Down: Asymmetric Predictions of Ascent and Descent in Rankings. *Journal of Behavior and Decision Making* 28: 491–503

Deluga, R. J. (1997). Relationship among American presidential charismatic leadership, narcissism, and rated performance. *The Leadership Quarterly*, 8, 49–65.

DeVito, J.A. (1986). *The Interpersonal Communication Book*. New York: Harper and Row.

DeVito, J.A. (1994). *Human Communication: The Basic Course*. New York, NY: HarperCollins.

Douge, B. (1999). Coaching adolescents: To develop mutual respect. *Sports Coach*, Summer, 6-7.

End, C. M., Dietz-Uhler, B., Harrick, E. A., & Jacquemotte, L. (2002). Identifying with winners: A reexamination of sport fans' tendency to BIRG. *Journal of Applied Social Psychology*, 32, 1017-1030.

Farmer, S. H., & Aguinis, H. (2005). Accounting for subordinate perceptions of power: An identity-dependence model. *Journal of Applied Psychology*, 90, 1069–1083.

Galinsky, Adam D., and Maurice Schweitzer. *Friend & Foe: When to Cooperate, When to Compete, and How to Succeed at Both*. N.p.: Crown Business, 2015. Print.

Goethals, George R., and Scott T. Allison. "Making Heroes: The Construction of Courage, Competence, and Virtue." *In Advances in Experimental Social Psychology*, edited by J.M. Olson and M.P. Zanna, 183-235. Vol. 46. San Diego: Elsevier, July 2012.

Goleman, Daniel. *Emotional Intelligence*. New York: Bantam, 1995. Print.

Gleason, T.A. (2015). Psychology of Training Football Players: Improved Performance and Success. *Strength & Conditioning Journal*, 27, 102-108.

Grant, Adam. "Goodbye to MBTI, the Fad That Won't Die." *Psychology Today*. 8 Sept. 2013. Accessed 8 May 2015.

Greene, R. (2012). *Mastery*. New York, NY: Viking.

Holt, N.L., Black, D.E., Tamminen, K.A., Mandigo, J.L., and Fox, K.R. (2008). Levels of social complexity and dimensions of peer experience in youth sport. *Journal of Sport and Exercise Psychology* 30, 411-443.

Honeywill, R.(2015). *The Man Problem: Destructive Masculinity in Western Culture*. New York, NY: Palvgrave Macmillan

Jehn, K., & Mannix, E. (2001). The dynamic nature of conflict: A longitudinal study of intragroup conflict and group performance. *Academy of Management Journal*, 44, 238 –251.

Jowett, S. (2007). Interdependence analysis and the 3+1Cs in the coach-athlete relationship. In S. Jowett and D. Lavallee (eds), *Social Psychology in Sport*. Champaign, IL: Human Kinetics.

Jowett, S. and Poczwardowski, A. (2007). Understanding the coach-athlete relationship.

In S. Jowett and D. Lavallee (eds), *Social Psychology in Sport*. Champaign, IL: Human Kinetics.

Judge, T. A., & LePine, J. A. (2007). The bright and dark sides of personality: Implications for personnel selection in individual and team contexts. In J. Langan-Fox, C. Cooper, & R. Klimoski (Eds.), *Research companion to the dysfunctional workplace: Management challenges and symptoms* (pp. 332–355). Cheltenham, UK: Edward Elgar Publishing.

Judge, T.A., Piccolo, R.F., Kosalka, T., (2009) The bright and dark sides of leader traits: A review and theoretical extension of the leader trait paradigm. *The Leadership Quarterly* (20) 855-875.

Kahnemann,D. (2011). *Thinking Fast & Slow.* New York, NY: Farrar, Straus and Giroux

Kaplan, R.M. & Saccuzzo, D.P. (2009) *Psychological Testing Principles, Applications, and Issues.* 7th Edition.

Kashdan,T, and Biswas-Diener,R. (2014). *The Upside of Your Dark Side: Why Being Your Whole Self— Not Just Your "Good" Self— Drives Success and Fulfillment.* New York, NY: Hudson Street Press.

Kavussanu, M., & Roberts, G.C., (2001). Moral functioning in sport: An achievement goal perspective. *Journal of Sport and Exercise Psychology* 23, 37-54.

Kim, J., Allison, S. T., Eylon, D., Goethals, G., Markus, M., Hindle, S. M., & McGuire, H. A. (2008). Rooting for (and then abandoning) the underdog. *Journal of Applied Social Psychology*, 38, 2550-2573.

Knowles,A.M., Shanmugam,V., and Lorimer,R. (2015). *Social Psychology in Sport & Exercise: Linking Theory to Practice.* New York, NY: Palgrave Macmillan.

Kouzes, J. M., & Posner, B. Z. (2003). *Credibility: How Leaders Gain and Lose it, Why people Demand It.* 2nd Edition. San Francisco, CA: John Wiley & Sons, Inc.

LaVoi, N.M. (2007). Interpersonal communication and conflict in the coach-athlete relationship. In S. Jowett and D. Lavallee (eds), *Social Psychology in Sport* (29-40) Champaign, IL: Human Kinetics

Lawrence, Paul R., and Nitin Nohria. *Driven: How Human Nature Shapes Our Choices.* San Francisco: Jossey-Bass, 2001.

Leary, M. R., & Kowalski, R. M. (1990). Impression management: A literature review and two-component model. *Psychological Bulletin*, 107, 34-47.

Lerner, M. J. (2003). The justice motive: Where social psychologists found it, how they lost it, and why they may not find it again. *Personality and Social Psychology Review*, 7, 388-399.

Marks, Susan. *Finding Betty Crocker: The Secret Life of America's First Lady of Food.* New York: Simon & Schuster, 2005. Print.

Mellers, B., Schwartz, A., Ho, K., and Ritov, I. (1997). Elation and disappointment: Emotional responses to risky options. *Psychological Science*, 8, 423-429.

Montgomery, B. (1988). Overview. In S. Duck (ed.), *Handbook of Personal Relationships: Theory, Research and Interventions.* Chichester: Wiley.

Nettle, D. (2006). The evolution of personality variation in humans and other animals. *American Psychologist*, 61, 622–63.

Nicholls, J. (1989). *The Competitive Ethos and Democratic Education.* Cambridge, MA: Harvard University Press.

Northouse, P. G. (1997). *Leadership: Theory and Practice.* Thousand Oaks, CA: Sage Publishing.

Parr, B. (2015). *Captivology: The Science of Capturing People's Attention*. San Francisco, CA: Harper One.

Paunonen, S., Lonnqvist, J., Verkasalo, M., Leikas, S., and Nissinen, V. (2006). Narcissism and emergent leadership in military cadets. *The Leadership Quarterly*, 17, 475–486.

Pells, Eddie, March (2015). Science shows March Madness fans cannot resist a underdog. Retrieved November 29th, 2015, from http://collegebasketball.ap.org/article/science-shows-march-madness-fans-cannot-resist-underdog

Petty, R.E., and Cacioppo, J.T. (1981). *Attitudes and Persuasion: Classic and Contemporary Approaches*. Dubuque, IA: Brown Company Publishers

Pink, D.H. (2012). *To Sell is Human: The Surprising Truth About Motivating Others*. New York, NY: Riverhead Books

Poczwardowski, A., Barott, J.E., and Henschen, K.P. (2002). The athlete and coach: Their relationship and its meaning. *International Journal of Sport Psychology* 33, 116-140.

Pope, J.P. and Wilson, P.M. (2012). Understanding motivational processes in university rugby players: A preliminary test of the hierarchical model intrinsic and extrinsic motivation and the contextual level. *International Journal of Sports Sci Coaching*. 7: 89-107.

Rahim, M. (2002). Toward a theory of managing organization conflict. *International Journal of Conflict Management*. 12 (3), 206-235.

Roberts, G.C., & Ommundsen, Y. (1996). Effects of achievement goal orientations on achievement beliefs, cognitions, and strategies in team sport. *Scandanavian Journal of Medicine and Science in Sport*, 6, 46-56.

Rosenthal, S. A., & Pittinsky, T. L. (2006). Narcissistic leadership. *The Leadership Quarterly*, 17, 617–633.

Russell, Bertrand. *Why Men Fight*. London: Routledge, 2010. Print.

Shepperd, J.A., & McNulty, J.K. (2002). The affective consequences of expected and unexpected outcomes. *Psychological Science* 13, 85-88.

Smith, R.E., Smoll, F.L., and Cumming, S.P. (2007). Effects of a motivational climate intervention for coaches on young athletes' sport performance anxiety. *Journal of Sport and Exercise Psychology* 29, 39-59.

Skeptic. (n.d.). Oxford English Dictionary. Retrieved December 09, 2015 from OED.com website, http://www.oxforddictionaries.com/us/definition/american_english/skeptic

Snyder, C. R., Lassegard, M., & Ford, C. E. (1986). Distancing after group success and failure: Basking in reflected glory and cutting off reflected failure. *Journal of Personality and Social Psychology*, 51, 382-388.

Takahashi, H., Kato, M., Matsuura, M., Mobbs, D., Suhara, T., & Okubo, Y. (2009). When your gain is my pain and your pain is my gain: neural correlates of envy and Shadenfreude. *Science*. 323, 5916 937-939.

Tamir, D.I., and Mitchell, J.P. (2012). Disclosing information about the self is intrinsically rewarding. *Proceedings or the National Academy of Sciences of the United States of America*. 21, 8038-8043

Tajfel, H., & Turner, J. C. (1986). The social identity theory of intergroup behavior. In S. Worchel & W. G. Austin (Eds.), *The social psychology of intergroup relations* (pp. 7-24). Chicago: Nelson Hall.

"The Master Impostor: An Incredible Tale." LIFE Magazine. 1952-01-28. Retrieved 10/17/2015

"Time" Accessed July 3rd, 2016 http://www.merriam-webster.com/dictionary/time.

Uhl-Bien, M., Marion, R., & McKelvey, B. (2007). Complexity Leadership Theory: Shifting leadership from the industrial age to the knowledge era. *The Leadership Quarterly,* 18, 298–318.

Underdog. (n.d.). Online Etymology Dictionary. Retrieved December 03, 2015 from Dictionary.com website, http://dictionary.reference.com/browse/underdog

Van de Pol, P.K.C., Kavussanu, M., and Ring, C. (2012). Goal orientations, perceived motivational climate, and motivational outcomes in football: A comparison between training and competition contexts. *Psychology of Sport and Exercise* 13, 491-499.

Vandello, J. A., Goldschmied, N., & Richards, D. A. R. (2007). The appeal of the underdog. *Personality and Social Psychology Bulletin,* 33, 1603-1616.

Vazou, S., Ntoumanis, N., and Duda, J.L. (2005). Peer motivational climate in youth sport: A qualitative inquiry. *Psychology of Sport and Exercise* 6, 497-516

Why Hogan?|Hogan Assessments www.hoganassessments.com. Retrieved 2016-09-25.

ABOUT THE AUTHOR

Brett Bartholomew is a strength and conditioning coach, consultant, and founder of the performance coaching and consulting company, Bartholomew Strength. His experience includes working with collegiate teams, professional teams, and individual clients. Taken together, Brett has coached a diverse range of athletes from across 23 sports at levels ranging from youths to Olympians. He's supported Super Bowl and World Series Champions, along with several professional fighters, including those competing in the UFC. He has also worked with members of the United States Special Forces community. His coaching and speaking has spanned the globe, from China to Brazil and numerous other stops in between.

As an entrepreneur, Brett has proudly served as a teammate and supporting partner in the strategic growth of two separate performance companies and is a highly sought-after consultant and mentor for many others across the United States and abroad. Additionally, his work and expertise has been featured in numerous local and national media outlets.

Brett is a member of the National Strength and Conditioning Association (NSCA) where he holds both their CSCS*D & RSCC*D distinctions. He is a proud graduate of Kansas State University, where he obtained a Bachelor of Science degree in Kinesiology, and Southern Illinois University-Carbondale, where he obtained a Master of Science in Education in exercise science with an emphasis on motor behavior, cueing, and attentional focus in human performance.

Made in the USA
San Bernardino, CA
11 October 2017